FROM MANY STRANDS
Ethnic and Racial Groups in Contemporary America

THE POPULATION OF THE UNITED STATES IN THE 1980s

A Census Monograph Series

FROM MANY STRANDS
Ethnic and Racial Groups in Contemporary America

Stanley Lieberson
and
Mary C. Waters

for the
National Committee for Research
on the 1980 Census

RUSSELL SAGE FOUNDATION / NEW YORK

The Russell Sage Foundation

The Russell Sage Foundation, one of the oldest of America's general purpose foundations, was established in 1907 by Mrs. Margaret Olivia Sage for "the improvement of social and living conditions in the United States." The Foundation seeks to fulfill the mandate by fostering the development and dissemination of knowledge about the political, social, and economic problems of America. It conducts research in the social sciences and public policy, and publishes books and pamphlets that derive from the research.

The Board of Trustees is responsible for oversight and the general policies of the Foundation, while administrative direction of the program and staff is vested in the President, assisted by the officers and staff. The President bears final responsibility for the decision to publish a manuscript as a Russell Sage Foundation book. In reaching a judgment on the competence, accuracy, and objectivity of each study, the President is advised by the staff and selected expert readers. The conclusions and interpretations in Russell Sage Foundation publications are those of the authors and not of the Foundation, its Trustees, or its Staff. Publication by the Foundation, therefore, does not imply endorsement of the contents of the study.

Library of Congress Cataloging-in-Publication Data

Lieberson, Stanley, 1933–
    From many strands: ethnic and racial groups in contemporary
    America / by Stanley Lieberson and Mary C. Waters for the National
    Committee for Research on the 1980 Census.
        p.   cm. — (The Population of the United States in the 1980s)
    Bibliography: p.
    Includes index.
    ISBN 0-87154-543-8
    1. Ethnology—United States. 2. United States—Population.
I. Waters, Mary C. II. National Committee for Research on the 1980
Census. III. Title. IV. Series.
E184.A1L48 1988
305.8'00973—dc19
                                      88-9651
                                          CIP

Cover and text design: HUGUETTE FRANCO

10 9 8 7 6 5 4 3 2 1

The National Committee for Research on the 1980 Census

The committee is sponsored by the Social Science Research Council, the Russell Sage Foundation, and the Alfred P. Sloan Foundation, in collaboration with the U.S. Bureau of the Census. The opinions, findings, and conclusions or recommendations expressed in the monographs supported by the committee are those of the author(s) and do not necessarily reflect the views of the committee or its sponsors.

Foreword

From Many Strands is one of an ambitious series of volumes aimed at converting the vast statistical yield of the 1980 census into authoritative analyses of major changes and trends in American life. This series, "The Population of the United States in the 1980s," represents an important episode in social science research and revives a long tradition of independent census analysis. First in 1930, and then again in 1950 and 1960, teams of social scientists worked with the U.S. Bureau of the Census to investigate significant social, economic, and demographic developments revealed by the decennial censuses. These census projects produced three landmark series of studies, providing a firm foundation and setting a high standard for our present undertaking.

There is, in fact, more than a theoretical continuity between those earlier census projects and the present one. Like those previous efforts, this new census project has benefited from close cooperation between the Census Bureau and a distinguished, interdisciplinary group of scholars. Like the 1950 and 1960 research projects, research on the 1980 census was initiated by the Social Science Research Council and the Russell Sage Foundation. In deciding once again to promote a coordinated program of census analysis, Russell Sage and the Council were mindful not only of the severe budgetary restrictions imposed on the Census Bureau's own publishing and dissemination activities in the 1980s, but also of the extraordinary changes that have occurred in so many dimensions of American life over the past two decades.

The studies constituting "The Population of the United States in the 1980s" were planned, commissioned, and monitored by the National Committee for Research on the 1980 Census, a special committee appointed by the Social Science Research Council and sponsored by the Council, the Russell Sage Foundation, and the Alfred P. Sloan Foundation, with the collaboration of the U.S. Bureau of the Census. This committee includes leading social scientists from a broad range of fields—

demography, economics, education, geography, history, political science, sociology, and statistics. It has been the committee's task to select the main topics for research, obtain highly qualified specialists to carry out that research, and provide the structure necessary to facilitate coordination among researchers and with the Census Bureau.

The topics treated in this series span virtually all the major features of American society—ethnic groups (blacks, Hispanics, foreign-born, European ancestries); spatial dimensions (migration, neighborhoods, housing, regional and metropolitan growth and decline); and status groups (income levels, families and households, women). Authors were encouraged to draw not only on the 1980 census but also on previous censuses and on subsequent national data. Each individual research project was assigned a special advisory panel made up of one committee member, one member nominated by the Census Bureau, one nominated by the National Science Foundation, and one or two other experts. These advisory panels were responsible for project liaison and review and for recommendations to the National Committee regarding the readiness of each manuscript for publication. With the final approval of the chairman of the National Committee, each report was released to the Russell Sage Foundation for publication and distribution.

The debts of gratitude incurred by a project of such scope and organizational complexity are necessarily large and numerous. The committee must thank, first, its sponsors—the Social Science Research Council, the Russell Sage Foundation, and the Alfred P. Sloan Foundation. The long-range vision and day-to-day persistence of these organizations and individuals sustained this research program over many years. The active and willing cooperation of the Bureau of the Census was clearly invaluable at all stages of this project, and the extra commitment of time and effort made by Bureau economist James R. Wetzel must be singled out for special recognition. A special tribute is also due to David L. Sills of the Social Science Research Council, staff member of the committee, whose organizational, administrative, and diplomatic skills kept this complicated project running smoothly.

The committee also wishes to thank those organizations that contributed additional funding to the 1980 census project—the Ford Foundation and its deputy vice president, Louis Winnick, the National Science Foundation, the National Institute on Aging, and the National Institute of Child Health and Human Development. Their support of the research program in general and of several particular studies is gratefully acknowledged.

The ultimate goal of the National Committee and its sponsors has been to produce a definitive, accurate, and comprehensive picture of the U.S. population in the 1980s, a picture that would be primarily descriptive but also enriched by a historical perspective and a sense of the challenges for the future inherent in the trends of today. We hope our readers will agree that the present volume takes a significant step toward achieving that goal.

CHARLES F. WESTOFF

Chairman and Executive Director
National Committee for Research
on the 1980 Census

Acknowledgments

Reynolds Farley, Charles Hirschman, Michael J. Levin, and Robin M. Williams, Jr., served on the advisory panel for this volume and provided many extremely useful comments and suggestions based on their careful readings of the first draft. Charles F. Westoff, Chairman and Executive Director of the National Committee for Research on the 1980 Census, also read the draft with great care and provided an extensive set of criticisms. The final product has been greatly improved by the comments from these colleagues. David L. Sills, of the Social Science Research Council, who served as staff to the committee, provided broad guidance on more than one occasion, and he was most encouraging about the timely completion of this volume. In addition, we are indebted to Michael Hout—ever generous in his advice and time—who provided a number of helpful comments and suggestions. Thanks are due also to several other members of the informal "Oakland School of Sociology"—David Matza and Michael Burawoy for discussions about several substantive issues, and Richard Ofshe for guidance through the more intricate elements of the computer environment at Berkeley. Glenn Carroll, Richard F. Curtis, Andrew Greeley, Jerome Karabel, and Tom Smith provided useful comments and leads at various points in the project. In addition, Mark Scarbecz (at the outset of the project) and Eleanor Bell (at its very end) both provided excellent research assistance which we gratefully acknowledge. We also thank Robert Freeland for his last-minute computing assistance.

A special note of thanks is due to Lawrence Santi. Early in the project, when the senior author was at the University of Arizona, he invited Santi to spend a year there, working full-time on the project. Santi came, but he left early for a longer-term position before the 1980 data were available. However, his important work on the nativity-ancestry cross-tabulation led to a publication which is cited at several points in the text.

As the massive job of undertaking the data processing for the 1980 one percent Public Use Microdata Sample tapes began, we learned that no such effort had previously been undertaken at Berkeley and we were obliged to confront special problems faced in processing such a data set. It was not an easy task, but it was manageable only because Ward Bell gave freely of his time in providing extraordinarily deep understanding of data processing and programming languages. It is our great pleasure to express gratitude for Ward's help, good humor, and patience.

Much of the project was conducted at the Survey Research Center of the University of California, Berkeley. Percy Tannenbaum and James A. Wiley, director and assistant director, respectively, were exceptionally supportive and helpful. Christine Day, Ilona Einowski, and Ann Gerken of the State Data Program at the Center, provided many hours of help in coping with the difficulties encountered in mounting and running sample tapes, as well as in the use of published materials. Finally, they were extremely accommodating with their own PC during a period when one of the authors' PC repeatedly crashed (thereby managing to keep one of us from crashing as well). Sally Elliott and Amy Kimball did everything possible to run the project from the Survey Research Center with the greatest of ease and the least possible inconvenience.

A study of this nature is not done without substantial monetary support. In addition to the core research support provided by the Russell Sage Foundation through the Committee for Research on the 1980 Census, we acknowledge with gratitude funds received from the Survey Research Center, as well as from the Departments of Sociology at both the University of Arizona and the University of California, Berkeley. In addition, the second author received support at Berkeley from both the Survey Research Center and the Graduate Group in Demography (through Grant T32-HD07275 from NICHD).

Finally, in a certain sense the coauthors are themselves testimony to the remarkable ethnic changes described in this volume. One need not go back too many generations for either author to find ancestors who almost certainly would have been unable to work together with someone of another ethnic group in the manner necessary to create this book, let alone in the comfortable and harmonious way that we have experienced. It is the joy of America that these changes have come about for so many people from so many different sources who are increasingly free to emphasize or ignore their ancestry as they choose—it is the tragedy of America that it has yet to include all of us.

STANLEY LIEBERSON
University of California, Berkeley

MARY C. WATERS
Harvard University

Contents

List of Tables

1

MEASURING ETHNIC ANCESTRY

THE UNITED STATES is peopled almost entirely by migrants and their descendants. Only 3 percent of the population in 1980 report origins that are at least partly indigenous: American Indian, Eskimo, Aleutian Islander, and Hawaiian. The overwhelming majority of the population are from elsewhere on the globe: Africa, Southeast Asia, the Indian subcontinent, the Middle East, Latin America, the Caribbean, Canada, and virtually every part of Europe. In addition, the nation also includes groups formed in the New World, such as Mexicans and Puerto Ricans, in some cases living in areas that were later conquered or purchased by the United States. This country has received more immigrants than any other in the world and consists of a wide variety of different racial and ethnic groups.

At the time of their arrival, the groups differed on a wide variety of critical attributes, such as culture, social organization, power, economic position, prestige, education, urban and industrial background, kinship structure, and the attitudes of earlier Americans toward them. They also differed in the forces propelling them to come: slavery, famine and starvation, political upheaval, social oppression, military conscription, impending war; dissenters seeking religious freedom, sojourners initially intending to return, criminals avoiding the reach of the law; others pursuing superior professional opportunities or temporary employment, a higher level of living, and better opportunities for themselves and their offspring. Moreover, the timing of arrival and concentration of immigration are distinctive for each group.

The history of the nation, therefore, is also the history of these diverse racial and ethnic groups superimposed on one another, occupying widely different social, political, economic, and cultural positions, and arriving under radically different conditions and at different periods. Some of the intergroup contacts were marked by competition and conflict at times and places that by the standards of the present day can only be described as barbaric. Yet for many groups there are periods of relative harmony, cooperation, and progressively improving conditions on both objective and symbolic dimensions. This facet of the nation's history is by no means over; in the years ahead there is every reason to expect shifts both in composition and in relations among groups. As in the past, relatively large numbers of immigrants to the United States continue to arrive, both legally and illegally. Moreover, the groups' positions vis-à-vis one another are changing or, at the very least, under constant challenge.

Understandably, there is considerable interest at present in the severe obstacles and difficulties encountered by peoples of non-European origin in the United States: blacks, American Indians, Eskimos, various Hispanic groups, Asians, and Pacific Islanders. In a society where whites constitute 83 percent of the population in 1980 and clearly dominate, it is appropriate that specific monographs in this series be devoted to analyzing the census materials available for these non-European peoples.[1] Yet there is a danger in overlooking the white groups themselves, in particular the *relative* ease and speed with which the nation incorporated remarkably large numbers of different European groups. While the United States is not unique in absorbing different ethnic groups, we should not take these events for granted, especially in comparison to white ethnic patterns in many other parts of the world.[2] Even in the United States, the formation of a white population in which ethnic divisions are minimal is far from complete and is accompanied by considerable conflict and internal divisions, albeit of a different magnitude from that experienced by blacks and some other non-Europeans.[3]

Moreover, the white groups of the United States are of interest simply because of the extraordinary numbers who live in this country.

[1]See, for example, Frank Bean and Marta Tienda, *The Hispanic Population of the United States* (New York: Russell Sage Foundation, 1988).

[2]See Stanley Lieberson, "A Societal Theory of Race and Ethnic Relations," *American Sociological Review* 26 (1961): 902–10. Donald L. Horowitz, *Ethnic Groups in Conflict* (Berkeley: University of California Press, 1985.

[3]Stanley Lieberson, *A Piece of the Pie: Blacks and White Immigrants Since 1880* (Berkeley: University of California Press, 1980).

Thanks to massive emigration streams from various parts of Europe, along with increases since arrival, the United States is the homeland of vast numbers of people who can trace their ancestry to different European nations. The population reporting Irish origin in the United States in 1980 is about eight times the combined population of Ireland and Northern Ireland, the Scottish population is double that of Scotland, and the number of persons in the United States reporting at least some English ancestry is several million greater than the population of England. Other groups are also very large relative to the numbers living in their ancestral homelands: Norwegians in the United States are about 85 percent of the number of residents in Norway, Germans are 63 percent of the combined populations of West and East Germany, Swedes are about half the number found in Sweden, and the Dutch are close to half of those in the Netherlands. The number of Italians, Poles, and French living in this nation are from 20 to 25 percent of their number in Italy, Poland, and France, respectively—with the percentage even higher for the Danes, Czechs, and Hungarians.

In recent decades, the census has been of decreasing value in helping us learn about white ethnic groups in the United States. This is surprising not only because of the numerical and social significance of white ethnic groups in the nation, but also because of the long-standing historical interest in them. Hutchinson[4] cites a memorandum from the American Philosophical Society in 1800, signed by Thomas Jefferson, and another in that year from the Connecticut Academy of Arts and Sciences—both proposing that Congress include a birthplace question in the second census then under consideration.

It was not until 1850, however, that a question on birthplace was added to the census, thus allowing identification of the *first* generation—people whose birthplace was outside the United States. With the introduction in 1880[5] of a question on birthplace of the respondent's parents it was possible to identify the *second* generation—people who were themselves born in the United States but with at least one parent who was an immigrant to the United States. Until 1980 the first and second generation were the only members of these white ethnic groups identifiable in census materials. The *third* generation and later—the grandchildren of immigrants and their descendants—were "native white of native parentage" and thus we had no information on their ethnic backgrounds.

This procedure was once reasonably adequate for examining various

---

[4]E. P. Hutchinson, *Immigrants and Their Children: 1850–1950* (New York: Wiley, 1956), p. 1.

[5]The second generation was first counted in the 1870 census (but not by specific country of parental birth). Hutchinson, *Immigrants and Their Children*, app. B, provides an excellent detailed review of the nativity data in earlier censuses.

white ethnic groups in the United States as long as most members were either of first- or second-generation residence in the nation. However, certain difficulties existed even then. For one, birthplace does not always correspond with ethnic group. Hence in most censuses one cannot separate German Swiss from Italian or French Swiss or separately classify the various ethnic groups with a common country of birth—for example, Serbs born in Yugoslavia have the same birthplace as Croats from that nation. In some circumstances, there is a reasonably close correspondence between birthplace and ethnic origin, but in others it is poor.[6] Another difficulty stems from the changing boundaries in Europe, which are probably not fully taken into account by respondents who had migrated earlier or whose parents had. Also, the nativity procedure was never adequate for persons of mixed nativity; generally, the scheme does not allow for multiple classification—rather the Census Bureau classified respondents' country of origin on the basis of father except when he was of American birth and the mother of foreign origin. Finally, and most significant, the nativity procedure was never applied to whites with three or more generations' residence in the country (native whites of native parentage). Accordingly, such persons could not be classified by birthplace or any other white ethnic delineation.

These nativity data are of diminishing value for the analysis of non-Hispanic white groups in the United States. With the decline of immigration from Europe, an increasing proportion of the population of European origin is of three or more generation's residence in the United States. Since the nativity data are restricted to the first two generations, they do not permit classification of such persons by origin. Accordingly, our knowledge of these groups has decreased over the years. Moreover, the rather high levels of intermarriage within the white population (see Chapters 6 and 7) make the simple nativity classification of decreasing value even if it were applied to later generations. We know that initially these European groups were very different from one another—but until 1980 we were hindered in our ability to study how later generations of these groups have changed.

Our lack of knowledge is justifiable if it can be assumed that these whites of European origin more or less merge and assimilate after only a few generations' residence. However, in recent decades the validity of this simple melting pot theory has been questioned; the argument has been made that diversity and pluralism are still found among these white ethnic groups such that they remain distinctive and by no means

---

[6]Stanley Lieberson and Laurence Santi, "The Use of Nativity Data to Estimate Ethnic Characteristics and Patterns," *Social Science Research* 14 (1985): 31–56.

entirely assimilated long after their first few generations of residence in the United States.[7]

Resolution of this debate has been greatly helped by the introduction in 1980 of a new question on the ethnic ancestry of the population. For the first time in a decennial census, all segments of the population can be classified by their ethnic ancestry, regardless of the number of generations of residence in the nation. There is now an opportunity to use census data to address the melting pot–pluralism debate.[8] If white ethnic groups are entering what Alba[9] has called, "the twilight of ethnicity," it is now possible to examine this in a manner that was hitherto impossible. If, on the other hand, ethnic origin still "matters," its form must be different from what existed when the European groups first arrived and were distinct in obvious ways such as language, dress, names, and cultural features. Our analysis of these new data provides evidence of a complicated nature, with developments in ethnicity that are not anticipated by either theory.

At issue, of course, is more than simply a resolution of the pluralism–melting pot debate, as important as this may be. This volume focuses on the current status of the vast majority of the population of the United States, dealing with one of the most fundamental experiences in the creation of a nation: namely, the merger of peoples whose initial dealings with one another were characterized by antipathy, if not outright antagonism. The 1980 census data provide basic evidence about the current situation for these ancestry groups—as well as a reference point to measure changes over time. As best as we can determine, the present patterns are not entirely in harmony with the speculations that have been made by researchers in this field prior to these data becoming available. In view of the existence of other monographs dealing with non-European groups, emphasis is appropriately directed toward the white ethnic populations, but we have also included data on the leading non-European populations in order to provide the reader with a broad overview applying to all of the groups, permitting comparisons that are of considerable interest at present. In effect, this volume examines all of

---

[7]For an excellent review of the literature on the melting pot debate, see Charles Hirschman, "America's Melting Pot Reconsidered," *Annual Review of Sociology* 9 (1983): 397–423.

[8]Of course, the ancestry question in the 1980 census, by combining second-generation individuals with later-generation individuals, poses another problem—the inability to separate individuals for whom ethnic ancestry is still a strong identity and those for whom ethnic ancestry is merely a label or a distant genealogical memory. This issue is addressed in much greater detail in Chapters 2 and 8.

[9]Richard D. Alba, *Italian Americans: Into the Twilight of Ethnicity* (Englewood Cliffs, NJ: Prentice-Hall, 1985b), chap. 7.

the major ethnic and racial groups in the United States, emphasizing social and economic conditions for which the census is an appropriate source.

The ancestry data used in this monograph are largely obtained from the new question on ethnic ancestry in the 1980 census. Since, to our knowledge, this is the first monograph to employ these data in such an extensive way, it is important that we review the conceptual problems involved in this question and its coding, as well as guide potential users through some of the difficulties encountered in using the data.

While usually such discussions of the wording of the ethnic question and the coding and analysis decisions are of interest only to specialists or are reserved for a "technical appendix," the following discussion is relevant to many general readers because some of the "technical" issues we describe are actually complications and difficulties that reflect the substantive nature of race and ethnic relations in the United States at present.

The 1980 Ancestry Question

The 1980 ethnic ancestry data are based on responses to the following new question: "What is this person's ancestry?" It is an open-ended question in the sense that respondents are asked to fill in a blank line. Under the blank line, the Census Bureau illustrated appropriate responses with the following: "(For example: Afro-Amer., English, French, German, Honduran, Hungarian, Irish, Italian, Jamaican, Korean, Lebanese, Mexican, Nigerian, Polish, Ukrainian, Venezuelan, etc.)" In addition, respondents were advised to see the instruction guide if they were uncertain about how to report ancestry. How many actually bothered to look through the guide is not known, but the instructions are reproduced below:

> Print the ancestry group with which the person *identifies.* Ancestry (or origin or descent) may be viewed as the nationality group, the lineage, or the country in which the person or the person's parents or ancestors were born before their arrival in the United States. Persons who are of more than one origin and who cannot identify with a single group should print their multiple ancestry (for example, German-Irish).

> Be specific; for example, if ancestry is "Indian," specify whether American Indian, Asian Indian, or West Indian. Distinguish Cape Verdean from Portuguese, and French Canadian from Canadian.

> A religious group should not be reported as a person's ancestry.

This question, and its treatment by the Census Bureau, is both a remarkably bold innovation and an endeavor marred by some serious deficiencies. It is a bold innovation because of its open-ended character such that the respondent is basically free to list as many groups as seems appropriate. It also requires the census to undertake a complicated and expensive coding procedure in order to reduce the different responses to a workable number. For example, Sicilian, Tuscan, Umbrian, Lombardian, Piedmontese, and Calabrian are among the responses obtained in the census that have to be combined under the "Italian" rubric.[10] Although the Census Bureau must necessarily be somewhat arbitrary in determining what groups should go together, one particularly questionable step by the bureau should be mentioned. Persons are classified as English if they report their ancestry as "British Isles" or "British (United Kingdom)." Although it is certainly appropriate to include English in either of these categories, it is not appropriate to assume that persons describing themselves as British are necessarily English; persons of Scottish, Welsh, and Northern Irish origin could be appropriately classified as British without implying English ancestry. This may or may not be a serious problem since the number responding as British is unknown.[11] A lesser problem of this sort reflects the census decision to pool "Belgian," "Flemish," and "Walloon" under the single rubric of "Belgian." This makes sense only if relatively few respondents indicate either of the last two responses; otherwise a basic ethnic distinction within Belgium is lost.

An admirable feature in 1980 is the way multiple responses are treated. For each respondent, the census records the second ancestry listed (if any) as well as the first, whenever both are *usable*, that is, acceptable responses in terms of the criteria to be discussed below. Thus, for example, we can learn the number of people who report themselves to be Greek-Swedish, Irish-Italian, and so on. Persons who report a single ancestry can be analyzed separately from those who report the same ancestry along with one or more others (multiple or mixed ancestry). This is often of great value; for example, the mates selected by persons of wholly Italian origin can be compared with those selected by persons who are part Italian. In addition, the 17 triple-ancestry combinations most frequently reported in previous Census Bureau surveys

---

[10]See U.S. Bureau of the Census, *1980 Census of Population and Housing,* Public Use Microdata Samples, Technical Documentation (Washington, DC: U.S. Government Printing Office, 1983e), app. E.

[11]In the future, the census should record and make available the frequency count for each of the specific responses that were later pooled.

were delineated by the census.[12] (However, if a person gave three responses which were not among these 17 common triple ancestries, only the first two ancestries mentioned were coded by the census.) The most frequent triple-ancestry combination is that made up of the three most common white ancestry groups: English-German-Irish (1.6 million people).

This is a useful data set for the 17 triple-ancestry combinations, but it does warp to some unknown degree the total counts for each group. For example, one third of all of the triple-ancestry responses would not have been included if such responses were limited to the first two, as is the case for other combinations. As a consequence, the groups and combinations included have a certain numerical advantage over other groups and combinations that are excluded. For example, if the English-German-Irish combination were not included and if each of the three groups were mentioned last in equal number, about 500,000 fewer Irish, English, and Germans would be recorded in the census (1.6 million divided by 3). Thus, all we know about someone reported as Greek-Swedish is that these were the first two ancestries listed; the response is indistinguishable from someone who added additional origins or who only gave these two.

Special Problems with the New Question
Inferring Longitudinal Changes

One of the great advantages of using census data is the possibility of examining changes over time based on responses to more or less comparable questions in different decades. This is readily apparent to readers acquainted with other volumes in this series. Obviously, it is an impossibility here since we are dealing with a new question for a decennial census. This is not a handicap for describing the current state of affairs for these groups, but two special procedures are necessary in order to estimate changes over time. First, we often use earlier data available for immigrants and/or the second generation, classified by country of birth or parental country of birth. This allows patterns for the groups in an earlier period to be compared with the present time, but it does mean moving from a nativity classification, restricted to the first two genera-

---

[12]U.S. Bureau of the Census, *1980 Census of Population*, Supplementary Report, "Ancestry of the Population by State: 1980," PC80-S1-10 (Washington, DC: U.S. Government Printing Office, 1983a), p. 6.

tions of residence in the United States, to the 1980 ethnic ancestry data that are based on all generations and not on country of origin.[13]

A second special procedure involves the use of age-specific cross-sectional data to infer longitudinal changes. This must be done with great care and caution; otherwise there is a danger of drawing conclusions about longitudinal societal changes which are due to changes in the life cycle.[14] We pursue this approach only when there can be reasonable confidence, based on the substance of the topic, that the differences between age cohorts reflect true changes that cannot be explained merely by shifts in the life cycle.

Interpreting Specific Responses

The responses to the ancestry question are largely in ethnic terms, but some clearly reflect country of origin rather than ethnic ancestry. For example, about one fourth of those answering "Swiss" gave no other ancestry—an extremely unlikely response for the descendants of immigrants from a country that has an intense awareness of the German, French, Italian, and Romansch components of the native population. Such a response reflects either an intentional downplaying by the respondent of a more precise ethnic marker and/or generational changes such that later American generations are unaware of ethnic distinctions within the Swiss population that were almost certainly important to their ancestors at the time of immigration. Likewise, about half of those responding as "Yugoslavian" did not modify their answer with one of the specific ethnic groups in the country; nearly 500,000 responded as "Scandinavian" rather than one of the specific groups in that category; and half of those giving "Canadian" as a response did not modify it with any specific ethnic origin. These responses are not really discouraged since the instructions to respondents view ancestry as, among other possibilities, "the country in which the person or the person's parents or ancestors were born before their arrival in the United States." These responses also suggest to us a possible shift over time in a population's

---

[13]The discrepancy between nativity and ethnic ancestry responses is a problem of varying significance, depending on the group (see Lieberson and Santi, "Use of Nativity Data"). The generational issue varies as well. For many of the southern-central-eastern European groups, combined first and second generation data in an earlier period—say, 1900—probably included the vast majority of the group living in the United States. For many of the northwestern European groups, this was probably rather inadequate even then, although obviously perfectly suitable for describing the social characteristics of recent immigrants from such sources.

[14]For relevant criticism, see Stanley Lieberson, *Making It Count* (Berkeley: University of California Press, 1985a), pp. 179–83.

ethnic conceptions—a matter that we will return to later in discussing the general shifts within the white population.

Distinguishing Religious Subsets

Because the U.S. Census does not ask a question on religion, it is impossible to subdivide ethnic groups by this characteristic. Thus, German Catholics are indistinguishable from German Protestants, Irish Catholics from Irish Protestants, and so on. This is unfortunate, particularly for those ethnic groups in which at least two major religions are represented in substantial numbers and where there is reason to expect behavioral differences between these religious subsets. Using National Opinion Research Center (NORC) General Social Survey data that provide information on both ethnicity and religion, Greeley[15] has shown that substantial differences may exist within an ethnic group along religious lines. Among Irish Protestants, for example, 29 percent live in rural counties, whereas this applies to only 5 percent of Irish Catholics. Although the gap is smaller, it also exists between German Protestants and German Catholics (25 versus 16 percent). In similar fashion, Greeley has demonstrated a wide variety of other differences between religious subsets of persons reporting the same ethnic ancestry—political attitudes, education, occupation, and income.

Identifying Jews

The Census Bureau is prohibited by law from collecting information on religion. Thus, it is impossible to directly obtain data on Jews; although it would be appropriate to view this population as both an ethnic group and a religious group—with a fairly high correspondence between the two questions. In Canada, for example, where "Jewish" is an acceptable response in both their ethnic and religion questions, 94 percent of those giving a Jewish ethnic response also give a Jewish religious response (the next most common response for "ethnic Jews" is no religion).[16] Researchers using U.S. census data in the past have custom-

---

[15]Andrew M. Greeley, *Ethnicity in the United States* (New York: Wiley, 1974), chap. 2.

[16]Derived from Statistics Canada, *1981 Census of Canada, Population*, vol. 1: *Ethnic Origin* (Ottawa, Ontario: Statistics Canada, 1984), table 5. The overlap in the opposite direction is not quite as close (89 percent of persons indicating they are Jewish on the religion question also indicate Jewish ethnicity), but it is still substantial. The somewhat weaker correspondence may reflect any or all of the following factors: non-Jews who have taken up the religion through intermarriage; persons who report another ancestry on that question because of their national origins; offspring of mixed marriages who are raised as Jews but report a non-Jewish ethnic ancestry.

arily relied on the population of Russian birth to indicate the behavior of Jews.[17] The assumption is widely made that a substantial proportion of the Russian first- or second-generation population are Jews and that a substantial proportion of Jews are of Russian birth. Because this procedure has been used by previous researchers and because we would like to be able to describe trends among Jews in the United States, we examine here the strengths and weaknesses of this approximation. How valid is this procedure generally and particularly when ethnic ancestry data are being used?

Based on an analysis of the NORC General Social Survey data (which reports both origin and religion of respondents) as well as census mother tongue data, there is no question that a substantial segment of the population reporting Russian origin is Jewish and, moreover, that a substantial segment of all American Jews reports Russian origin. On the other hand, the correspondence between the two has probably been overestimated by many earlier researchers. A majority of the Russian-origin population appears to be Jewish, but the majority of the Jewish population do not indicate a Russian ancestry. The correspondence may be stronger than this, however, since an unusually large number of Russians report no religion (these may be Jews—in ethnic terms—who chose to report no religious affiliation or participation). Likewise, it may well be that Jews whose ancestors came from Russia do not report this any longer since it is not a salient characteristic to them. At any rate, our experiments with the use of Russian-origin data as a surrogate for Jews in the United States indicate that, if anything, the relatively favorable socioeconomic position occupied by Jews is underestimated when the population reporting Russian origin is used as a surrogate for all Jews. Of course, these are national data and the correspondence between the two categories almost certainly varies between different subareas of the nation. (A detailed review of our analysis is provided in an appendix to this chapter.)

Handling Multiple-Origin Data

A substantial segment of the population reports more than one ethnic ancestry (nearly 40 percent of all those giving at least one specific ancestry in 1980 also reported at least a second one). The handling of such complicated data is by no means obvious. Under some circumstances, each combination of ancestral origins should be treated as a

---

[17]See Lisa J. Neidert and Reynolds Farley, "Assimilation in the United States: An Analysis of Ethnic and Generation Differences in Status and Achievement," *American Sociological Review* 50 (1985): 840–50, and the literature cited therein.

separate entity. If, say, there are 33 groups of interest, we can visualize 561 entries, one for each of the 33 unmixed ancestry combinations as well as the 528 different possible pairings. Such detailed analysis is sometimes critical—for example, in Chapter 7, when marriages of persons of mixed origin are examined, it is important to know the precise origins of the mates. But keeping track of all the specific combinations gets cumbersome and often involves combinations with extremely limited numbers, even when using the 1980 1 percent Public Use Microdata Sample (the source of the data used here when obtained from unpublished sources). For many problems, it is therefore suitable merely to subdivide each ancestry into those of single or unmixed origin and those of mixed origin. For example, we report the behavior of persons of unmixed Dutch origin and the behavior of those of mixed Dutch origin (in effect, combining all those reporting Dutch along with at least one other origin). For other purposes, we have simply pooled all persons of a given origin, regardless of whether they are of mixed or unmixed ancestry.[18]

[18]One possible alternative is to use the procedure which Neidert and Farley ("Assimilation") adopted. This procedure has certain advantages when detailed cross-tabulations are not wanted because it is easier to pool the data. Persons listing multiple ancestries are classified by the one that they first reported. "A man who listed French-Norwegian, for example, was treated as French" (p. 843). There is something to be said for such a procedure because the data for each group can be added in a very simple and straightforward way since each person appears only once. It is also easy to administer. A minor disadvantage is that it is awkward to use with persons in any of the triple-ancestry entries because the census does not indicate which of the ancestries was listed first. Each multiple would have to be divided into three equal parts. Somewhat more serious is the difficulty caused when there is a nonrandom ordering of the groups in a given combination. For example, for persons of multiple XY origins, if it was chance which origin was listed first, we would expect roughly half of the population to respond XY and roughly half to respond YX. Some trials with the 1979 CPS data indicate this does not occur, although in some cases the gaps are moderate. But if there is some systematic difference between the XYs and the YXs, this distortion will affect the description of each group. This, we think is probably a modest problem in most cases (see, however, the Scotch-Irish discussed below), and actually is no problem if the researcher randomly assigns XYs and YXs, half to X and half to Y, regardless of the order given. (Or if one wishes to argue that the first listed is indeed most preferred and hence somehow more relevant, then the procedure used by Neidert and Farley would cause no difficulty.)

A serious problem with this procedure remains; namely, the description of each group is disproportionately weighted more by the unmixed than the mixed components. If 60 percent of the population reporting some X ancestry are unmixed Xs and 40 percent are of mixed origin, the division of the mixed Xs into two subsets (based on either first ancestry reported or the random assignment procedure) will mean that the ratio of unmixed to mixed in group X is 3:1 (60/20) rather than 1.5:1 (60/40) if all persons with some X origin are included. Since, in general, persons of mixed ancestry differ from single-ancestry compatriots, estimates of the group characteristics are affected. Moreover, this distortion is not of equal magnitude for all groups, since it is affected by the relative sizes of the mixed and unmixed components. In short, this alternative approach has a number of attractive features, and researchers should consider if these more than outweigh some difficulties that follow from its use, keeping in mind that none of the ways for handling multiple-origin respondents is without some shortcomings.

A special problem exists when the data arc pooled, as described in the second and third procedures above. Namely, someone of mixed ancestry—say, English-German—is counted twice, once as English and once as German. This causes no problem as a description of either ancestry group. We present information about all persons of English ancestry (in whole or part) and again we provide information about all persons with known German origins. This can cause certain difficulties if the researcher is not careful. First, comparisons between any two groups involve a part-whole problem because the two groups include some of the same people; second, the data for such groups have to be summed carefully. If, for example, we ask what percentage of the population belongs to each ancestry category, the sum will be well in excess of 100. Furthermore, pooling of the data to obtain a national total requires some care; it is necessary to weight persons by dividing them by the number of times they appear under various ancestries. Finally, the data cannot always be added in a simple and direct manner when persons appear more than once. If, in Hawaii, 27 percent of the residents are Japanese, 15 percent Filipino, and 10 percent Chinese, it does not that follow that 52 percent of the population belong to one of these groups since there could easily be a certain amount of overlap such that some persons are being counted more than once.

Dealing with the Scotch-Irish Combination

The treatment of one of the mixed combinations, the Scotch-Irish, is especially problematic. As the Census Bureau itself observed:

> The response Scotch-Irish can refer to the unique single-ancestry group from Northern Ireland or to the multiple-ancestry group (both Scotch and Irish ancestry). Since the unique single response could not be distinguished from the multiple response, Scotch-Irish was treated as a multiple origin group and tabulated in both categories "Scotch" and "Irish." . . . It will never be possible, however, to determine whether respondents intended to report a single response or a multiple-ancestry response.[19]

The Census Bureau procedure was also followed in this monograph, although on further reflection it may be questionable. The number of mixed persons reporting Scottish and Irish ancestry in that order is 4.7 times larger than the number giving the response in the opposite order,

[19]U.S. Bureau of the Census, "Ancestry of the Population," p. 6.

an extraordinary difference unmatched by any other combination examined.[20] This suggests that much of the response is of people who are really picking a single group, the Scotch-Irish. Accordingly, classifying all people reporting those two groups in that order as belonging to a single ethnic population, the Scotch-Irish, may be more accurate than treating them as two separate groups.

Clarifying Terminology

We sometimes use the terms "European" and "white" interchangeably just for stylistic purposes. In fact, "white" is not the same as "European," although it is common enough to encounter their everyday usage as synonyms. It is true that the vast majority of persons who describe themselves as white on the race question also report a European ancestry. However, that only reflects the enormous European migration to the United States. Obviously, most persons answering "Canadian" to the ancestry question are white, and a fair number of persons reporting various Spanish origins (including Mexicans) also describe themselves as white. Further, there are significant segments of the Middle Eastern population who are white.

Likewise, we use the term "ethnic" at times in a restricted sense, applied to various white or European groups, a not uncommon usage that is followed here for easy communication. However, the reader should keep in mind—census procedures notwithstanding—that there is no reason for applying the term "race" to blacks, Asians, or virtually any other group in the United States. It is equally appropriate to call such populations "ethnic groups." In terms of the classical meaning of race, cocker spaniels and German shepherds are races; blacks, whites, and so on, are not. However, it is the case that groups defined as nonwhite in racial terms have historically been at a disadvantage in their treatment in the United States.

Much will be said later in this volume about the "American" response to the ethnic ancestry question. We find it to be an extremely interesting response—all the more so because it was discouraged by the Census Bureau and tended to be ignored in their cross-tabulations—and leads us to speculate later about the future of ethnic groups in the United States. At any rate, "American" was recorded by the Census Bureau when it was the only response given; any combinations of American and some other group—for example, Mexican American or Italian

[20]Based on an analysis of 1979 CPS data.

American were recorded as single-ancestry responses of Mexican and Italian, respectively. Finally, the "White/Caucasian" response is reported separately in most of our tables, although it is not that frequent in number, because the census includes within that category a number of responses that we find people are curious about: Anglo, Anglo-Saxon, Appalachian, Aryan, Hillbilly, Swamp Yankee, WASP, White.

Other Ethnic/Racial Information in the 1980 Census

The ancestry question, asked in a random sample of approximately 19 percent of the nation's housing units, is not the only source of ethnic and racial information in the 1980 census. There is also a race question which asks, "Is this person?" and then gives some specific choices, such as White, Black or Negro, Japanese, Chinese, etc. It is called a "race" question by the Census Bureau, although the term was not used in the actual question (it had been in the 1970 census and in other earlier censuses).[21] This Census Bureau practice is unfortunate because labeling such response categories as Korean, Vietnamese, and American Indian as races is no more justifiable than referring to Danes, Swedes, and Norwegians as races—a practice which certainly has historical roots in the United States, but which stopped long ago.[22]

Another relevant question asks, "Is this person of Spanish/Hispanic origin or descent?" The choices are:

No (not Spanish/Hispanic)
Yes, Mexican, Mexican-Amer., Chicano
Yes, Puerto Rican
Yes, Cuban
Yes, other Spanish/Hispanic

Obviously, there is a certain amount of overlap in the wording of this question and the general one for ethnic ancestry. Indeed, we could make a case for including all of the Spanish/Hispanic information in one basic ancestry question—except for the fact that the Spanish/Hispanic question provides specific response categories rather than depending on an open-ended ancestry response. The Spanish/Hispanic question was introduced a decade before the ethnic ancestry item, and it yields larger counts of these groups (a fact that may be attractive to some interested

---

[21]U.S. Bureau of the Census, "Ancestry of the Population," pp. 8–9.
[22]See, for example, Oscar Handlin, *Race and Nationality in American Life* (Garden City, NY: Doubleday Anchor Books, 1957), pp. 83–6.

parties regardless of the technical reasons for its occurrence), and provides an official special recognition. The census is a political event, as well as a demographic and legal product of the federal government. As such, there are pressures operating on the Census Bureau in terms of the subjects covered and the construction of the questions.[23]

The census has designated the "race" item as the "primary" source of data for whites, blacks, American Indians, Eskimos and Aleuts, and Asian and Pacific Islanders. The Spanish/Hispanic-origin question is designated by the census as the primary source for those groups. For some ethnic and racial groups, the results obtained from one of these questions differ substantially from those obtained from the ancestry item. In those cases, three questions are raised about such discrepancies: What causes them? Which figure should be used? Do these discrepancies suggest that the new ancestry question in the census is seriously flawed?

The most significant discrepancy is in the American black response. In 1980, 26.5 million people reported themselves as black on the race item, but only 21 million identified themselves as Afro-American or black on the ancestry item. The exact source of this discrepancy is not known, but it is probably due to a sizable number of blacks omitting a response to the ancestry question since they had already indicated they were black on the race question which occurs earlier in the census. This difficulty is resolved in this study through a simple and pragmatic approach; all persons were classified as "black" if they either checked off "Black or Negro" on the race item or described themselves as such on the ancestry item. Since almost all of the persons indicating the latter had also indicated black on the race item, this total is not very different from what is obtained from relying on the race item alone, but it is harmonious with the ancestry item. For those blacks (in either sense) who indicated some white ancestry as well on the ancestry item, we included them in both the black and other ethnic ancestry counts. These increments are modest but consistent with the goal of not interfering with the self-description of respondents and, moreover, they reflect mixing that has occurred from the very outset of slavery in the New World.

As for the discrepancies between the numbers obtained through the Spanish/Hispanic item and the ancestry question (examined in Chapter 2), several factors lead us to use the latter. Obviously, all things being equal, we prefer the ancestry item, simply in the interests of consistency. Moreover, although the number of Latino responses is larger in

[23]See, for example, Harvey M. Choldin, "Statistics and Politics: The 'Hispanic Issue' in the 1980 Census," *Demography* 23 (1986): 403–18.

the Spanish/Hispanic item than in the ancestry question, evidence gathered in 1982 indicates a certain amount of overreporting of Spanish/Hispanic responses in the former question (93 percent of blacks reporting Mexican origin and 33 percent of whites reporting Mexican origin were rejected by the Census Bureau in a postenumeration survey of Mexican responses in certain selected parts of the nation).[24] This, of course, excludes errors for those who were initially judged as acceptable under the edit rules and hence not subject to a follow-up. Of course there is an opposite type of error that was not considered in the 1982 study—namely, those not reporting Mexican origin, but who might have been labeled Mexican by other criteria. Further, the error rate may not have been as high for those living in states with major Mexican populations. But the point is simply that a larger number is not necessarily an indicator of greater accuracy—unless a purely political position is taken whereby size of response is itself a measure of accuracy.

The smaller number giving a Spanish response in the ancestry question could also reflect several other factors. First, a respondent of mixed origins (one or more of them being Spanish), might list other ancestries first, or even instead of, Spanish origin. If a Spanish ancestry was given third, it would not be included since none of the 17 triples includes a combination with one of the Spanish groups. Second, since the Spanish question comes earlier in the questionnaire than does the general ancestry question, some respondents may well have felt that they had answered the question or at least that the question did not apply to the Spanish elements of their ancestry.[25] Finally, the Spanish-origin item is not open-ended, and hence responses are not elicited through a comparable procedure to that obtained from the ancestry question. Although instructions to respondents are similar in the two questions (emphasis on identification, nationality group, lineage, or country of birth), the two items differ in a critical way. In the Spanish question, the respondent is given a set of specific choices and asked to respond to them; in the ancestry item, the respondent is given a blank line and told to fill it in. Therefore, the ancestry item requires a somewhat stronger degree of attachment to one of the Spanish groups than does the Spanish item

[24]See U.S. Bureau of the Census, *1980 Census of Population*, Supplementary Report, "Persons of Spanish Origin by State: 1980," PC80-5-7 (Washington, DC: U.S. Government Printing Office, 1982b), table E3.

[25]It would be a useful experiment to examine the Spanish/Hispanic results that would be obtained on the ancestry question if no special Spanish/Hispanic question is first asked. In similar fashion, if the substantially smaller number of black responses to the ancestry item reflects their earlier response to the race question—as is currently suspected—this, too, could be tested by experimenting with a second version of the questionnaire in which the race item is omitted.

simply because the former does not point the respondent in a certain direction. In that regard, the Spanish/Hispanic results obtained through the ancestry question are more consistent with the remainder of the ethnic data. At any rate, the use of ancestry data to determine the Spanish/Hispanic groups involves excluding people who should be included (and were in the separate question) counterbalanced by the exclusion of people who should not be classified as Spanish/Hispanic by the criteria used in the general ancestry approach (and who were by this criterion incorrectly included in the special question). Since the numbers falling into each circumstance are unknown, the simplest solution is to be consistent with the general ancestry item.[26]

There is also a major discrepancy between the American Indian count obtained from the race item (1.4 million) and the ancestry item (6.7 million). The ancestry item yields the larger response because there are many people who have some American Indian ancestry but who are functioning in the society as whites. As a consequence, they check off white on the race question—rather than Indian—but then indicate Indian ancestry in the later question. There is nothing inappropriate when whites indicate an American Indian ancestry in response to the ethnic origin question. Essentially, a narrower and broader definition of American Indian exists; the choice between them cannot be made on the basis of which is generally better—rather the choice has to be made in terms of the appropriateness for a given purpose. It is critical that a researcher be clear about what the goals are, decide accordingly, and then not be confused by the data set.[27] Again, consistent with the intent of the ancestry item, we have adopted the ancestry definition of American Indian. Thus, we include people who report at least some American Indian ancestry. As is the case for those reporting German ancestry, the magnitude and nature of their identification should be an empirical question, not the basis for deciding whether the respondent should be so classified.

[26]The preference given for the Spanish/Hispanic question by the Bureau of the Census at the moment has to be seen as a political decision as much as any other. It does increase the total number of persons in the country who are of Spanish origin. However, from a scientific perspective, the basic question is really the same as that intended for the remaining groups in the country and measured via the ancestry question. In order to reach a scientific basis for deciding which question is better for measuring these specific groups, it would be necessary to develop appropriate criteria for deciding what a "correct" answer is and then determine which of the two questions generates the least number of errors—and both types of errors have to be considered: inclusion of respondents who should not be listed as Spanish/Hispanic, as well as omission of those who should be included.

[27]For example, Richard D. Alba and Reid M. Golden, "Patterns of Ethnic Marriage in the United States," Social Forces 65 (1986): 202–23, treat American Indian data from the ancestry question as if this is essentially a nonwhite population. However, the vast majority of persons defined as "American Indian" are white.

Finally, for the various Asian groups, there are relatively small differences between the counts obtained from the race and the ancestry questions. Notwithstanding the census preference, we have elected to use the tabulations based on ancestry since they are consistent with the general data set. Moreover, the ancestry question should prove superior in the decades ahead if there is substantial intermarriage among different Asian groups or between Asians and whites. As is the case for the Spanish/Hispanic question the "race" question does not adopt well to mixes since both questions instruct the respondent to fill only one circle.

The 1979 Current Population Survey

The same 1980 ancestry question was also asked in 1979, as part of the Current Population Survey (CPS). There are some substantial differences in the results, even though the surveys are only one year apart. The Census Bureau noted that (1) more people reported multiple ancestry in 1979 than 1980 (38 versus 31 percent); (2) twice as many persons in 1980 reported single English ancestry than in 1979 (23.7 versus 11.5 million); (3) in general, the numbers reporting multiple origins dropped between 1979 and 1980 for the early European groups, such as Irish, Scottish, German, English, Dutch, and French, and for American Indians.

The Bureau of the Census has two speculations about the cause of these discrepancies.[28] First, the 1979 survey used interviewers to administer the questionnaire (unlike the census which uses a mailout-mailback approach), which may have increased the chances of people reporting multiple origins. Second, English was given greater emphasis in the 1980 census; the ancestry question immediately followed a question on language which gave prominence to the term "English," and English was the second example listed under the ancestry question (the 1979 CPS gave no examples).

In addition to these factors, we speculate that the drop-off in multiple-origin responses is due to their discouragement in the 1980 census—relative to 1979—and the possible neglect or ignorance of written instructions in the 1980 census as opposed to the instructions given by the trained interviewers themselves in the 1979 CPS. Regarding the first issue, none of the 16 examples given under the 1980 question were en-

[28]U.S. Bureau of the Census, *Statistical Abstract of the United States: 1980* (Washington, DC: U.S. Government Printing Office, 1984), p. 5.

tries that would have been coded as "multiples" by the Census Bureau. The respondent had to read the specific instructions (a step encouraged for those uncertain how to report ancestry) and then find the last sentence in the first paragraph indicating: "Persons who are of more than one origin and who cannot identify with a single group should print their multiple ancestry (for example, German-Irish)." Even here, the instructions are to give multiple origins *only* if respondent cannot *identify* with one group. By contrast, instructions issued to the trained enumerators in the 1979 CPS are receptive to multiple-ancestry responses. The introductory paragraph indicates: "The answer does not have to be a single ancestry. Multiple ancestries are acceptable and are to be entered in the space provided."[29]

Other evidence exists which supports our conjecture that special guidelines had more of an impact in 1979 because they were read by the trained interviewers, whereas the 1980 instructions were less likely to have an impact because they depended on the initiative of the subject. In 1980, a respondent had to get to the last line in the instruction guide in order to learn that "a religious group should not be reported as a person's ancestry." By contrast, interviewers in the 1979 CPS were instructed to "ask for country of origin or nationality group" if a respondent gave a religious group. There are only 195,000 persons in the unclassifiable category in the 1979 CPS (which includes religious and other responses), whereas there are 1.8 million in the 1980 census, when respondents had to go out of their way to learn not to use religion, a difference of somewhat more than 1.5 million. Moreover, and relevant to the discussion of Jews and Russians earlier, there were about 700,000 more persons of Russian ancestry reported in the 1979 CPS than in the 1980 census. This reversal is exactly what one would have expected since, in 1979, interviewers would have urged Jewish respondents to give an alternative whereas it would not have been so obvious in 1980 that Jewish was an inappropriate response. Of course, this hardly accounts for all of the gap, but this decline in the number of Russians is actually in the opposite direction from that experienced by a number of other European groups; for example, there were about 400,000 more Italians in 1980 than in 1979 and 200,000 more Ukrainians in the latter period. In the ethnic case, these results suggest that instructions destined for the respondent lose, at the very least, a substantial part of their impact.

At this point, it is impossible to tell which is the "better" enumeration, although our suspicions favor the 1979 data. However, for the

[29]U.S. Bureau of the Census, *November 1979 CPS Interviewer's Instructions*, CPS Interviewer's Memorandum no. 79-18 (Washington, DC: U.S. Bureau of the Census, 1979), p. 7.

most part, only modest differences exist in the numbers enumerated for a given group (likewise only slight differences exist between their 1979 and 1980 geographic distributions). As a consequence, the 1980 data are used throughout because of the larger sample sizes involved. The only exceptions are the tabulations by three generations, available only in the 1979 CPS. Also, for the broad population data, we favor the 1979 percentage mixed for the English ancestry group.[30]

An Evaluation of the 1980 Ancestry Question

In evaluating the ancestry question, we have two basic concerns: How well does it measure what it seeks to measure? Is what it seeks to measure an appropriate goal?

As for the first question of validity, it is impossible to determine how accurately the ancestry question measures what it is intended to measure. The ancestry reported by a sample of subjects in the 1980 census was matched in the Census Reinterview Study with their responses to a special postenumeration survey of the birthplaces of their ancestors on both sides.[31] Although the postenumeration survey yields a fairly close correspondence for many of the ancestral responses in the 1980 census, in our estimation the test is less than fully adequate. The discrepancies between birthplace and ethnic ancestry discussed earlier are not a problem since they actually operate against finding a high level of consistency. But there are two key issues of concern. First, the construction of the census question itself contains certain ambiguities and inconsistencies that make it impossible always to decide if the responses are appropriate or not. This is discussed below in detail, but obviously a follow-up question in the postenumeration survey does not quite get at this issue. Second, the procedure is biased in favor of finding a match-up; for those reporting mixed ancestry on the census question and/or more than one country of origin in the postenumeration survey, it was considered a satisfactory result if any of the census responses matched any of the reinterview responses. Thus, a match-up means that there is some connection between the two responses, but how much is not known for those giving multiple responses in either survey. Since multiple responses are quite common, this is not a trivial issue.

The relatively favorable results from the postenumeration survey

---

[30]The percentage mixed among those who report English origins declined from 71.3 in 1979 to 52.1 in 1980; whereas the respective figures are 66.8 and 63.5 for Germans, 77.7 and 74.3 for Irish, and 83.2 and 77.7 for Dutch.

[31]U.S. Bureau of the Census, 1986, pp. 38–40, 102.

are not to be taken as strong evidence that the ancestry question is valid; on the other hand, discrepancies between the ancestry counts for some groups and those obtained from the Spanish/Hispanic or "race" question should not be attributed to inadequacies in the ancestry question. For reasons discussed earlier, there are no grounds for assuming that the validity of the ancestry item is questionable when its results differ from those obtained with the other items.

Conceptual Issues and the Ancestry Question

There are four ways of viewing each subject's ethnic origin or ancestry.[32] (1) What are the true ancestral roots of the respondent if we could trace them back through time to a given year—say, 1500—or a given event—say, when each ancestor reached the New World? (2) What does the respondent believe his/her ancestry to be? (3) With what origin(s) does the respondent identify? (4) What ancestry do others attribute to the respondent—for example, when governmental bodies classify and label people or when ethnicity is attributed to persons on the basis of their surname? This is a complex matter, but presumably all four of these dimensions are associated with one another in varying degrees. The strength of these associations need not remain fixed over time, or even between places. They probably become progressively weaker in a social system where assimilation occurs as persons are increasingly removed in generations from the base year to which ancestry is being traced. In that respect, the association between the true ancestral roots and any of the other three ways of measuring ancestry should be progressively weaker, albeit always positive.

Since the typical respondent in the United States and many other societies will not normally "know" his/her roots in the sense of having anything remotely like documentary evidence, obviously the subject can respond to such a question only in terms of his/her beliefs about them. However, for the purposes of conceptual clarity, the census question should not needlessly confuse these four different responses—even though the respondents will typically be affected by the other dimensions. In other words, true roots can be most closely approximated by asking the respondent to indicate what they are. Self-identification is a separate dimension; identification imposed by others is yet another pathway, not particularly appropriate in the United States in 1980, although it was used in the past for certain ambiguous situations. At one

[32]For a fuller discussion, see Stanley Lieberson, "Unhyphenated Whites in the United States," *Ethnic and Racial Studies* 8 (January 1985b): 159–80.

22

time, for example, persons were officially defined as "black" rather than "white" even when their predominant origins were overwhelmingly European and without regard to their own dispositions. Although each dimension will be imperfectly measured, it will be even *more* imperfect if the dimensions are confused and mixed in the structure of the question or in the instructions provided with the question.

The basic 1980 question appears to be directed toward obtaining each respondent's best answer to true roots: "What is this person's ancestry?" It is a bit weak in not specifying the time period or point of origin; for example, the 1981 Canadian census asks, "To which ethnic or cultural group did you or your ancestors belong on first coming to this continent?"[33] However, the instruction guide does have a reference to country prior to arrival in the United States. This is not a satisfactory substitute for a more precise initial question because those reading the instructions will not be a random sample of respondents and, moreover, may well be only a small proportion of relevant respondents.

More distressing is the first sentence in the instruction guide's discussion of the ancestry question: "Print the ancestry group with which the person *identifies*" (italics are those of the Census Bureau). This is clearly an invitation not to respond in terms of what one believes one's true roots to be, as implied by the initial census question, "What is this person's ancestry?" Rather, if the respondent is uncertain about it, the Census Bureau seems to be implying that he/she try a different tack, namely, ethnic identification. The only virtue of this question is to reduce the population falling into the "No response" or "Unknown" categories. But it is at the expense of fusing two basic questions that should be given separately. Moreover, if there is an interest in the ancestral roots of the nation's population and the social conditions associated with each ancestry, people who do not know their roots are of considerable interest. Statistics Canada, in contrast to the Census Bureau, intentionally avoided using an identification and/or affiliation conception of ethnicity.[34]

On this score, the census question is inferior to the revised ethnic question used by NORC in its yearly General Social Survey; it asks respondents, "From what countries or part of the world did your ancestors

[33]Australian Bureau of Statistics, *The Measurement of Ethnicity in the Australian Census of Population and Housing* (Fyshwick, A.C.T.: Canberra Reprographics, 1984), pp. 73–75. This publication also has an excellent review of the ethnic question used by a number of nations, as well as important experiments tried in Australia. "Continent" is rather undesirable for the U.S. Census since it would eliminate Mexican as an acceptable response and, if taken literally, would cause problems for indigenous peoples.

[34]John M. Kralt, "Ethnic Origin in the Canadian Census, 1871–1981," in W. R. Petryshyn, ed., *Changing Realities: Social Trends Among Ukrainian Canadians* (Edmonton, Alberta: Canadian Institute of Ukrainian Studies, 1980).

come?" and records up to three different groups, in the order mentioned. On the other hand, the question emphasizes *country* of origin rather than *ethnic* origin, a procedure that might cause problems for those persons whose ethnicity is not coterminous with political nation. Of special appeal is a separate question, which asks about the country toward which the respondent feels closest.[35] Hence origin and identification are not confused or pooled. This is not the case for an earlier NORC ethnic question which refused to accept multiple origins, instead asking such respondents to indicate which country they felt closer to—a procedure that probably confused origin and identification even more than does the census approach.[36] In the case of the census, it is probably helped somewhat because identification is not mentioned except in the special instruction sheet and hence many people never read it; also the census does not request multiple-origin persons to choose and, therefore, does not force the question into an identification issue as quickly as did NORC.[37]

Substantive Sources of "Difficulty"

In discussing the validity and reliability of the ancestry question, difficulties created by inadequate questionnaire construction, coding procedures, interviewer effects, and the like, must be distinguished from problems that are caused, instead, by ongoing social phenomena. The first source of difficulty involves technical issues of one sort or another; the second is a substantive matter dealing with the nature of ethnicity and tells us something about the society. The ethnic question in the census is a mixture of both—a design that is not entirely satisfactory, coupled .vith a social phenomenon that guarantees that there cannot be a fully adequate question, if by "adequate" we mean results that show a level of reliability and clarity comparable to questions on year of birth

[35]National Opinion Research Center, *General Social Surveys, 1972–1986: Cumulative Codebook* (Chicago: NORC, 1986), p. 49.

[36]National Opinion Research Center, *General Social Surveys, 1972–1980: Cumulative Codebook* (Chicago: NORC, 1980), p. 41.

[37]The ethnic question used in the National Election Study also avoids the confusion between origin and identification, asking separate questions on these matters—Center for Political Studies, *American National Election Study, 1984 Appendix: Notes and Questionnaire* (Ann Arbor, MI: Inter-university Consortium for Political and Social Research, 1986), questions Y52 and Y52a. A major difficulty with the ancestry question ("In addition to being American, what do you consider your *main* ethnic group or nationality group?") is that the emphasis is on *main* group. Hence, although multiple group entries are accepted, the wording does not encourage such responses. Also the term "consider" might imply to some respondents an "identification" query rather than an effort to determine the main roots of respondent.

or level of educational attainment. As we shall see, apparent inconsistencies actually are reflecting ethnic processes occurring in the society as well as technical issues about the adequacy of the questions or the enumeration procedures themselves.

There is much to be learned if we move away from the traditional view of ethnic and racial groups as an invariant set of categories, with membership fixed in one simple and correct way over a person's lifetime or even intergenerationally. This means that errors are caused not only by inadequate procedures or intentional distortions by respondents. Such problems exist and are to be avoided in racial and ethnic enumerations with the same intensity as one proceeds with questions on age or marital status or occupation. In addition, the dynamic and fluctuating nature of ethnic and racial membership in the society also operates to create a "problem" for the census taker. And, from our perspective, this is a basic finding about the nature of race and ethnic relations. Consider the English ethnic population in the United Kingdom. At one time their origins consisted of peoples from a variety of groups—for example, Normans, Saxons, Angles, and Danes. If they are now "English" it certainly did not occur in a brief period such that in one year the population would have responded uniformly as English, whereas one year earlier they would have described themselves in the aforementioned detail. Almost certainly there was a period of "error" and inconsistency and flux, and it would have been a great mistake to have chosen to ignore the variation in response. Thus, difficulties in the responses to the ethnic question provide us with information about current ethnic and racial relations in the United States.

Appendix: Detailed Analysis of Russian Data

Among the foreign-born in the United States in 1920 with either a Yiddish or Hebrew mother tongue, nearly three fourths were born in Russia (Poland and Austria were runners-up with about 10 percent each). On the other hand, Yiddish or Hebrew is the mother tongue of nearly 60 percent of immigrants born in Russia, and there is reason to believe that a considerable proportion of the 26 percent reporting Russian are also Jewish.[38] Although this seems to indicate that most Jews were of Russian birth *and* most Russians were Jewish, this is not entirely convincing because Jews arriving from elsewhere in Europe may have been less likely to have a Yiddish mother tongue (say, perhaps

[38]See Niles Carpenter, *Immigrants and Their Children: 1920*, Census Monograph 7 (Washington, DC: U.S. Government Printing Office, 1927), tables 58 and 157.

those of German birth); and earlier Jewish immigration was almost certainly not of Russian origin, and their demographic contribution to the current set of Jews might be larger because of greater length of residence in the country.

The linkage between the Russian ethnic response and Jews can be more directly estimated by using the NORC General Social Survey, (GSS) which does measure both attributes (albeit their ethnic question is somewhat different from that used in the census). As for the cross-tabulation between Russian and religion, we observe (for those aged 20 and over, 1972–1985 GSS) that the majority of persons reporting themselves as Russian were raised as Jews (139/250), but obviously a substantial number were not. Moreover, less than half of those reporting themselves as raised as Jews were listed as Russian (139/400). These results suggest a weaker correspondence between Jews and Russians, but they may reflect certain special conditions which underestimate the correspondence. First, among those Russians not reporting themselves as Jewish, the number indicating they were raised with no religion is relatively large compared with the remainder of the U.S. population. Hence it is at least possible that many of these are—in *ethnic* as opposed to *religious* terms—Jewish. Second, as for the large number of Jews who are not reported as Russian on the ethnic question, it is hard to know how much this reflects the different wording in the NORC procedure, particularly with its emphasis on *identification*.[39]

As a consequence, we tried a simple and direct comparison for a basic socioeconomic variable, the educational attainment of the groups. First, using data gathered by NORC, we can compare the educational distribution of Russians with all other whites. This more or less duplicates the typical approach used with census data. In turn, using the NORC data for Jews, we can then examine the difference found between them and all non-Jewish whites to see if a Russian–non-Russian comparison can serve as a close approximation to what is the correct gap between Jews and non-Jews. The index of Net Difference (ND) is used to summarize the educational gaps; ND determines the outcome that would occur if the educational attainment of every member of one group (X) were to be compared with that for every member of another group (Y). Three possibilities exist: pairings in which both persons have the same educational attainment, pairings in which X exceeds Y, and pairings in which Y has the higher education. The value of ND gives

---

[39]More recently, NORC has changed its question but through much of the period there was considerable emphasis on identification for those indicating multiple countries.

the proportion of all pairings in which X education is higher *minus* the proportion of pairings in which the opposite inequality holds.[40]

The ND for education between Jews and non-Jews (both sexes combined) is .40, which means that if the educational attainment of every non-Jew is compared with that of every Jew, the proportion of pairings in which Jews exceed non-Jews is 40 points greater than the opposite inequality. Assuming that no information on religion exists in GSS, what would be the results if Russians and non-Russians were compared (as would be the practice in the census)? ND favors Russians, but it is only .20, half of the value obtained through a Jewish–non-Jewish comparison. What happens is that a large educational gap exists between Russian Jews and Russian non-Jews (ND is .33), which reduces the overall educational distribution of the Russian population because a substantial minority in the NORC data on Russians are not Jews. The net effect, based on this trial with NORC data on educational attainment, is to suggest that the gaps between Russians and others in the census may well substantially *underestimate* the attainment of Jews relative to the remainder of the population.

[40]For more details about this index, see Stanley Lieberson, "Rank-Sum Comparisons Between Groups," in David Heise, ed., *Sociological Methodology 1976* (San Francisco: Jossey-Bass, 1975).

2

THE ETHNIC AND RACIAL
COMPOSITION
OF THE UNITED STATES

T HE ETHNIC and racial makeup of the United States in 1980 is only one point in a long and continuously changing history of race and ethnic relations in the nation. In order to understand the contemporary composition of the United States, it is necessary to appreciate several key historical features. First, government immigration policies have been very restrictive toward some groups while simultaneously encouraging other groups. Second, the sources of immigration have also varied because of the influences of changing opportunities in the United States, shifts in the push to emigrate in the host countries, and the relative difficulty and cost of transportation. Third, earlier immigrant groups have a greater impact on the current ethnic makeup of the United States than do immigrant groups of comparable size who arrived later. Fourth, differences between groups in their intrinsic rates of natural increase in the United States, as well as in the age and sex composition of the immigrant populations, affect the growth or contraction of a group's relative position in later generations. (An historical examination of ethnic differences in fertility is postponed until Chapter 4.) Finally, the ethnic composition of the United States has also been affected by the groups living in the territories that were conquered, purchased, or otherwise obtained as the nation's boundaries spread outward from its initial beginnings on the Atlantic Coast. Groups such as Puerto Ricans, Mexicans, Spanish, French, Russians, many different American

Indian tribes, Eskimos, and Hawaiians were either brought within the national population or received important numerical increases through various territorial expansions. The last factor requires no elaboration here. But the first three factors, all dealing with various facets of the immigration history of the United States, are central to understanding the present-day ethnic and racial makeup of the United States and how it has changed through the years.

Changing Patterns of Immigration

All nations attempt to exercise some control on the numbers and nature of immigrants allowed to cross their borders. In exercising this control, governments often consider potential immigrants in terms of the existing ethnic and racial composition of the country. Through much of the nation's history, receptivity toward further immigration has had a strongly European tilt: Of the 49 million immigrants who arrived in the United States between 1820 and 1979, nearly three-fourths were from Europe and another 8 percent from Canada. All of Asia (including countries in the Middle East) contributed only 6 percent through 1979, most having arrived since the end of World War II. Mexico has contributed less than 5 percent of all immigrants, and Africa has contributed a scarce 0.3 percent.[1] Blacks provide the most extreme example of immigration barriers. Although slaves were still smuggled in after their legal importation ended in 1807, immigration of free blacks was not encouraged. The growth of the black population in the United States occurred almost entirely through an excess of births over deaths in the nineteenth century, with only modest immigration recorded from either Africa or the West Indies. Until the beginning of this century, there was no decade in which more than 900 immigrants came from Africa or more than 35,000 from the West Indies.[2] Because white growth was also aided by enormous immigration flows during much of the nation's history, the black component of the American population declined from 19 percent in the first census of 1790 to a low of just under 10 percent in 1930 and has increased to about 12 percent in 1980.[3] Asians were also specifically excluded by U.S. immigration law. In an earlier era, there was a relatively brief period when Chinese and Japa-

---

[1]U.S. Bureau of the Census, *Statistical Abstract of the United States: 1980* (Washington, DC: U.S. Government Printing Office, 1983d) p. 91.

[2]U.S. Department of Justice, *1970 Annual Report, Immigration and Naturalization Service* (Washington, DC: U.S. Government Printing Office, 1971), table 13.

[3]Richard T. Schaefer, *Racial and Ethnic Groups*, 2nd ed. (Boston: Little, Brown, 1984), p. 209.

nese were allowed into the United States, but the flow was shut off in 1882 and 1907, respectively, after relatively small numbers had immigrated. Prior to 1970, the largest number of Chinese immigrants reported in a census of the mainland United States was 107,000 in 1890, when they amounted to little more than 1 percent of the foreign-born in the nation; the numerical high point for Japanese prior to World War II was 82,000 in 1920, when they were barely more than 0.5 percent.[4]

Even with respect to European immigrants, white groups that arrived earlier have been apprehensive whenever there have been substantial shifts in the sources of immigrants. Benjamin Franklin was much concerned about what he saw as the growing number of Germans in Pennsylvania; the Irish immigrants of the mid-nineteenth century created an enormous stir, in no small way due to the fears of Catholicism, and were met with open antipathy and severe discrimination.[5] The changing sources of immigration, and the fears precipitated by their presence, began to intensify after 1880, when the Europeans from southern-central-eastern (SCE) Europe started to arrive in substantial numbers.[6] These reactions eventually led, in 1924, to a sharp restriction in the numbers of SCE Europeans allowed entry. The old-new distinction between immigrants from northwestern and SCE Europe is based on the period that a particular category of immigrants first came in sizable numbers, not on those who later followed. Thus, British immigrants arriving in 1910 would be considered "old" whereas Greeks arriving ten years earlier would be considered "new." In reviewing the origins of this distinction, and the conceptual difficulties and inconsistencies, one of the present authors observed:

> There appears to be no formal theory of old-new behavioral differences. Rooted in late nineteenth century nativism and based upon the racist notions then prevalent, the northwestern Europeans were viewed as peoples with a culture closer to Americans, more adaptable, better workers, less likely to provide social problems, and inherently more assimilable than populations from southern, central, and eastern Europe. . . .
>
> There are conceptual difficulties in the old-new dichotomy. For example, several new groups had sizable numbers in the nation long before the 1880's. This would obviously be the case for the Spanish, as well as

[4]Based on U.S. Bureau of the Census, *Historical Statistics of the United States: Colonial Times to 1970*, Bicentennial Edition, pt. 1 (Washington, DC: U.S. Government Printing Office, 1975a), pp. 117–18.

[5]Maldwyn Allen Jones, *American Immigration* (Chicago: University of Chicago Press, 1960), p. 20; Oscar Handlin, *Boston's Immigrants*, rev. and enl. ed. (Cambridge, MA: Belnap Press, 1959).

[6]See Stanley Lieberson, *A Piece of the Pie: Blacks and White Immigrants Since 1880* (Berkeley: University of California Press, 1980), p. 20.

. . . the Bohemians and Poles. By contrast, several Scandinavian and other northwest European countries were both numerically and proportionately more important sources of immigration between 1880 and 1920 than in preceding decades. . . . Germany is included among the old groups whereas Austria is placed with new central European sources.[7]

Nevertheless, these distinctions between European groups, although extremely important, are modest compared with the concerns about non-European groups found through much of the nation's history. After all, the nation remained accessible for a remarkably long period to immigration of Europeans from places quite different from those of the earlier white settlers. Even though the immigration of the newer groups was reduced in 1924 to a point where they would no longer be seen as a threat to the earlier white groups, this was only after those arriving from these newer sources began to reach remarkable numbers. As we have seen, by contrast the tolerance and admission of non-Europeans was minimal.

Even without governmental interference, changes in the sending countries, as well as shifts in the economy of the United States, helped greatly to alter the ethnic composition of immigrants to the nation. In 1850, for example, Ireland and Germany together sent two thirds of the 370,000 immigrants arriving in the United States in that year (Ireland, 44 percent; Germany, 21 percent). By contrast, the remainder of central and eastern Europe sent just 51 immigrants, and Italy sent only 431. There were about 16,000 from the rest of the Americas, of which Canada contributed about 60 percent; the West Indies were of lesser importance, and Mexico provided 597 of the recorded immigrants. China in that year sent 3 and Japan none. The largest number of immigrants—1.3 million—ever to arrive in the nation in a single year arrived in 1907. However, in that year, immigrants from Ireland and Germany were actually smaller in number than they had been 64 years earlier and together amounted to about 6 percent of all immigrants. On the other hand, Italy, Czarist Russia (including also the small Baltic states), and central Europe (excluding Germany) each contributed more than 250,000 immigrants.[8] These shifts reflect changing political, demographic, and economic forces in the sending countries and changing opportunity structures in the United States.

The timing of immigration has an effect on the nation's ethnic composition in profound ways. A given rate of natural increase (excess

[7]Stanley Lieberson, "The Old-New Distinction and Immigrants in Australia," *American Sociological Review* 28 (1968b): 550–65.

[8]Based on U.S. Bureau of the Census, *Historical Statistics*, pt. 1, pp. 105–9.

of births over deaths) for early immigrants to the United States will have more long-term impact on the nation's ethnic composition than will the same rate for a more recent immigrant group of comparable size. This is because the groups which immigrated earlier have had more generations to reproduce in the nation than have the more recent groups. For example, between 1820 and 1979 Italy was the second most important source of immigration to the United States, 5.3 million compared with 7.0 million from Germany. But Italians are the fifth largest white ethnic group in the nation in 1980, with about 25 percent of the number reported as either German or English and about 30 percent of the number of Irish. This is true even though there were about 600,000 fewer Irish than Italian immigrants during the period. The reason is simple enough; the earlier groups had far more time in the United States to grow and multiply beyond their original numbers than do the more recent groups, assuming broadly similar fertility rates and rates of return migration.

There is an additional reason that timing of immigration has a bearing on the ethnic composition of the nation—a factor that becomes increasingly important as the nation grows in number. Through much of the nation's history, the number of immigrants admitted has been rather large relative to the host population at the time. The high point was the first decade of this century, when 8.8 million immigrants were admitted, a rate of 10.4 newcomers per 1,000 residents[9]—that is, one new immigrant admitted per 100 residents during each year of the decade. The rates were nearly as high in the 1850s (9.3), 1880s (9.2), and 1840s (8.4). To be sure, not all immigrants remained in the United States and there were repeat migrants who inflate the figures. Still it is clear that the numbers arriving were very large relative to the host population, and therefore any shifts in the sources of immigrants would have an impact on the ethnic composition of the nation. As the population of the United States grows, however, it takes increasingly larger numbers of immigrants from new sources to have the same impact on the ethnic makeup of the nation. The population at the time of the first census in 1790 was 4 million; it was 23 million in 1850, shortly after the waves from Germany and Ireland had started in substantial numbers; it was 50 million in 1880, a period marking the beginning of a radical increase in migration from SCE Europe; and it was getting close to 230 million people in 1980. In the 1980 census year, there were more than 500,000 recorded legal immigrants, a number matching the increases during the 1880s, but the population is so much larger now that

[9]U.S. Bureau of the Census, *Statistical Abstract*, p. 88.

the ratio of immigrants to total U.S. population is one quarter of the ratio observed then.

Ethnic Composition in 1980

Table 2.1 lists the major ethnic and racial groups in the United States in 1980: first, in descending numbers, the 16 European-origin groups with at least 1 million compatriots; then, the numerically most important non-European groups; and, finally, the most important residual ethnic and racial categories. Wherever appropriate, the data are drawn from the official census counts; otherwise data are based on the 1 percent sample tapes.

By a wide margin, the three most common ancestries are all from northwestern Europe: English and German each reported by nearly 50 million persons, and Irish reported by 40 million.[10] Black occupies fourth place, with 27 million.[11] The next most frequent responses are French (nearly 13 million), and Italian and "American," both given by nearly 12 million persons.[12] If the 200,000 giving "United States" as their ancestry as well as the 650,000 responding "White/Caucasian" are added to the American response, it means that up to 13 million (5.7 percent of the population) are whites giving an essentially new ethnic response, that is, a response that reflects experience since the immigration of their ancestors to the United States. In addition, 20 million people did not report an ancestry (close to 9 percent of the population), which means that about 14.5 percent of the nation's population are whites who are unable or unwilling to report their European origins.[13] Altogether, the number of whites with no avowed sense of any ethnic

[10]The same person will be reported more than once if they are of multiple origins *and* both ancestries are listed in the table. Thus, someone of part German and part Dutch origin will be included for both groups; hence the total number for Table 2.1 is far in excess of the population in the nation. (See Chapter 1 for a discussion of these coding procedures.)

[11]This is slightly in excess of the official census count for blacks based on the "race" question because it includes persons who indicate black ancestry even though they do not call themselves black on the "race" question. The figure is considerably in excess of the number obtained solely by ancestry count because many blacks did not specify an ancestry after indicating that they were black on the earlier question (see Chapter 1).

[12]This is calculated conservatively because the census used this response only if no other ancestry was reported and, additionally, we do not include those respondents who had indicated "black" on the earlier race question.

[13]The number listed as "no response" in Table 2.1 is less than the number of "not reported" in the 1980 census because persons not responding to the ancestry item were excluded if they answered black on the "race" question.

TABLE 2.1
Ethnic and Racial Composition of the United States, 1980
(in thousands)

Ancestry	Number	Percentage of Population
English	49,598	21.9%
German	49,224	21.7
Irish	40,166	17.7
French	12,892	5.7
Italian	12,184	5.4
Scottish	10,049	4.4
Polish	8,228	3.6
Dutch	6,304	2.8
Swedish	4,345	1.9
Norwegian	3,454	1.5
Russian*	3,489	1.5
Czech	1,892	.8
Hungarian	1,777	.8
Welsh	1,665	.7
Danish	1,518	.7
Portuguese	1,024	.5
Black*	26,858	11.9
Mexican	7,693	3.4
Puerto Rican	1,444	.6
Spanish—Other*	4,251	1.9
American Indian	6,716	3.0
American*	11,961	5.3
United States*	216	.1
White/Caucasian*	650	.3
North American Other*	1,243	.5
Other SCE European*	5,869	2.6
Other Northwestern European*	1,993	.9
Middle Eastern/North African*	894	.4
African, Caribbean, Pacific*	1,400	.6
South Asian*	369	.2
Other Asian*	3,255	1.4
No Response*	20,084	8.9
All Other*	1,379	.6

SOURCE: All other data from U.S. Bureau of the Census, *1980 Census of Population,* Supplementary Report, "Ancestry of the Population by State: 1980," PC80-S1-10 (Washington, DC: U.S. Government Printing Office, 1983), table 1.

NOTE: Percentages are of total U.S. population who give the ancestry specified. They sum to more than 100 because of persons who indicate more than one ancestry.

*Derived from 1980 1 percent sample tapes.

ancestry is in excess of all white ancestral responses except for the three largest groups.

In addition to the three specific European ancestries mentioned above, another 13 were selected by at least 1 million people in 1980. However, their numerical size declines rapidly compared with the three most frequent responses. The only remaining ancestries reported by at least 10 million residents are French (nearly 13 million), Italian (12 million), and Scottish (10 million). A quick inspection of these 16 largest European ancestral responses in Table 2.1 makes clear the overwhelming northwestern European character of the white population of the United States. The three largest SCE European responses are Italian, Polish, and Russian (12, 8, and 3.5 million, respectively).[14] All three of these groups together are smaller than any one of the three most commonly reported ancestries. The numerical importance of the largest ethnic groups is apt to be lost when one considers the relative emphasis in the literature on different groups; in particular, the Irish and British groups are studied less frequently than some of the numerically smaller groups.[15] There are many other European groups that we would like to include here and in the analyses to follow, but issues of space and sample size for later analyses restrict our presentation. In particular, Austrians and Greeks are both just under 1 million, and Finns, Lithuanians, Slovaks, and Ukrainians number from about 600,000 to 750,000 in 1980.[16] As is the case for Table 2.1, data are reported in many places for persons in the residual northwestern and SCE European categories.

Although distinctively smaller in number than blacks, Mexicans and American Indians are the next most commonly reported non-European groups indicated in the census (respectively, 7.7 and 6.7 million). As noted in Chapter 1, census figures for various Spanish/Hispanic groups are somewhat lower with the ancestry question than with the

---

[14]Besides the groups included under the "Russian" rubric in the census procedure, codes 140-156—(U.S. Bureau of the Census, *1980 Census of Population and Housing,* Public Use Microdata Samples, Technical Documentation (Washington, DC.: U.S. Government Printing Office, 1983e), app. E, pp. 125, 131—we have included Georgian, Ruthenian (Little Russian, Malo-Russian), Carpathian (Carpatho), Ukrainian, and Belorussian (White Russian). Obviously these should all be treated as separate ethnic groups if the respondents were accurate. But some of the responses are already combined by the census under the "Russian" rubric—for example, Yakut and Tartar. Accordingly, we combined the above groups as well, maintaining only the Armenians as a separate entry. Even here there may be an underestimation of that group if members responded "Russian" to indicate country of origin (see U.S. Bureau of the Census, *1980 Census of Population,* Supplementary Report, "Ancestry of the Population by State: 1980," PC80-51-10 (Washington, DC: U.S. Government Printing Office, 1983a), p. 7.

[15]Thomas J. Archdeacon, "Problems and Possibilities in the Study of American Immigration and Ethnic History," *International Migration Review* 19 (1985): 112–34.

[16]The interested reader can obtain numerical and locational details for a large number of groups by consulting U.S. Bureau of the Census.

Spanish-origin question: The number of Mexicans is smaller by about 1 million, Puerto Ricans by 600,000, and Cubans by about 200,000. Altogether, all persons answering affirmatively in the specific Spanish/Hispanic origin question is 14.6 million, still far less than the number of blacks in the nation. The "Other Spanish" residual category numbers more than 4 million people, including 600,000 Cubans, 171,000 Dominicans, and 156,000 Colombians. But the largest single category of "Other Spanish" are the 2.7 million persons responding as Spanish or Hispanic, and this encompasses a variety of ancestry groups, as well as probable errors.

Data are also given in Table 2.1 for other major ancestry groups, based on the census delineations.[17] Within the Middle Eastern/North African category, the most common ancestry responses are Lebanese (295,000), Armenian (213,000), Iranian (123,000), and Syrian (106,000). Some of these groups have remarkable levels of spatial concentration: 50 percent of all Armenians in the United States reside in either California or Massachusetts; 43 percent of Iranians are located in California or New York. Lebanese and Syrians are less concentrated, although relatively large percentages of the former are found in California, Michigan, New York, and Massachusetts. The next category—"African, Caribbean, Pacific"—combines Subsaharan Africa, non-Spanish peoples living in the Caribbean and Latin America, and those of Pacific origin (American blacks are reported separately). In 1980, Nigerians (48,000) are the largest specific Subsaharan group in the nation. Jamaicans (253,000) and Haitians (90,000) are the largest specific groups in the United States with origins in the non-Spanish parts of the Caribbean and Latin America. Also, the majority of persons in the Pacific category are the 202,000 reporting Hawaiian ancestry, in whole or part. The largest North American group (other than American Indians who are reported separately) are those responding as French Canadians or Canadians. Asia was divided into several subsets by the census; Southwest Asia is a large part of the Middle East and was included along with Africa north of the Sahara in a residual category discussed above. The remainder of Asia was divided into South Asian and Other Asian. The former is essentially the Indian subcontinent, and the 300,000 Asian Indians make up the vast majority of persons shown in Table 2.1 in that category. The larger groups in the Other Asian category are the Chinese (900,000), Filipinos and Japanese (each about 800,000), Koreans (375,000), and Vietnamese (200,000). Although several have continued to increase rapidly since the last census, in 1980 they are all smaller than either the Austrian or Greek groups.

[17]See U.S. Bureau of the Census, *1980 Census,* Public Use Microdata Samples, app. E.

For those interested in the questions of what is the most commonly reported ancestry in the United States, it would be unwise to conclude that the answer is English rather than German. The gap between the two in 1980—374,000—is remarkably small for groups that number about 50 million each. When we consider that the census chose to classify persons as English if they reported their ancestry as "British" or "United Kingdom," such a small difference could easily reflect this questionable classification procedure (it assumes that persons reported as British are only of English origin, rather than of Scottish, Welsh, or Northern Irish ancestry—or some mixture thereof). But even more significant is the discrepancy between the data obtained in the 1979 CPS and the 1980 census. The earlier enumeration yielded 51.6 million German responses and 40 million English responses (the single most important discrepancy between the CPS and the decennial census). If the discrepancy between the CPS and the census reflects even a modest distortion in 1980 due to the prominence of the term "English" in the immediately preceding language question, there would be grounds for concluding that German would be the most commonly reported ancestry in 1980. Also, German ancestry could have been denied during two major wars against Germany—a pattern documented by Ryder[18] for the Canadian census.

On the other hand, there may well be a significant undercount of the English-origin population because of a disproportionate contribution of such people to the "American" response or those who are unable to report any ancestry. Quite likely a sizable segment of the white population reporting themselves as "American" are some sort of British origin—that is, they are disproportionately southern Protestants with at least four generations of residence in the United States.[19] Moreover, since the "triple" entries have somewhat fewer English responses than German responses, the differential use of triples may somewhat inflate the latter group more than the former in the 1980 figures. Finally, if the English-origin population has a longer average residence in the nation than those of German ancestry, the former may well be truly more mixed by now—as opposed to what is recorded in the census. The potential consequences are unclear since it depends on whether English and German differ in being underreported by the descendants of mixed parents. There are some distortions in each direction, and it is difficult to determine their relative impact. In either case, these are self-reported descriptions of ancestry, not what would be ascertained if the true an-

---

[18]Norman B. Ryder, "The Interpretation of Origin Statistics," *Canadian Journal of Economics and Political Science* 21 (1955): 466–79.

[19]Stanley Lieberson, "Unhyphenated Whites in the United States," *Ethnic and Racial Studies* 8 (January 1985b): 159–80.

cestral roots of individuals could be traced. As a consequence, it would be best to simply conclude that English and German are the two most frequently reported ancestries in the nation, but the numbers are too close and/or inconsistent to permit any more precise statement about their relative sizes in the American population.

Earlier Ethnic Composition

The pre-Revolutionary British colonial censuses are of little value for distinguishing between different white groups—although, as Wells observes,[20] race was often enumerated. Moreover, for most of the nation's history since independence, there are no census or survey data giving the ethnic composition of the white population. Two major estimates exist of the white ethnic composition of the United States in 1790, at the time of the first census. Both are based on a classification of the surnames obtained in the original census records. The first estimate, which is believed to be less accurate, reported that about 82 percent of whites in 1790 were of English or Welsh origin, 7 percent Scottish, 6 percent German, 2.5 percent Dutch, 2 percent Irish, 0.6 percent French, and 0.3 percent other and unassigned.[21] The English contribution probably was overestimated because the procedure attributed English ancestry to all names other than those that could be specifically allocated to one of the categories indicated above. It also meant that distortions due to Anglicization of surnames would be ignored.

The results obtained from a second analysis of these data, by the American Council of Learned Societies,[22] that attempted to deal with these objections are shown in Table 2.2. Although the estimate is considerably lower than the previous one, the English are still estimated to be 61 percent of the white population, far in excess of any other group. Indeed, despite the different histories of the former colonies, the English are estimated to be a numerical majority in all but New Jersey and Pennsylvania. Even in those two states, they are the largest single group, albeit barely edging out the Germans in Pennsylvania. The Irish, Germans, and Scots are the next largest white groups, all distinctly smaller

[20]Robert V. Wells, *The Population of the British Colonies in American Before 1776* (Princeton, NJ: Princeton University Press, 1975), p. 267.

[21]U.S. Bureau of the Census, *A Century of Population Growth: 1790–1900* (Washington, DC: U.S. Government Printing Office, 1909), p. 121.

[22]American Council of Learned Societies, "Report of Committee on Linguistic and National Stocks in the Population of the United States," *Annual Report of the American Historical Association, 1931*, vol. 1 (Washington, DC: U.S. Government Printing Office, 1932).

TABLE 2.2

Estimated Nationality Distribution of the White Population, 1790

Area	Total	English	Scottish	Irish		German	Dutch	French	Swedish	Spanish	Unassigned
				Ulster	Free State						
Total States	100.0%	60.9%	8.3%	6.0%	3.7%	8.7%	3.4%	1.7%	0.7%		6.6%
Maine	100.0	60.0	4.5	8.0	3.7	1.3	.1	1.3			21.1
New Hampshire	100.0	61.0	6.2	4.6	2.9	.4	.1	.7			24.1
Vermont	100.0	76.0	5.1	3.2	1.9	.2	.6	.4			12.5
Massachusetts	100.0	82.0	4.4	2.6	1.3	.3	.2	.8			8.4
Rhode Island	100.0	71.0	5.8	2.0	.8	.5	.4	.8	.1		18.6
Connecticut	100.0	67.0	2.2	1.8	1.1	.3	.3	.9			26.4
New York	100.0	52.0	7.0	5.1	3.0	8.2	17.5	3.8	.5		2.9
New Jersey	100.0	47.0	7.7	6.3	3.2	9.2	16.6	2.4	3.9		3.7
Pennsylvania	100.0	35.3	8.6	11.0	3.5	33.3	1.8	1.8	.8		3.9
Delaware	100.0	60.0	8.0	6.3	5.4	1.1	4.3	1.6	8.9		4.4*
Maryland (including the District of Columbia)	100.0	64.5	7.6	5.8	6.5	11.7	.5	1.2	.5		1.7
Virginia (including West Virginia)	100.0	68.5	10.2	6.2	5.5	6.3	.3	1.5	.6		.9
North Carolina	100.0	66.0	14.8	5.7	5.4	4.7	.3	1.7	.2		1.2
South Carolina	100.0	60.2	15.1	9.4	4.4	5.0	.4	3.9	.2		1.4
Georgia	100.0	57.4	15.5	11.5	3.8	7.6	.2	2.3	.6		1.1
Kentucky and Tennessee	100.0	57.9	10.0	7.0	5.2	14.0	1.3	2.2	.5		1.9
Other Areas											
Northwest Territory	100.0	29.8	4.1	2.9	1.8	4.3	.3	57.1			
Spanish, United States	100.0	2.5	.3	.2	.1	.4				96.5	
French, United States	100.0	11.2	1.6	1.1	.7	8.7		64.2		12.5	

SOURCE: U.S. Bureau of the Census, *Historical Statistics of the United States: Colonial Times to 1970, Bicentennial Edition,* pt. 2 (Washington, DC: U.S. Government Printing Office, 1975b), p. 1168.

NOTE: Maine was a part of Massachusetts until it became a state in 1820.

*Corrected figure; does not agree with source.

than the English (9.7, 8.7, and 8.3 percent of whites). The Irish contribution may be overstated with these figures because some segment of the Irish are actually Scotch-Irish, particularly among those from Ulster (there were also English-Irish emigrants). Surname analysis indicates that the Scotch-Irish population of Ulster were more likely to emigrate than were the Celtic-Irish, and the English-Irish occupied an intermediate position. The American Council of Learned Societies estimated that 6.3 percent of the population was of "Celtic-Irish stock" in 1790.[23] Nevertheless, it is reasonable to conclude from these estimates that perhaps 5 percent or so of the white population in 1790 were Irish, as opposed to either English- or Scotch-Irish. Finally, the figures in Table 2.2 appropriately refer to the ethnic makeup of the white population. If the sizable black component were included in the calculations, not only is it by far the second largest group in the United States in 1790 (just short of 20 percent), but the English component of the entire population is actually 49 percent. Of course, the combined groups from the British Isles are well in excess of half.

Table 2.2 shows substantial differences between states in their ethnic makeup. Some of these locational patterns are still observed in 1980. The Germans, for example, are about 39 percent of the population of Pennsylvania in 1980 reporting any specific ancestry, a figure far in excess of their position in the remainder of the Northeast. Similarly, the Scots were relatively concentrated in the South Atlantic states in 1790, and they are still somewhat more concentrated at present in that area, particularly in the Carolinas (albeit virtually none for Georgia). On the other hand, the early position of the Dutch in New York and New Jersey is not at all the same at present, and the relatively large number of Swedes once found in Delaware is no longer significant; in 1980 there were only 7,426 persons with Swedish ancestry in that state. (The relatively large percentage of Swedes found in the Delaware population of 1790 reflects the settlement in 1638 of what is now Wilmington by a Swedish mercantile company coupled with the presence of only 46,000 whites in Delaware in 1790. There was only modest emigration from Sweden prior to the loss of the colony to the Dutch in 1655; the estimate works out to only about 4,000 persons of Swedish origin in Delaware in 1790.)[24]

Of particular interest are the changes since 1790 in the reported ethnic composition of whites in the nation. Of the major early groups, only the groups from Great Britain have experienced a decline, but it is

[23]American Council of Learned Societies, pp. 115–18.
[24]Historical materials on the Swedes based on Ulf Beijbom, "Swedes," in Stephan Thernstrom, ed., *Harvard Encyclopedia of American Ethnic Groups* (Cambridge, MA: Belnap Press, 1980), p. 971.

one of spectacular magnitude. Although about 60 percent of the white population were English in 1790, only about 27 percent of the white population reported this ancestry in 1980. Likewise, Scots have declined from about 8 to 5 percent during this span. Assuming that those either not knowing their ancestry or giving "American" as a response include a sizable segment from the British Isles, the decline is overestimated in terms of what the true origins are of the American population. But even allowing for such a sizable distortion, the drop in the English component reflects a true shift in the ethnic makeup of the white population.

None of the increases in specific groups is comparable to the decline of the English, but they are still quite substantial (this means that there was more diversity among the gainers than among the losers). Germans increased from 9 to 26 percent during this span, the Irish from 10 to 21 percent, and the French from 2 to 7 percent. Since immigration from France was modest during the period (750,000), this reflects the acquisition of French territories, in particular the Louisiana Purchase of 1803 and the movement of French Canadians into the United States. Swedes also gained, from an estimated 0.7 percent in 1790 to 2.3 percent in 1980. The Dutch remain more or less at about the same relative size they were in 1790. As for gains among groups that were small in number in 1790, one need simply look down the list of leading groups in 1980 in Table 2.1; Italians, Poles, Norwegians, Russians, Czechs, Hungarians, Welsh, Danish, and Portuguese. All of these were too small in number to be singled out in the estimates for 1790, but they are now among the ancestries most frequently mentioned by whites in 1980. Finally, the data for the Spanish are not comparable, but persons in the United States with at least some Spanish roots in 1980 are far greater than the 0.7 percent estimated for 1790.

Another significant estimate of the population is that provided for 1920 by the Secretaries of State, Commerce, and Labor in connection with the immigration quotas of 1924.[25] However, in light of the results obtained for 1980, we are inclined to view many of these estimates with suspicion. For example, they estimated that 41.4 percent of the white population had origins in the United Kingdom, 11.2 percent in Ireland, and 16.3 percent in Germany. Since immigration from all three of these sources (indeed most European sources) has been relatively modest since that period, it is hard to believe that the distributions for these three major groups could change so radically from that period through differences in natural growth and modest immigration. Thus, for certain key groups, it appears more or less impossible for the 1980 census and the

---

[25]Reported in Warren Thompson and P.K. Whelpton, *Population Trends in the United States* (New York: McGraw-Hill, 1933), p. 91.

1920 estimates both to be reasonably correct. In particular, if Germans in 1980 roughly equal the population originating in England and if the Irish are not far behind either of these groups, there is no way that the estimate for 1920 could be reasonably accurate. Although this is hardly conclusive evidence, we should keep in mind that this estimate for 1920 was developed in order to influence the immigration quotas at a time when there was considerable agitation about the European sources of immigration.[26]

The English, as we noted earlier, are no longer the numerical majority of the whites in the United States—indeed, they are far from it. Still, they remain the first or second largest group in the United States. Moreover, their impact on the American people has hardly disappeared. This reflects three key factors. First, the non-English population did not arrive in full force overnight. As a consequence, the native white population always outnumbered the newcomers at any given time. As long as the earlier non-English groups were largely assimilated to the ways of the dominant English, progressive changes in the ethnic and racial makeup of the population did not have the same consequence as would be expected solely on the basis of the numbers.[27] Second, the ethnic and racial changes in the composition of the country were largely due to the introduction of migrant groups from Europe and elsewhere, who initially were politically and economically subordinate. Compared with subordinate *indigenous* groups, immigrants are far more likely to assimilate to the existing social order, accepting its fundamentals and seeking only to reform rather than revolutionize it.[28] Third, the forces necessary for the establishment of English traditions in the United States are not necessarily symmetrical, such that the removal of these demographic conditions does not necessarily lead to a reversal of outcomes.[29] That is, social institutions and customs have a life of their own and will tend to continue long after their initial causes are removed. Clearly, the United States reflects the influence of far more than the English settlers and descendants. On the other hand, the influence of the English is greater than their present-day numbers suggest, simply because of their numer-

[26]The Johnson-Reed Act established that these estimates of the national origins in 1920 of the white population would be the basis for immigrant quotas after 1927. See John Higham, *Strangers in the Land* (New Brunswick: NJ: Rutgers University Press, 1955), p. 324.

[27]The analysis of group continuity through blood relationship by Simmel is relevant here; Georg Simmel, "Social Interaction as the Definition of the Group in Time and Space," in Robert E. Park and Ernest W. Burgess, eds., *Introduction to the Science of Sociology* (Chicago: University of Chicago Press, 1921), pp. 351–52.

[28]Stanley Lieberson, "A Societal Theory of Race and Ethnic Relations," *American Sociological Review* 26 (1961): 902–10.

[29]Stanley Lieberson, *Making It Count* (Berkeley: University of California Press, 1985a), chap. 4.

ical and political predominance in the early years of the nation. This is
reflected in a variety of institutions such as the law and political heritage, in cultural features such as language and the measurement system,
and in a wide variety of other ways.

Timing of Arrival, and Mixed Origins

Generation

The nation's population in 1979 is not only overwhelmingly of native birth, it is also primarily a population with at least three generations' residence in the nation; 81 percent were born in the United States
of parents who were themselves *both* born in the nation. The second
generation in 1979 was only 11 percent of the population (persons born
in the United States, but with one or both parents of foreign birth), and
5 percent were foreign-born.[30] These figures reflect the decline of immigration relative to the population of the nation; in the first few decades of this century, about one third of the population were either immigrants or their American-born offspring.[31] For some groups, virtually
everyone in 1980 is of at least third generation: 98 percent of American
Indians, 96 percent of blacks, and 94 percent of Puerto Ricans (it would
be even higher for American Indians if analysis were restricted to persons of unmixed Indian origins). Of particular note, 98 percent of the
population indicating "American" ancestry also have at least three generations' residence, supporting the notion that this type of response is
especially likely among those of long-standing residence in the nation.
(Using NORC survey data, we find that 97 percent of whites unable to
name an ancestry or choosing "American" are of at least four generations' residence in the United States—well in excess of the 57 percent
of the population for the nation as a whole.[32]) Also, at least 90 percent
of most of the old European groups specified in Table 2.3 are of at least
three generations' residence in the country (the figures are in the middle
to low 80s for Scandinavians and Swiss). The concentration of immigration in more recent periods for the SCE European groups is reflected in
their generational distribution: They range from about 70 percent at

---

[30]Data for 1979 must be used here in order to separate the population of U.S. birth
into those whose parents were foreign-born and those whose parents were U.S.-born. The
1980 census distinguishes only between the population of foreign and U.S. birth (the first
as opposed to the second generation).

[31]See Niles Carpenter, *Immigrants and Their Children: 1920*, Census Monograph 7
(Washington, DC: U.S. Government Printing Office, 1927), p. 5.

[32]Lieberson, "Unhyphenated Whites," p. 175.

least three generations' residence (Poles and Czechs) to 45 percent (Greeks). Mexicans were even less likely to be of at least three generations' residence in 1979—41 percent—followed by even lower figures for the three largest Asian groups. However, the Japanese (whose immigration was more concentrated in the period before World War II) exceed the other two Asian groups by a considerable margin.

Timing of Arrival

Another indicator of length of residence can be derived from each group's immigration history in the United States, coupled with the estimates of their size in 1790. For some of the groups, we can obtain the number immigrating from a specified homeland in each decade from 1820 through 1970. In addition, we also employ the estimated number of each ethnic group who were living in the United States in 1790. Combining all of these figures, we obtain a frequency distribution for each of the groups shown in Table 2.3. Employing the Index of Net Difference (ND), we compare the distribution of each group with the distribution for the population from England and Wales. A negative value indicates that the group overall had a more recent migration-settlement pattern; a positive value (not found for any of the groups) would occur if the population's settlement pattern was earlier than the English.[33] Of course, we have no breakdown for migration prior to 1790 and the period between 1790 and 1820—to say nothing about differentials in return migration and fertility and the imperfect overlap between ethnic origin and the designated countries of origin. With these cautions in mind, the ND values vary widely in the crudely estimated recency of the groups: the Irish being rather long-standing; Scots and Germans somewhat more recent, but all being of distinctly longer residence than some of the Scandinavian groups; and they in turn being less recent than Italians, Poles, Russians, Greeks, and Romanians. The Spearman rank-order correlation between the two measures of length of residence, ND and generation, is high (Spearman rho is .91, $P < .0001$), suggesting further confidence in the ND index as a crude indicator of relative average length of residence. (Our use of tests of significance here and elsewhere in the monograph is not based on a naive assumption that the data can be viewed in any form as a random sample from a larger uni-

[33]For a discussion of ND, see Stanley Lieberson, "Rank-Sum Comparisons Between Groups," in David Heise, ed., *Sociological Methodology 1976* (San Francisco:Jossey-Bass, 1975). It was assumed that each of the groups present in very minimal numbers in 1790 was 5 percent of the residual population shown in Table 2.2.

TABLE 2.3

Timing of Arrival, Generation, and Mixed Origins

Origins	Percentage Three or More Generations' Residence	Net Difference	Percentage Mixed	Old-New
Specific European				
English	93%	.00	72%	Old
German	91	−.22	64	Old
Irish	93	−.06	74	Old
French	90	−.24	76	Old
Italian	65	−.60	44	New
Scottish	91	−.20	88	Old
Polish	70	−.63	54	New
Dutch	93	−.29	78	Old
Swedish	84	−.39	70	Old
Norwegian	84		63	Old
Russian	57	−.55	50	New
Czech	69	N/A	58	New
Hungarian	60	N/A	59	New
Welsh	92		81	Old
Danish	82	−.41	72	Old
Portuguese	60	N/A	40	New
Belgian	N/A	−.49	66	Old
Greek	45	−.69	36	New
Romanian	N/A	−.57	55	New
Swiss	82	−.36	76	Old
Other				
Black	96			
Mexican	41			
Puerto Rican	94			
American Indian	98			
American	98			
Japanese	35			
Chinese	20			

NOTES: From 1820 to 1868 immigration data for Norway and Sweden were combined. Accordingly, the Norwegian and Swedish groups were combined on the basis of their relative numbers for other variables when correlated with ND. Likewise, because the immigration data combined England and Wales, correlations with ND also combined the data for those two groups (however, for reasons discussed in Chapter 1, the mixed percentage for the English is based on 1979 data). N/A-not available.

verse. Rather, we use the tests of significance (single-tailed unless indicated to the contrary) to determine the probability of observing the given rank-order statistic *if* the rank data for the variables had been randomly shuffled.)

Multiple Origins

Multiple ancestry of a group reflects several basic factors: the degree of intermarriage among ancestors, the fertility of intermarried couples, the propensity for mixed offspring themselves to intermarry, and the retention of this information by later generations so that they know that they are of mixed origins—as opposed to truncating their origins into a single ancestry. (The intermarriage of a respondent does not affect the level of ethnic mix in the population—it is affected only through offspring produced through mixed marriages.) The new census question in 1979 and 1980 allows persons to indicate multiple ancestral origins or identification—except for the cases discussed in Chapter 1. A rather substantial segment of the U.S. population reports at least two ancestral origins. In 1980, among those reporting at least one specific ancestry, 37 percent reported at least a second ancestry as well; the figure was 46 percent in 1979. In either case, the rates are even higher for the white groups since the data for the United States include blacks, who are less likely to report mixed ancestral origins. As Table 2.3 shows, the percentages vary widely between the groups but are almost universally higher than the 37 percent observed for the entire population in 1980. Of the groups specified, only Greeks—whose immigration is concentrated in a relatively recent period for a European group—have a lower percentage of mixed.

Holding all factors constant, we expect number of generations to be positively related to the degree of mix in a group, since there is more exposure to the possibility that some ancestor will have outmarried. This is borne out empirically; groups of European origin whose average member has relatively long-standing residence in the United States (as measured by the percentage reporting at least three generations' residence or the ND index dealing with their timing of arrival) are also groups that tend to have a larger percentage whose members are of mixed origins. The Spearman rank-order correlations, rho, between the percentage mixed and the two measures of a group's age are .81 ($P <$ .0001) and .78 ($P =$ .0002), respectively. At least for the white population, we can conclude that the ancestry groups become increasingly hybridized as a function of length of residence in the United States.

Old-New Distinction

The data in Table 2.3 indicate that the old-new distinction still differentiates the groups. There is no overlap between the old and new groups with respect to their ND index of recency of arrival, the percent-

age with three or more generations' residence, and the percentage reporting mixed ancestry (the Mann-Whitney tests are all significant at
the .001 level). This means that the various European ethnic components of the white population still differ considerably from one another
in several straightforward demographic characteristics that have a bearing on current behavior. In particular, there are major differences between the various groups in their generational distribution within the
United States. From the perspective of any assimilation model, generation obviously makes a great difference, particularly in the first few generations after arrival. Accordingly, insofar as assimilation is operating in
the United States, the groups differ on their fundamental generational
distribution in ways that greatly affect comparisons between them.

Furthermore, the white groups differ considerably from one another
in the degree to which their members are of single origin compared with
mixed origin. As we shall see in Chapter 7, marital patterns and age-
specific differences observed in 1980 lead us to expect that mixing will
expand in the future. This has potentially great consequences for the
maintenance of the groups themselves, to say nothing of the ability of
the white segment of the population to accurately report their origins.
Indeed, insofar as the census follows a procedure of classifying only the
first two origins reported (except for certain specified cases), an increasing multiplicity of ancestral roots for the average person will mean either distortion and selectivity in what ancestries are recognized and reported; and/or a need for recording more than two ancestries from the
entry into the census tapes; and/or a new form to the ethnic question
which allows for preferences or predominance of ancestries. In any case,
the white ethnic groups differ in their degree of mix at present, probably
reflecting generational factors as much as anything. This has relevance
for old-new comparisons because northwestern European groups are on
the average of longer residence in the United States than are SCE European groups and therefore differ in their degree of mix.

Reliability of Responses

Early in the 1970s the U.S. Census made a remarkable effort to examine the consistency of reporting of ethnic origin. Information on the
ethnic origin of the same persons was obtained through surveys in successive years (the March 1971, 1972, and 1973 Current Population Surveys). Table 2.4 shows the consistency of response in 1972 for those
reporting a given ethnic origin in 1971. Part of the inconsistency can be
explained by factors somewhat irrelevant to the issue at hand—namely,
the possibility that different adults in the same household were enum-

TABLE 2.4

Consistency of Ethnic Origin Response, 1971 and 1972

Origin Reported In 1971	Percentage Consistent in 1972
Puerto Rican	96.5%
Black	94.2
Mexican	88.3
Italian	87.8
Polish	79.2
German	66.1
Russian	62.3
French	62.1
Irish	57.1
English, Scottish, or Welsh	55.1
Don't know	34.9

SOURCE: Charles E. Johnson, Jr., *Consistency of Reporting of Ethnic Origin in the Current Population Survey*, Technical Paper no. 31, Current Population Survey (Washington, DC: U.S. Government Printing Office, 1974), table E.

erated in successive years—but the ethnic/racial differences in consistency are of interest since they suggest that substantive factors were operating as well. It is our impression that the rank ordering of consistency is harmonious with two factors: First, non-European groups are far more consistent about who they are: Puerto Ricans, blacks, and Mexicans are exceptionally high in their consistency. Second, white groups that have been here for the longest time and have substantial mixed components are less consistent than less mixed groups with shorter spans in the country. Thus, Italians and Poles are far more consistent than are the British, Irish, French, and Germans. The Russians appear to be an exception, but we speculate that this may reflect the possibility of inconsistency for Russian Jews such that a considerable number bounce back and forth between reporting themselves as "Russian," in a question such as the one used in these surveys, and "Jewish." In this regard, the overwhelming majority of Russians in 1971 who did not report themselves as such in 1972 were classified as "Other" by the census.[34]

Also consistent with these conclusions about variations in the reliability of responses by ethnic groups is the result for those who said "Don't know" in 1971. Nearly two thirds gave a different answer one

[34]A category which also incorporates persons reporting an origin that is not in the small census list used in these surveys.

year later. Of special interest is that a substantial number were reported one year later as either one of the British groups (20 percent), Irish, (6 percent) or German (6 percent). By contrast, Italian, Polish, and Russian were virtually never picked by such persons a year later (less than 0.5 percent for each of these responses). These differences in the consistency of ethnic/racial responses, in short, are further evidences of the impact of generational, mixing, and racial forces in the behavior of ethnic groups in the country. It is also further evidence of our contention in Chapter 1 that difficulties in the responses to the ethnic question are not merely reflections of the inadequacy of the enumeration procedures, but due to the current nature of ethnic relations.

The Years Ahead

The ethnic and racial makeup of the nation is not etched in stone— as our review of the nation's history indicates. The United States remains an exceptionally attractive destination for large numbers of potential immigrants. Although the economic outlook has been less sanguine in recent years than it had been in many earlier periods, we expect the United States to continue to be an attractive destination for a substantial segment of the world's population presently living in areas with poorer alternatives and opportunities. Changes in the future ethnic and racial makeup of the nation will be affected by the same factors that altered the nation's composition in the past: government policy toward the number of immigrants accepted, the enforcement of these policies, the tilt of policies in favor of some ethnic/racial groups as opposed to other groups, economic opportunities in the United States, and the differentials between potential sending countries in the relative attractiveness of the United States as a destination compared with the homeland. For immigration substantially to alter the ethnic and racial composition of the United States, however, it will take progressively larger numbers of newcomers of a given ancestry.[35] As the nation's population increases, a constant number of immigrants has a progressively smaller impact on the overall composition of the nation. Thus, increasingly larger and larger numbers of immigrants would have to arrive in order to reach any specified percentage of the national population. Groups

[35]This ignores differentials in the intrinsic rate of natural increase after arrival, as well as the short-term fertility consequences when the immigrants are in the young adult ages that favor a higher crude fertility rate. There is every reason to assume that in a relatively small number of generations, initial fertility differences will be dampened considerably (see Chapter 4).

that were relatively rare in the nation can, of course, suddenly be visible through relatively heavy immigration over a short period of time, coupled with publicity and with concentration in a limited number of residential locations or in highly visible occupational niches. But it is another matter whether these shifts will alter substantially the ethnic makeup of the nation.

We can expect the percentage with at least three generations' residence to increase rapidly in the years ahead for most groups. The only exception are groups whose new immigration is large relative to the number of compatriots currently living in the United States. The old-new distinction, while clearly relevant at present, should matter much less as the older immigrant and second-generation populations die off and are not replaced by comparable numbers of newcomers.[36] To be sure, the northwestern European groups will still have a larger average number of generations in the United States, barring some radical shift in immigration flows. But these gaps will be of decreasing importance if we assume that the first few generations matter a great deal for all sorts of assimilation and cultural issues, but that the differences between succeeding generations rapidly become relatively minor for many social phenomena after a few generations of residence in the United States. This does not mean that ethnic differences within the European population will disappear—far from it—but it does mean that generational factors will not be the cause for their existence.

Finally, we observe that a substantial segment of the white population are "unhyphenated whites"—to use a term that has been applied elsewhere—namely, they either report themselves as "American" or are unable to indicate their ancestry.[37] Since the ethnic origins question is a new one, there is no basis for projecting changes into the future. But if the level of mixing continues, such as to cause a rapid increase in the segment of the white population with complicated mixed origins, and if the generational gap from their European ancestors grows, we can expect decreasing accuracy in the responses to the origins question and a shift toward a new white subset of the population who are essentially unaware of their European origins. The development of an increasingly mixed white population, along with apparent shifts in the ancestries reported, is a topic that we will return to in several of the ensuing chapters.

---

[36]See Richard D. Alba, *Italian Americans: Into the Twilight of Ethnicity* (Englewood Cliffs, NJ: Prentice-Hall, 1985), p. 113.

[37]Lieberson, "Unhyphenated Whites."

3

SPATIAL PATTERNS

W E EXPECT every ethnic group in the United States—or in any
other nation—to exhibit a distinctive locational pattern. As observed in Chapter 2, the groups came to this nation for a variety
of reasons and under changing conditions. Each of these forces has ramifications for their settlement patterns. The spatial pattern of conquered
people, such as American Indians, results from their location at the time
of their conquest, as well as from movements that were forced upon
them later. This combination of initial location and later changes also
applies to people whose territories were acquired in other ways as the
United States expanded westward—for example, the groups living in the
Louisiana Territory purchased from France. Since most blacks arrived in
the nation as slaves, their initial locations reflected the decisions of
their masters and the distinctive economic niches intended for them.

Unique patterns of geographic distribution are also to be expected
among the descendants of peoples who migrated to the New World by
choice because the locations of economic opportunity change constantly
in the United States and the groups arrived in different periods. Moreover, areas also differ in the kinds of opportunities offered, an important
fact since the groups vary in their skills, resources, and background at
their time of arrival. For example, not all migrant groups were equally
likely to pursue the agricultural opportunities available during the period when relatively cheap farm lands were available. Each group's spa-

tial pattern within this nation is also affected by the proximity of their homeland to different points in the United States (say, Mexico versus Cuba; Japan versus Sweden).

These influences not only operate for recent immigrants to the United States, but also are relevant for understanding the descendants of earlier immigrants. The concentration of some central and eastern European peoples in the industrial Midwest and Northeast reflects developments of heavy industry (for example, in the steel and automobile producing cities) late in the nineteenth century and early in the twentieth century, coupled with the minimal skills that many possessed at the time of arrival. About 5 percent of the population in 1980 reporting an ancestry live in Ohio, but it is the home state of 15 percent of the nation's Croatians, 14 percent of the Hungarians, 8 percent of the Romanians, 15 percent of the Serbs, 22 percent of the Slovaks, and 45 percent of the Slovenes.[1]

Similarly, Germans migrated in significant numbers at a time when they were able to take advantage of the agricultural opportunities opening in the upper Midwest; and their present-day concentrations still reflect this historic development. In the West North Central states (Minnesota, Iowa, Missouri, the Dakotas, Kansas, and Nebraska), 40 percent of all residents report at least some German ancestry. This is more than double the next largest white ancestry group—the English. The variation in the country is quite striking. For example, if we exclude our analysis to only those defined by the census as reporting an ancestry (see footnote 1), then 56 percent of Wisconsin's residents report some German ancestry and only 14 percent have some English ancestry; in Utah, by contrast, 61 percent are English and 17 percent are German.

The pronounced early concentration of various Asian groups on the West Coast reflects the ports of entry and the location of economic opportunities for them, just as migrant groups from Mexico, Cuba, and French Canada are affected by the proximity of their countries to different parts of the United States. Special conditions operated for blacks, who were concentrated initially in the South. Groups such as Hispanos in New Mexico and elsewhere and the French in Louisiana found themselves suddenly living in territories that were either conquered or purchased as the United States extended its boundaries across the continent. This, too, helped to develop distinctive locational patterns when these areas and peoples were incorporated into the nation. The distinc-

---

[1]State and regional data used in this section of the chapter are for 1980 and are partly derived from U.S. Bureau of the Census, *1980 Census of Population, Supplementary Report,* "Ancestry of the Population by State: 1980," PC80-S1-10 (Washington, DC: U.S. Government Printing Office, 1983a), tables 2, 3, and 4. "Population reporting an ancestry" is defined by the census as excluding "American" or "United States" responses, religious groups, unclassifiable answers, as well as those not reporting.

tive geographic pattern of Native Americans reflects the differential demise of some tribes at the hands of the whites, the resettlement patterns due to the establishment of reservations, and the efforts of Native Americans to escape the white onslaughts.

What are these regional patterns at present in the United States? How do they compare with earlier periods? For our major metropolitan areas, what are (and were) their distinctive ethnic makeups? Which groups live in Denver, Los Angeles, Boston, and Dallas? In some cases we have stereotypes—the Irish in Boston, Jews in New York, Poles in Chicago. But are these stereotypes correct? For other cities, we do not even have stereotypes of what we might expect.

Location is not a trivial question; it has ramifications far beyond the simple description of where our groups live. We are not merely dealing with a fundamental fact about ethnic and racial patterns in the nation; spatial concentrations also affect assimilation, intermarriage, political power, visibility, and interaction with others. The ethnic and racial composition of the population also seem to influence the occupational distributions a group exhibits as well as the gap between a group's income and other groups in the same location.[2] Indeed, the isolation of groups will also affect their potential for separatism. Although that is not an issue in the United States, it is in many other nations of the world.

Current Spatial Patterns

In varying degrees, each group has a unique spatial distribution and, likewise, each area has a unique ethnic composition. Some groups are concentrated in a narrow range of locations; others are located broadly throughout the nation. In 1980, of the 1 million persons of Portuguese ancestry living in the nation, 31 percent reside in California and 26 percent in Massachusetts. Indeed, nearly 75 percent are found in Massachusetts or Rhode Island on the East Coast or California or Hawaii in the West Coast. In the South as a whole English is by far the most frequently reported white ancestry, with 20 million persons reporting themselves as partly or wholly English compared with 13 and 11 million reporting at least some Irish or German ancestry. However, French is the most commonly reported European ancestry in Louisiana (29 percent of all persons reporting one or more specific ancestries).

In order to describe contemporary geographic ethnic patterns we ask

[2]Stanley Lieberson, *A Piece of the Pie: Blacks and White Immigrants Since 1880* (Berkeley: University of California Press 1980), chap. 10; Gary S. Becker, *The Economics of Discrimination* (Chicago: University of Chicago Press, 1957).

two questions: From the perspective of a specific part of the nation, what are the numerically important groups? From the perspective of the group itself, where are its members concentrated? Both questions are different ways of analyzing the same data set. The answer in the first case is affected by the size of the group in the nation as a whole; some groups are so large that it would take unusual conditions for them *not* to be numerically important everywhere and other groups are so small that even an exceptional level of concentration would not make them a numerically important group in one of the heavily populated parts of the nation. For instance, some 38 percent of the nation's Armenians live in California, but this amounts to only 82,000 people in a state containing more than one tenth of the nation's entire population.

From the second perspective, that of the group itself, the concentration of the remaining population affects the meaning of a given group's particular pattern. Numerically large groups can be important in parts of the country even if they are not concentrated in the area; conversely, numerically small groups can be heavily concentrated in one location but still not be very important in absolute numerical terms. A lot depends, of course, on the size of the pond; there are more Americans of Japanese and Filipino ancestry living in California than in Hawaii; but Hawaii's population is about 4 percent of California's. As a consequence, the number of both Japanese and Filipinos in Hawaii exceeds the number for any specific white ancestry—indeed, the Chinese are barely edged out by the English in that state. In Hawaii, more than 25 percent of the residents are Japanese, 15 percent Filipino, and 10 percent Chinese.

Both of these perspectives on the relative numbers of ancestries have strong sociological implications. Ignoring for the moment the important issues of the variation in the strength and meaning of ethnic identification across and within groups, the concentration or dispersion of a given group will affect their relative political power and visibility. Groups which are numerically small in national terms, but highly concentrated locally can have political and social influence beyond what one would expect given a simple demographic count. On the other hand, a larger ethnic group which is evenly dispersed throughout the country may have less electoral or political influence because of this dilution.

Leading Groups in Each Geographic Division

The ten most frequent ancestries reported in each of the nine main geographic divisions of the United States are shown in Table 3.1. There is considerable variation among divisions in their specific ethnic

TABLE 3.1

Ten Largest Groups in Each Geographic Division, Ranked by Percentage of Population with Each Ancestry, 1980

New England		Mid Atlantic		East North Central		West North Central		South Atlantic	
English	24%	German	22%	German	32%	German	40%	English	27%
Irish	23	Irish	19	English	20	English	20	Black	21
French	16	Italian	15	Irish	17	Irish	19	Irish	16
Italian	13	English	14	Black	11	Norwegian	7	German	15
German	9	Black	12	Polish	7	French	6	American	9
Polish	6	Polish	7	French	6	Swedish	6	Scottish	5
Scottish	5	French	4	American	5	American	5	French	4
Black	4	American	4	Italian	4	Black	5	American Indian	3
American	4	Scottish	3	Scottish	4	Scottish	4	Italian	3
Portuguese	3	Russian	3	Dutch	4	Dutch	4	Dutch	2

East South Central		West South Central		Mountain		Pacific	
English	31%	English	22%	English	29%	English	22%
Black	21	Irish	18	German	23	German	20
Irish	17	German	15	Irish	17	Irish	16
American	13	Black	15	Mexican	7	Mexican	11
German	11	Mexican	11	Scottish	6	Black	6
Scottish	4	French	8	French	6	French	6
American Indian	4	American	7	American Indian	5	Scottish	5
French	3	American Indian	6	Hispanic	5	Italian	4
Dutch	2	Scottish	4	American	4	American	4
Italian	1	Dutch	2	Swedish	4	American Indian	3

NOTE: Ranks based on percentage carried out further than shown in table. Individuals with multiple ancestries are counted more than once; thus, percentages in each division will add to more than 100. These figures are based on the entire population in the division, including the denominator persons not reporting any ancestry.

makeup, but the nation's largest groups are important everywhere, even though their relative positions vary greatly. Germans, Irish, English, Scottish, and French (five of the six largest groups in the country) are among the top ten in each division (Germans, Irish, and English are *always* among the top five); French are important in New England (16 percent of the population) and the West South Central states (due to the concentration in Louisiana), but elsewhere their percentages are modest, albeit they number among the top ten. Blacks appear among the ten largest in eight of the nine divisions, Italians in five divisions, and American Indians in seven divisions.

Although the nation's major subdivisions tend to have certain common ethnic features, the specific details vary in two important ways. First, the *relative* importance of these large groups varies greatly between divisions. German is the most frequently reported ancestry in the Mid Atlantic and North Central states (indeed, the percentage of Germans in the West North Central states is greater than that for any group in any divison of the nation). On the other hand, Germans are a weak fifth in New England (9 percent of the population), and in the East South Central states (Kentucky, Tennessee, Alabama, and Mississippi) they are only 11 percent. Indeed, in the remainder of the South, only about 15 percent report German ancestry. The Irish- and English-ancestry responses are most consistent throughout the nation. Irish ancestry is at least the second or third largest group in all divisions. The English are the most important group in six of the nine divisions: New England, South Atlantic, East and West South Central, Mountain, and Pacific. Persons of Dutch ancestry constitute another relatively large ethnic group and are fairly uniform in their modest presence throughout the divisions.

Blacks and Italians vary widely in their importance. Blacks range from 2 percent of the Mountain population and 4.5 percent of the West North Central population to 21 percent of the South Atlantic and East South Central populations (essentially the historic black belt of the United States).

In much of the nation, specific southern-central-eastern (SCE) European groups are not numerically important; indeed, no single SCE European group is prominent in all (or most) divisions of the United States. Even Italians, the most numerous of these groups, exhibit this pattern. In most parts of the nation, their numbers do not generally approximate the numbers reported for some of the groups discussed above. Italians are the only SCE group among the top ten in the South Atlantic states, but they occupy tenth place with only 3 percent. There are no SCE groups in the top ten in the remaining southern divisions. They are also weak in the Plains and Mountain states (where there are no representations among the top ten) and in the Pacific, where Italians are the eighth largest.

These SCE European groups are important only in New England, the Mid Atlantic states, and the industrial part of the Midwest. In the Mid Atlantic, Italians are the third largest group, while in New England, Italians are the fourth largest group, with Poles important in both, as well as Portuguese in New England, and Russians in the Mid Atlantic. In the East North Central states, Poles are the fifth largest and Italians eighth largest. The situation for these groups with respect to metropolitan areas is another matter, as will be seen below. And it may well be that their prominence in many of our leading metropolitan centers leads to overestimating their numerical position in the nation. Overall, however, we are impressed with the lesser numerical position occupied by most of the SCE European groups in the various major subdivisions of the United States.[3]

Some groups found in Table 3.1 are numerically important in only one or a few divisions. Norwegians and Swedes are important only in the Great Plains. Americans of Mexican ancestry are among the larger groups found in the western part of the United States, as well as the West South Central states (thanks to the large number in Texas). Likewise, Hispanics are one of the largest groups in the Mountain states, probably due to a relatively strong propensity among many persons of Mexican origin in New Mexico and Colorado to use that appellation. In the South, "American" without any other ethnic qualifier is one of the leading responses.

Geographic Concentration of Each Group

Another way of describing the same data is to consider the concentration of each ethnic group in the different census divisions of the country. This information, for the 35 largest groups in the United States, is provided in Table 3.2. Since the distribution of the entire population is also shown, the reader can ascertain if a group is concentrated in a division relative to the nation's entire population. For example, more persons with Irish ancestry live in the East North Central states than in any other part of the nation (18.0 percent of all Americans reporting such ancestry). But since 18.4 percent of all Americans reside in that division, the Irish are actually slightly underrepresented. In general, the current distributions reflect the historical settlement patterns of the groups. Germans and Scandinavian groups (Swedes, Norwegians, Finns, and Danes) are still located disproportionately in the Midwest; eastern and central European groups (Poles, Russians, Czechs, Hungarians, Austrians, Slavs, and Ukrainians) remain overrepresented in the Mid Atlantic and Midwest divisions; Italians and Greeks maintain their largest numbers in the Mid Atlantic. The largest Asian groups (Filipinos, Chinese, and Japanese) remain concentrated on the Pacific Coast. The Latino groups remain most numerous in their divisions of initial settle-

---

[3]Here and elsewhere the reader must keep in mind that there can be significant variation between the states, let alone cities, within a given region. Witness the earlier result with respect to the French in Louisiana compared with the entire West South Central region of which it is a part.

TABLE 3.2
Geographic Distribution of Ethnic Groups in the United States, 1980

Group	New England	Mid Atlantic	East North Central	West North Central	South Atlantic	East South Central	West South Central	Mountain	Pacific	Total	Index of Dissimilarity
U.S. Total	5.5%	16.2%	18.4%	7.6%	16.3%	6.5%	10.5%	5.0%	14.0%	100.0%	
American	3.6	10.7	16.1	6.3	24.2	13.9	13.1	3.6	8.4	100.0	19
American Indian	2.6	6.1	15.5	8.0	15.4	8.7	19.5	8.5	15.8	100.0	17
Austrian	5.4	38.1	17.1	5.2	10.8	1.1	3.0	5.2	14.2	100.0	22
Black	1.8	16.5	17.2	3.0	28.9	10.8	13.3	1.0	7.5	100.0	23
Canadian	28.3	14.1	16.2	2.7	10.5	1.3	3.4	4.3	19.1	100.0	28
Chinese	3.8	20.7	7.2	2.1	6.6	1.0	4.1	2.7	51.8	100.0	42
Cuban	1.8	22.2	3.7	.4	59.6	.4	2.6	1.0	8.4	100.0	49
Czech	2.6	15.2	29.3	19.9	6.6	.7	11.0	4.6	10.0	100.0	24
Danish	3.1	6.3	16.2	21.4	5.4	.9	3.5	19.0	24.3	100.0	38
Dutch	2.1	15.9	24.9	10.6	12.6	4.7	8.9	5.7	14.7	100.0	11
English	5.9	10.6	16.5	6.8	19.9	9.1	10.6	6.6	14.1	100.0	11
Filipino	1.3	8.8	9.0	1.7	7.5	.8	2.9	2.2	65.8	100.0	52
Finnish	9.3	6.5	30.7	18.7	5.8	.8	2.1	5.6	20.5	100.0	34
French	15.4	10.8	18.7	8.3	9.9	3.2	14.3	4.9	14.5	100.0	16

TABLE 3.2 (continued)

Group	New England	Mid Atlantic	East North Central	West North Central	South Atlantic	East South Central	West South Central	Mountain	Pacific	Total	Index of Dissimilarity
French Canadian	34.5	12.1	17.9	4.9	7.9	1.1	4.4	4.0	13.3	100.0	29
German	2.2	16.8	27.2	13.9	11.5	3.2	7.1	5.4	12.6	100.0	21
Greek	12.7	27.7	21.1	3.2	12.3	1.5	3.6	4.3	13.5	100.0	22
Hispanic	3.1	19.8	5.9	1.8	13.1	1.2	11.9	20.4	22.8	100.0	30
Hungarian	4.8	34.7	29.9	3.1	10.1	1.0	2.3	3.0	11.0	100.0	30
Irish	7.2	17.1	18.0	8.3	14.9	6.4	10.4	4.7	13.0	100.0	4
Italian	13.1	43.8	14.0	2.3	8.3	1.1	3.3	3.0	11.0	100.0	37
Japanese	1.3	5.7	5.6	1.9	4.7	1.0	3.0	4.5	72.3	100.0	58
Lithuanian	16.6	30.6	27.4	2.6	9.6	.6	1.8	2.3	8.6	100.0	35
Mexican	.1	.7	7.5	1.6	1.3	.2	33.1	10.2	45.2	100.0	61
Norwegian	1.9	4.7	19.7	35.3	3.9	.7	2.7	8.2	22.9	100.0	42
Polish	8.9	31.7	33.3	5.0	8.0	.8	2.7	2.4	7.2	100.0	35
Portuguese	40.0	10.1	2.2	.8	4.0	.5	1.4	2.0	39.0	100.0	60
Puerto Rican	8.2	65.0	10.5	.4	6.4	.4	1.6	.8	6.7	100.0	52
Russian	8.3	39.6	12.9	4.2	13.0	.7	2.1	3.1	16.0	100.0	29
Scottish	6.6	12.0	15.7	7.2	18.7	6.1	9.9	6.6	17.0	100.0	9
Slavic	3.3	36.2	25.5	5.5	8.3	1.0	2.1	6.5	11.6	100.0	29
Swedish	6.6	8.6	20.4	22.1	6.4	1.3	4.1	9.4	21.2	100.0	30
Swiss	3.0	15.1	27.5	11.3	8.0	2.2	4.4	8.5	19.9	100.0	22
Ukrainian	6.8	48.3	20.2	3.0	8.5	.7	1.7	2.3	8.6	100.0	35
Welsh	3.5	21.2	19.4	7.4	13.0	2.9	5.7	8.9	18.0	100.0	14

ment—Mexican Americans in the Southwest, Puerto Ricans in the Northeast, and Cubans in the Mid Atlantic and South Atlantic. Despite the massive northward migration of blacks throughout much of this century, they are still found in disproportionate numbers only in the South (albeit very slightly in excess of the Mid Atlantic total).

Of special interest is the overall measure of dispersion presented in the last column of Table 3.2. This is the index of dissimilarity (D) between the divisional distribution of a given ancestry response and the distribution of the remainder of the U.S. population. D ranges from 0 to 100, with 0 occurring if a group's divisional distribution is identical to that of the rest of the population; the opposite extreme of 100 would occur if a group's distribution was so different from the rest of the population that its members were located in divisions where nobody else was found. (The latter condition is essentially impossible, except for the largest groups, but it does provide a scale on which to measure the dissimilarity of each group from the remainder of the population.)

Groups vary greatly in their locational dissimilarity. The divisional distributions of the Irish, English, Scottish, and Dutch most closely resemble that of the U.S. population as a whole (their indexes range from 4 to 11).[4] At the other extreme are the groups with values of 50 or more—the Portuguese, Japanese, and Mexican populations. In general, the ten groups with divisional distributions most closely approximating the remaining U.S. population are ones whose presence in sizable numbers dates back to the colonial period (the Czechs are the only exception). This makes sense if the forces generating idiosyncratic locational patterns are strongest at the time of initial settlement. After that, the groups probably tend to disperse in response to a variety of social and economic changes occurring within the nation, leading the groups to respond similarly to other populations in terms of regional developments. Likewise, over time, changes within the group will probably diversify the population and hence open them up to a variety of locational pulls. If this is correct, we would expect the groups to be most distinctive in their spatial distribution at the initial points of settlement and to spread out over time.

Empirical support for this interpretation is provided in Table 3.3. Data limitations restrict the analysis to those European groups for which it is possible to estimate average length of residence in the United States compared with persons of English and Welsh ancestry (this approach was discussed in Chapter 2). The first column provides the index of net difference (ND) between a given group's arrival pattern

---

[4]The D values have been corrected to take into account that group's contribution to the U.S. total, so that there is no part-whole problem here.

TABLE 3.3

Average Length of Residence (ND)
and Dissimilarity in Spatial Distribution (D)

Group	ND	D
Irish	−.06	4
Scottish	−.20	9
Dutch	−.29	11
French	−.24	16
German	−.22	20
Norwegian-Swedish	−.40	36
Swiss	−.37	22
Russian	−.55	29
Greek	−.70	21
Italian	−.60	37
Polish	−.63	35
Danish	−.42	38

NOTES: ND is a measure of the average "age" of the groups in the United States relative to the English and Welsh. The estimated number of English and Welsh in the United States in 1790 was combined with the number of immigrants from these sources in succeeding decades. The percentage distributions derived from this is then compared with analogous figures for each of the groups specified. Relative recency is indicated by increasingly negative values of ND. For example, ND of −.70 for Greeks means that their arrival pattern is considerably more recent than the base group (−1.0 would occur if all Greeks arrived later than all English and Welsh). See Stanley Lieberson, "Rank-Sum Comparisons Between Groups," in David Heise, ed., *Sociological Methodology 1976* (San Francisco: Jossey-Bass, 1975).

The D values for Norwegian and Swedish are an average of the two groups' individual D values.

and the arrival pattern for the population from England and Wales (see details in the notes to Table 3.3). The more negative the ND value, the more recent is the group's period of arrival in the nation; a positive value would occur if the group's settlement pattern was earlier than the English.[5] The second column shows the index of dissimilarity for each group's divisional distribution compared with the remainder of the nation. The correlation (r) is −.72, suggesting that length of residence in the United States does lead to greater dispersion of the members of these groups over time in a form resembling the entire population. The regression coefficient, −.43 of D on ND, suggests a fairly substantial decline across the range of values.

[5]For a description of ND, see Stanley Lieberson, "Rank-Sum Comparisons Between Groups," in David Heise, ed., *Sociological Methodology 1976* (San Francisco: Jossey-Bass, 1975).

The spatial patterns for both American Indians and blacks appear to run counter to this generalization. The latter group, with a modal number of generations in the nation that exceeds virtually any of the white groups, has an index of dissimilarity of 23, and the index for American Indians is not much lower—17. Although the indexes for these groups are the 7th and 13th lowest of the 35 groups examined (see Table 3.2), we might expect them to be even lower. In the case of blacks, however, the overwhelming majority were slaves until the end of the Civil War and were therefore not free to migrate until then. As a consequence, if the starting point is really postbellum South, their dispersion toward the national pattern has not been unusually slow. For example, D is lower than that found among any of the new European groups and for some of the old European groups as well. The value for Indians probably reflects their relative isolation from the society introduced by the white conquerers and the effort among many—whether by choice or imposition is another question—to maintain a life closer to their traditional one. In many nations it is not at all uncommon for subordinate *indigenous* groups to be slower in participating in the national economy and thereby to remain isolated.[6]

Historical Patterns

An inspection of historical data for immigrants in the United States provides support for two fundamental contentions about the spatial distribution of ethnic groups: first, there is variation among areas and over time in their attractiveness to immigrants; second, the early immigration patterns still affect the ethnic makeup of various areas of the nation. Information is available on the divisional patterns of the foreign-born as far back as the 1850 census, a point well within the first great wave of massive immigration in the nineteenth century. Table 3.4 shows how the foreign-born percentage of the nation's population has fluctuated considerably through this period, peaking late in the last century and again early in this century and declining persistently since 1910 (affected first by World War I and then by the quotas introduced in 1924). Although the nation still receives relatively large numbers of permanent immigrants compared with the remainder of the world, the number of immigrants admitted to the nation (according to official statistics) is less than it used to be and the number enumerated in the

[6]Stanley Lieberson, "A Societal Theory of Race and Ethnic Relations," *American Sociological Review* 26 (1961): 902–10.

TABLE 3.4

Percentage Foreign-Born, by Geographic Division

Year	New England	Mid Atlantic	East North Central	West North Central	South Atlantic	East South Central	West South Central	Mountain	Pacific	United States
1850	11.2%	17.3%	12.2%	11.3%	2.2%	1.5%	9.3%	5.8%	21.6%	9.7%
1860	15.0	20.8	17.3	16.0	3.0	2.5	7.3	13.8	34.9	13.2
1870	18.6	21.3	18.2	17.4	2.9	2.4	6.4	27.6	33.5	14.4
1880	19.8	19.3	17.1	16.2	2.3	1.7	5.4	24.6	30.4	13.3
1890	24.3	21.6	18.6	17.3	2.4	1.6	4.6	21.2	27.2	14.7
1900	25.8	21.5	16.4	14.8	2.1	1.2	4.1	18.0	22.5	13.6
1910	27.9	25.1	16.8	13.9	2.5	1.0	4.0	17.2	22.8	14.7
1920	25.5	22.3	15.1	11.0	2.4	.8	4.5	14.0	20.3	13.2
1930	22.5	20.1	12.9	8.1	1.9	.6	3.6	10.1	16.5	11.4
1940	17.8	16.4	9.7	5.8	1.6	.4	2.2	6.3	11.9	8.7
1950	13.7	12.9	7.0	4.0	1.7	.4	2.3	4.7	8.6	6.7
1960	10.1	10.3	5.2	2.6	2.1	.5	2.1	3.7	7.9	5.4
1970	7.8	8.6	3.9	1.8	2.9	.5	2.0	3.0	7.8	4.7
1980	7.8	9.6	4.2	2.0	4.7	1.0	4.3	4.3	12.8	6.2

SOURCES: Niles Carpenter, *Immigrants and Their Children: 1920*, Census Monograph 7 (Washington, DC: U.S. Government Printing Office, 1927), table 8, U.S. Bureau of the Census, *1950 Census of Population*, vol. 2: *Characteristics of the Population*, pt. 1: *U.S. Summary* (Washington, DC: U.S. Government Printing Office, 1953), table 6; vol. 4: *Special Reports*, pt. 3, *Nativity and Parentage of the White Population* (Washington, DC: U.S. Government Printing Office, 1954), table 2; *1980 Census of Population*, *U.S. Summary*, "Characteristics of the Population," PC80-1-A1 (Washington, DC: U.S. Government Printing Office, 1983c), table 236; vol. 1: *General Social and Economic Characteristics*, pt. 1: *U.S. Summary* (Washington, DC: U.S. Government Printing Office, 1983f), tables 10 and 49.

NOTES: Figures for 1850–1920 and 1960–80 refer to foreign-born of all races, while the figures for 1930–50 refer to the white foreign-born only. (In all years, the denominator is the total population of all races.) Inasmuch as the nonwhite foreign-born represent a small proportion of all foreign-born, this is of minor consequence. Including nonwhite foreign-born in the U.S. total for 1930, 1940, and 1950 raises the percentage foreign-born to 11.6, 8.8, and 6.9, respectively.

censuses is small relative to the size of nation's population. As Simon[7] observes:

> Immigrants who arrived in the decade 1901–1910 constituted 9.6% of the population at the end of that decade; by comparison those who came in 1961–80 and 1971–80 constituted 1.6% and 2.0% of the population respectively. That is, relative to resident population, the rate of gross immigration . . . was 5 or 6 times greater in the earlier period than recently. [p. 18]

Much of the recent public attention to the number of immigrants has focused on the number of illegal immigrants in the United States. However, even if we include the estimate of Passel[8] of between 2.5 and 3.5 million undocumented immigrants, they constitute about 1 to 1.5 percent of the entire U.S. population (p. 188).

Divisions differ in the magnitude of the effect of immigration on them. For more than one hundred years, immigrants have been concentrated in the New England, Mid Atlantic, and Pacific divisions. In 1850, for example, just under 10 percent of the U.S. population was foreign-born, but the percentages were 11, 17, and 22, respectively, for the three divisions mentioned above. In 1890 and again in 1910, when 15 percent of the American population was foreign-born, about 25 percent of the residents in each of these divisions were of foreign birth. The South has been consistent in the opposite direction, with a relatively small percentage of its residents being of foreign birth throughout this period. Around the turn of the century, when close to 15 percent of the U.S. population was of foreign birth, the proportions ranged between 1 and 5 percent in the three southern divisions.

Some of the areas have shifted greatly during this period in the relative importance of immigrants. The less industrialized part of the midwestern region, the West North Central states, exceeded the national average during the second half of the nineteenth century (a period of relatively rapid growth there), but has not during this century. The Mountain states exceeded the national level between 1860 and 1920, and during part of this time to a far greater degree than was ever experienced in the Midwest (1870–90). Even among the divisions absorbing the largest number of immigrants there have been sharp changes in their relative positions. Throughout this century, one or the other of the northeastern divisions has had the largest foreign-born percentage; from

[7]Julian L. Simon, "Basic Data Concerning Immigration into the United States," *Annals of The American Academy of Political and Social Science* 487 (1986): 12–56.

[8]Jeffrey S. Passel, "Undocumented Immigration," *Annals of the American Academy of Political and Social Science* 487 (1986): 181–200.

1850 to 1890, however, the Pacific contained the largest percentage foreign-born, as much as a third of the population. Although the *absolute number* of immigrants in the Northeast was far larger, the total population was so much smaller in the Pacific states at that time that the *percentage* was greater. It is estimated that the total population of the Pacific division in 1850 was only 106,000; in 1860 it had increased to 444,000. The immigrant population had risen from 24,000 to 155,000 in this period, with the Chinese, Irish, and Germans contributing the largest specific immigrant increases. Until recently, the eastern half of the Midwest exceeded the national percentage of immigrants, albeit not by very much.

The initial settlement locations of the immigrants have a profound impact on the major ethnic groups currently found in each area. With very few exceptions, the groups that are currently among the five numerically most important in each division (referring to *all* generations, see last column of Table 3.5) were among the five largest immigrant groups living in the area in at least one of these years: 1850, 1900, 1920. For example, in the Mid Atlantic states, Germans are the largest and Irish the second largest of the ancestry groups in 1980. In all three periods—during the great wave of immigration in the middle of the nineteenth century, in the middle of the new wave from SCE Europe, and in 1920 shortly before the demise of massive immigration—German and Irish immigrants were among the five largest foreign-born groups living in the area (their immigrants were among the top five in the first two periods). The story is the same for the other leading groups in the division; Italian immigrants were particularly prominent in the second and third period, and Poles in the 1920 census. Table 3.5 shows that this relationship appears in all of the divisions. The only exceptions are the French (in the New England and East North Central states and the Scots in the Mountain states). Because these are groups with lengthy histories in North America and relatively small nineteenth-century immigrant populations, they do not appear as major immigrant groups during the 1850–1920 period even when they are currently one of the five largest ancestry groups in a division.[9]

Table 3.5 shows how the present-day areal distribution of racial and ethnic groups continues to bear the imprint of immigrant settlement

---

[9]The opposite exception occurs for the population of Canadian birth. They often appear as one of the largest birthplace groups even when they do not appear as a leading ancestry. This occurs, in no small way, because most of them and their descendants report themselves in terms of some ancestry prior to arrival in Canada, albeit some Canadian-born do report "Canadian" for their ancestry. (See Stanley Lieberson and Lawrence Santi, "The Use of Nativity Data to Estimate Ethnic Characteristics and Patterns," *Social Science Research* 14 (1985): 31–56.)

TABLE 3.5

Five Largest Immigrant Groups in Each Geographic Division, 1850, 1900, and 1920; and the Five Leading Ancestry Groups in 1980

Division	Largest Immigrant Groups			Largest Ancestry Groups 1980
	1850	1900	1920	
New England	Ireland	Canada	Canada	English
	Canada	Ireland	Ireland	Irish
	England	England	Italy	French
	Scotland	Germany	Russia and Lithuania	Italian
	Germany	Italy	England	German
Mid Atlantic	Ireland	Germany	Italy	German
	Germany	Ireland	Russia and Lithuania	Irish
	England	England	Poland	Italian
	Canada	Italy	Germany	English
	Scotland	Russia	Ireland	Polish
East North Central	Germany	Germany	Germany	German
	Ireland	Canada	Poland	English
	England	Ireland	Russia and Lithuania	Irish
	Canada	England	Canada	Polish
	Scotland	Sweden	Italy	French
West North Central	Germany	Germany	Germany	German
	Ireland	Sweden	Sweden	English
	England	Norway	Norway	Irish
	Canada	Canada	Russia and Lithuania	Norwegian
	France	Ireland	Canada	French

SOURCE: Niles Carpenter, *Immigrants and Their Children: 1920*, Census Monograph 7 (Washington, DC: U.S. Government Printing Office, 1927), table 162.

NOTE: Wales is separated from England; Canada birth data were not subdivided into "French" and "Other" until 1890.

patterns that occurred many years ago. It also reveals something of the historical sequence out of which the contemporary patterns emerged. In 1850, persons from the British Isles (Ireland, 43 percent; England, 12 percent; Scotland, 3 percent; Wales, 1 percent), Germany (26 percent), France (2 percent), and Canada (7 percent) constituted the vast majority of the foreign-born population of the nation—no other individual birthplace represented as much as 1 percent.[10] Persons of Mexican birth were a very important component of the immigrant population in some areas, but not in the nation as a whole. (The percentage of Mexican immi-

[10]U.S. Bureau of the Census, 1933a, table 4, p. 233.

TABLE 3.5 *(continued)*

| Division | Largest Immigrant Groups | | | Largest Ancestry Groups |
	1850	1900	1920	1980
South Atlantic	Ireland	Germany	Russia and Lithuania	English
	Germany	Ireland	Germany	Irish
	England	England	Italy	German
	Scotland	Russia	Poland	Scottish
	France	Cuba and West Indies	England	French
East South Central	Ireland	Germany	Germany	English
	Germany	Ireland	Italy	Irish
	England	England	Russia and Lithuania	German
	France	Italy	England	Scottish
	Scotland	Canada	Ireland	French
West South Central	Germany	Germany	Mexico	English
	Ireland	Mexico	Germany	Irish
	France	Italy	Italy	German
	Mexico	Austria	Czechoslovakia	Mexican
	England	Ireland	Russia and Lithuania	French
Mountain	Mexico	England	Mexico	English
	England	Germany	England	German
	Ireland	Canada	Canada	Irish
	Canada	Sweden	Germany	Mexican
	Germany	Ireland	Sweden	Scottish
Pacific	Mexico	Germany	Canada	English
	England	Canada	Italy	German
	Germany	Ireland	Germany	Irish
	Ireland	England	Mexico	Mexican
	France	Sweden	England	French

grants living in Texas, California, and the New Mexico Territory was quite high in 1850—respectively, 27, 29, and 66.[11] Nevertheless, in contrast to 1850, the figures for 1900, and more so for 1920, reflect the increasing numbers of immigrants from SCE Europe, as well as the important migration from Scandinavia.)

In summary, the geographical prominence of various groups in different areas of the United States at present reflects not only their nu-

[11]U.S. Bureau of the Census, *Seventh Census of the United States: 1850* (Washington, DC: U.S. Government Printing Office, 1853), table XV.

merical importance in the nation as a whole, but also the initital settlement patterns at the time of their arrival. Each area experiences a
certain "cumulative layering" in which newer immigrant groups leave
their mark on an area while those of earlier groups persist. Geographic
concentration declines over time, perhaps with dispersion occurring
through the generations. The 1980 spatial patterns still reflect the influence of earlier geographic variations in the nature of the economy and
the opportunity structure faced by each group. The current picture will
be considered later in this chapter.

Major Urban Centers
Historical Background

The ethnic composition of major urban areas has long been a topic
of considerable interest in the United States, and a topic with important
political and social ramifications. At present, we are fully aware of the
very large concentrations of blacks and Latino groups in the *central
cities* of many metropolitan areas. Less obvious is the fact that in earlier
periods other groups were massively concentrated in many of our urban
centers. As is the case today, this concentration of certain ethnic groups
generated great concern among some segments of the population at the
time. It is difficult to trace this feature through the years because the
metropolitan boundaries change and there are no true ancestry data for
earlier periods. But even a cursory glance indicates that there were great
concentrations of specific white groups in these centers in the late nineteenth and early twentieth centuries.

In the leading cities of 1890 (all of which are still leading cities) the
populations were very much of German and/or Irish origin. These two
groups (first and second generation combined) amount to 54 percent of
the entire population of New York (including Brooklyn), 45 percent of
Chicago, 41 percent of Philadelphia, 54 percent of St. Louis (primarily
owing to the 40 percent contribution from Germans), 45 percent of Boston (primarily owing to the Irish), and 34 percent of Baltimore.[12] (These
data refer only to the foreign-born or second-generation component of
the entire population; hence the role of these two groups is underestimated to the degree that members with such ancestry are third or later
generation.)[13]

[12]Based on data reported in U.S. Census Office, *Compendium of the Eleventh Census: 1890*, pt. 3 (Washington, DC: U.S. Government Printing Office, 1897) pp. 83, 111.
[13]On the other hand, this procedure underestimates the numerical importance of
groups that arrived in substantial numbers much earlier since they will tend to be concentrated in generations that are not measured with nativity data.

By 1920, the new immigrant groups from SCE European sources were filling up these same cities and changing the ethnic nature of the cities.

In Chicago, fully one-third of the residents were either immigrant or second generation members of these groups; approximately 40 percent of the residents of both Cleveland and Newark belonged to these groups. In New York City, the newcomers were less than 7 percentage points away from claiming an absolute majority of the population. In other leading industrial centers of the era, Boston, Buffalo, Detroit, Philadelphia, and Pittsburgh, one-quarter of the population were South-Central-Eastern European immigrants or their immediate descendants. To be sure, there were a number of other major cities, for example, Indianapolis, Washington, D.C., Kansas City, Cincinnati, and Seattle, where the new groups were a less substantial percentage. But clearly the enormous numbers coming from these parts of Europe, coupled with the economic opportunities available in the industrial centers of the Northeast, created fear among the older white settlers about the maintenance of the American Society.[14]

Current Situation

If one examines the present-day ethnic/racial composition of the large urbanized areas—as opposed to the central cities—one finds a concentration of groups that is quite different from that suggested by either historical concerns about the new Europeans or the current focus on the makeup of inner cities. Table 3.6 indicates the most common ethnic responses in each of 33 large urbanized areas in 1980.[15] (The sixth largest entry is shown for those areas where one of the five most common ancestry replies was "no response.") Data are provided for the 18 largest urbanized areas along with other large centers selected in part to provide

[14]Lieberson, *A Piece of the Pie*, pp. 23–24.

[15]"An urbanized area consists of a central city or cities and surrounding closely settled territory or 'urban fringe.' " U.S. Bureau of the Census, *1980 Census of Population, U.S. Summary*, "Number of Inhabitants," PC80-1-A1 (Washington, DC: U.S. Government Printing Office, 1983b), p. A-3. Urbanized areas are delineated by the Census Bureau to pool data together for urban centers that are integrated socially and economically and that together have a certain minimum population. Unlike the standard metropolitan statistical area delineation, urbanized areas provide a better separation of urban from rural in the surrounding area. (U.S. Bureau of the Census, "Number of Inhabitants," pp. A-3, A-4.) All of the 1980 data refer to these areas and hence any reference simply to a "city," "place," "urban area," and so on, is simply shorthand for the ubanized area. This is not the case for earlier periods, as discussed below. Also, for urbanized areas that have more than one place and/or state in their title—for example, "Los Angeles–Long Beach," "Chicago, Illinois–Northwestern Indiana," "Washington, D.C.–Maryland–Virginia"—at times reference will be to an abbreviated title, for example, "Los Angeles," "Chicago," and "Washington, D.C."

TABLE 3.6
Five Largest Ancestry Groups in Selected Urbanized Areas, 1980

City	First	Second	Third	Fourth	Fifth
Atlanta	Black 29%	English 27%	Irish 17%	German 12%	No Response 9%
Baltimore	Black 30	German 26	Irish 17 English 17		Polish 6
Boston	Irish 30	English 19	Italian 17	French 8	German 7
Buffalo	German 29	Polish 20	Irish 18	Italian 15	English 13
Chicago	Black 22	German 20	Irish 15	Polish 12	English 9
Cincinnati	German 39	English 20	Irish 19 Black 19		No Response 7
Cleveland	German 22	Black 20	English 14 Irish 14		Polish 12
Dallas–Fort Worth	English 27	Irish 20	German 16	No Response 10	Mexican 8
Denver	German 28	English 25	Irish 20	Mexican 8	No Response 7
Detroit	Black 23	German 21	English 16 Irish 16		Polish 12
Houston	English 20 Black 20		German 15 Irish 15		Mexican 14
Indianapolis	German 27	English 24	Black 19	Irish 18	No Response 9
Kansas City	English 26 German 26		Irish 23	Black 16	No Response 10
Los Angeles	Mexican 21	English 18	German 15	Irish 13	Black 10
Miami	Spanish 29	Black 18	English 10	German 8 Irish 8	

TABLE 3.6 (continued)

City	First		Second		Third		Fourth		Fifth	
Milwaukee	German	45	Polish	16	Irish	13			English	10
					Black	13				
Minneapolis–St. Paul	German	39	Irish	18	Norwegian	15	Swedish	14		
							English	14		
New Orleans	Black	36	French	22	German	16	English	13		
							Irish	13		
New York	Italian	18			Irish	15	German	12	English	7
	Black	18								
Oklahoma City	English	27	Irish	23	German	20	No Response	12	Black	11
Oxnard	English	23	German	21	Mexican	20	Irish	18	French	7
Philadelphia	Irish	23			German	19	English	13		
	Black	23					Italian	13		
Pittsburgh	German	31	Irish	23	English	15	Italian	13	Polish	9
Portland, OR	German	30	English	28	Irish	20	No Response	9	French	8
St. Louis	German	36	Irish	21			English	17	French	7
			Black	21						
Salt Lake City	English	54	German	15	Irish	11	Danish	8	No Response	7
San Antonio	Mexican	45	German	16	English	15	Irish	12	Black	7
San Bernardino–Riverside	English	23	German	21	Mexican	18	Irish	17	Black	7
San Diego	English	23	German	21	Irish	18	Mexican	14	No Response	7
San Francisco–Oakland	English	20	German	16			Black	13	French	6
			Irish	16					Asian	10
San Jose	English	23	German	19	Irish	17	Mexican	14	Asian	8
Seattle–Everett	English	28	German	25	Irish	19	Norwegian	9	French	8
									No Response	8
Washington, D.C.	Black	30	English	22	German	17	Irish	16	Scottish	5
									No Response	5

a broader geographic picture. Although the urban areas differ from one another in their ethnic makeup, they share certain features. Without exception, the largest five ethnic groups specified in every urbanized area include the nation's three largest groups: English, German, and Irish. However, the relative positions of the groups vary greatly.

English, for example, is the ancestry—in part or whole—of slightly more than half of the population in Salt Lake City. At the other extreme, it is reported by only 7 and 9 percent, respectively, of the residents of the New York and Chicago areas. Nevertheless, even in the latter cases, the English are still one of the five largest ethnic groups. The numerical importance of Germans likewise varies widely, ranging from 7 and 8 percent of the population in Boston and Miami, respectively, to 45 percent in Milwaukee and 39 percent in both Minneapolis–St. Paul and Cincinnati. The Irish range is not as great—ranging from 30 percent in Boston to 8 percent in Miami.

As for the single largest group in these urbanized areas, the results are somewhat different. The English and Germans are again very important, each occupying first place in 11 urbanized areas. However, the Irish are the single largest group in only two of the 33 areas, Philadelphia (where they are in a tie for first) and Boston. Blacks, on the other hand, are the largest group in nine of the urbanized areas. (Blacks are one of the five leading groups in many of the areas, although Table 3.6 shows that they are not as widespread as the three leading white groups.) Finally, Chicanos are also the largest in two areas.[16]

The geographical divisions are related to where the groups hold first place. Germans are the largest group through much of the Midwest (Cincinnati, Cleveland, Indianapolis, Kansas City, Milwaukee, Minneapolis–St. Paul, and St. Louis) and two industrial centers in the East (Buffalo and Pittsburgh). In addition, they are the largest group in Denver and Portland, Oregon. The pattern for the English is strikingly different. Kansas City, where the two groups tie, is the southern- and western-most edge of the German urban stronghold in the Midwest; by contrast, it is the upper edge of the English ethnic stronghold. The English are first in Dallas–Fort Worth, Houston, and Oklahoma City in the West South Central states and in much of the West (Oxnard–Ventura–Thousand Oaks, Salt Lake City, San Bernadino–Riverside, San Diego, San Francisco–Oakland, San Jose, and Seattle–Everett).

Blacks are the numerically most important group in those parts of the Midwest and industrial East where Germans occupy second place

---

[16]There are ties in some urbanized areas for the largest group, and therefore the total exceeds 33. The largest groups in the central cities of these urbanized areas would be another matter, given the concentration of some groups in the central cities. However, space does not permit examination of this matter here.

(Chicago and Detroit), and also edge out Germans in industrial Baltimore. They are also the largest single group in much of the Central and Atlantic parts of the South (Atlanta, New Orleans, Washington, D.C.). In addition, blacks tie with the English in Houston, with the Irish in Philadelphia, and with the Italians in New York. Latinos are the largest group in three of the cities examined. In the San Antonio urbanized area, 45 percent of the residents report at least some Mexican ancestry, and Mexicans are also the largest group in Los Angeles. In Miami, Cubans are the largest group (presumably they are the vast majority of the " Other Spanish" occupying first place). Italians are the only other group represented in the first position, being tied with blacks in New York.[17]

The "ethnic character" of a city is affected not only by the largest group in the area, and/or even the relative prominence of the nation's other major groups, or the intensity of the affiliation held by these persons—as important as these features may be—but also by other ethnic components. First, cities vary greatly in their degree of ethnic heterogeneity. As Table 3.6 shows, urbanized areas vary greatly in the percentage of the population belonging to the group achieving a given rank position. The English are the largest group in the Salt Lake City area, with 54 percent of the residents; likewise, they are the largest group in the San Francisco–Oakland and Houston urbanized areas, but amount to only 20 percent of the population. Irish ancestry is reported by 23 percent of the residents of Philadelphia, a level which ties them for first place; the same percentage in Kansas City puts them in third place. Thus, in many urbanized areas, there is considerable room for other groups to play an important role.

In addition, there are both contemporary and historical forces operating to affect the influence of a given ethnic group on an urban area. Most of the ethnic groups have been in the process of assimilating with respect to at least superficial characteristics such as language and dress. Hence an urban place that is the point of arrival for massive numbers of immigrants direct from their homeland is going to be differently affected by the same ethnic makeup as one which becomes populated only by later generations of the same ethnicity—say, the third or fourth generations. In this regard, the ethnic character of a city such as Los

[17]As indicated in Chapter 1, data on Jews are not available. Although Jews would certainly rank as one of the largest ethnic groups in the New York urbanized area, they are probably not the largest. The New York Standard Consolidated Statistical Area's boundaries are not radically different from the boundary for the urbanized area; the 1980 populations are, respectively, 16.1 and 15.6 million. Piecing together various Jewish population estimates for different subparts of the SCSA, it is estimated that 13 percent are Jewish—as defined and estimated by the various sources used by Alvin Chenkin, "Jewish Population in the United States, 1982," in Milton Himmelfarb and David Singer, eds., *American Jewish Yearbook, 1983* (New York: American Jewish Committee, 1983).

Angeles may be relatively more affected by its Asian and Chicano components than by some white groups who move westward after several generations of settlement elsewhere in the nation. On the other hand, once-prominent immigrant groups may have a lingering impact on the culture and traditions of a place long after their descendants have assimilated and changed.

Of special concern here, however, is the fact that many other ethnic groups have an important demographic impact on a limited number of places. Swedes and Norwegians, along with the massive German and substantial Irish component, help to give Minneapolis–St. Paul its distinctive ethnic character. But except for Norwegians in Seattle and Swedes in Salt Lake City, neither of these groups is especially important in any of the other urbanized areas considered. This is true of other groups as well; Italians are important in Boston, Buffalo, Philadelphia, and Pittsburgh, as well as in New York, but numerically they are a relatively minor group in many other places. Likewise, the French are the largest single white component in New Orleans (22 percent of the residents), but they are only a moderately important group in other places where they are among the top five (see Table 3.6). Poles constitute from 12 to 20 percent of the population in such industrial centers as Chicago, Detroit, Milwaukee, and Buffalo and they are important to a lesser degree in Cleveland, Pittsburgh, and Baltimore. American Indians are especially important in the Oklahoma City area, with 10 percent of the residents reporting this origin. Likewise, the Mexican-ancestry group is also important in various California areas (Oxnard, San Bernadino, San Diego, and San Jose) as well as in Houston, Dallas, and Denver in the areas of Old Mexico. (Detailed data for particular groups and/or areas are provided in Appendix Table 3.1.)

The variation in the location of the nation's largest groups, along with this concentration of some of the smaller groups, means that many urbanized areas have rather distinctive ethnic patterns. Miami, for example, has remarkably few Germans, English, and Irish; it is not uncommon in many areas to find one of these groups exceeding the combined percentage for all three in Miami (and that ignores the overlap between individuals in Miami). Other urban centers have distinctive features, reflecting the relative importance among the leading three white groups and/or the role of blacks and/or Latinos and/or the numerically important presence of relatively uncommon groups in a restricted number of places—for example, the French in New Orleans or Norwegians in Minneapolis–St. Paul. In other cases, the gaps are moderate but important. The populations in both Chicago and Detroit, for example, report 12 percent Polish ancestry and are within 1 percentage point of each other in the size of their black, Irish, and German components.

However, 9 percent of Chicago's population reports English ancestry whereas it is 16 percent in Detroit. This probably reflects the important migration of Appalachian whites to Detroit's assembly plants and the proximity of Detroit to Canada (there are also more French in Detroit and more Mexicans in Chicago).

In some cases, the historical and geographic forces combine to generate remarkably similar centers. Cincinnati and St. Louis, both older areas whose period of rapid growth peaked earlier than did some of the other Midwest centers, are similar in the relatively minor role of SCE Europeans; the paramount importance of Germans (respectively, 39 and 36 percent); the significant component of blacks (19 and 21 percent), English (20 and 17 percent), and Irish (19 and 21 percent).[18] Although "American" is the fifth largest specified group in Cincinnati (5 percent) and French the fifth largest in St. Louis (7 percent), the actual positions are similar as well; French ancestry is reported for 4 percent of Cincinnati and "American" is reported for 4 percent of St. Louis. Thus, these two areas are remarkably similar in the role of their leading groups.

The new European groups are of demographic importance only for a restricted range of major urban centers. This may be surprising to a number of readers, given the prominence of SCE European groups in sociological discussions of continued ethnic ties among white ethnic groups as well as the attention given to groups such as Italians and Poles in the mass media.[19] Although SCE European groups play an important role in many of the older centers of the Northeast and industrialized Midwest, they are a minor demographic force elsewhere.

The area termed the "Sunbelt" begins in the upper corner of the Southeast—Baltimore and Washington—and sweeps through the South (Atlanta, Miami, Oklahoma City, Dallas, Houston, San Antonio) and then moves westward, expanding upward into the Mountain States (Denver, Salt Lake City) and along the Pacific Coast (six urbanized areas in California, beginning with San Diego) to Portland and Seattle (two unlikely candidates for Sunbelt status but possessing a moderate winter).

---

[18]Although data on urbanized areas cannot be traced back to the relevant early periods, the city size data are relevant, particularly for earlier periods when the central city would almost certainly have been a very large part of the urbanized area. In 1850, Cincinnati was the 6th largest city in the nation; by 1910 it was 10th, and by 1980 it was 32nd (24th largest urbanized area). St. Louis , which moved from 8th to 4th place in the last half of the nineteenth century, was 26th in 1980 and the 11th largest urbanized area. Data are from U.S. Bureau of the Census, *1980 Census of Population, U.S. Summary*, "Characteristics of the Population," PC80-1-A1 (Washington, DC: U.S. Government Printing Office, 1983c), tables 28 and 35.

[19]Nathan Glazer and Daniel Patrick Moynihan, *Beyond the Melting Pot* (Cambridge, MA: MIT Press, 1963); Michael Novak, *The Rise of the Unmeltable Ethnics* (New York: Macmillan, 1971).

Except for Baltimore (which is really an older extension of the industrial belt) where 6 percent of the population is of Polish ancestry, there are no SCE European groups among the leading five specified ethnicities in any of the other Sunbelt urbanized areas. Blacks and Chicanos are among the leaders in many Sunbelt areas; Scots and French in some areas; Asians in two areas; Swedes, Danes, and Norwegians in one area each. In most cases, the new European groups do not amount to a sizable percentage even if we go further down the list, although Italians in New Orleans and San Francisco (8 and 7 percent, respectively) are among the rare exceptions. A full determination of the factors responsible for this is beyond this overview, but at least some clues will be provided below when we consider internal migration in the United States.

Trends in Mobility for Specific Ethnic Groups

Historically, the United States has been a nation of movers. Growth of the Sunbelt's population and the outmigration from the colder areas of the nation are the most recent forms of this long-standing feature of American society. It is not possible to determine the long-run consequences of the current migration patterns since there is little reason to expect them to continue unaltered through the years. But an analysis of the movement of Americans within the United States during the five years preceding the 1980 census is of value because it tells us something about the potential impact of present-day shifts for the long-term ethnic distributions in the nation. It also provides a dynamic, contemporary test of the interpretation offered earlier about the tendency—with time—for ethnic groups to lose their distinctive spatial distributions.

Since the data are restricted to the movement of persons living in the United States in both 1975 and 1980, the analysis is confined to persons aged 5 and over in 1980. The census determined where such persons lived in each period, and it is possible to compare their locations and thereby determine the "net" movements from one subarea of the United States to another for persons reporting a specific ethnic ancestry. (A standard limitation of such data is that movement is known only for changes from the beginning to the end of the period—all other movements within the period are not recorded.) No effort is made to separate persons of mixed or single ancestry. Thus, the data for English include persons of mixed English ancestry and the data for Italians similarly include those of partly Italian ancestry. A person of mixed Italian-English ancestry will appear in the information for both groups.

For each group, it is possible to determine the rates of change between areas of the United States during the 1975–80 period (a "transition matrix"). By applying these rates for a long span of time, eventually a stable pattern evolves in which there are no further changes between succeeding five-year periods. Contrary to what might be our intuitive expectation, the stable state that finally results is independent of the initial distribution of the U.S. population (the "vector"). This procedure is called a Markov Chain analysis and provides an interesting way of describing the contemporary patterns of internal migration even though we can be reasonably certain that the long-term consequences will never occur. It enables us to project the contemporary internal migration patterns of different groups as a way of learning intrinsic ramifications of their current behavior.[20]

A projection of the 1975–80 trends into the future, via this Markov analysis, makes it clear that there would be significant changes in the percentage of the nation's population found in each area if current rates for the entire population were to continue indefinitely. Declines occur throughout the Northeast and Midwest (the first four areas shown in Table 3.7), accompanied by particularly sharp increases in the West South Central, Mountain, and Pacific states, along with increases elsewhere in the Sunbelt. The gains in some areas coupled with the losses in others together yield some massive shifts. Both the industrial Mid Atlantic and the South Atlantic have about 16 percent of the population in 1980 (that is, the population aged 5 and over who lived in the United States five years earlier). If current rates were to continue into the future indefinitely, the Mid Atlantic percentage of the national population would decline from 16 to 7, whereas the South Atlantic would increase to 19. The long-term ramifications of net internal migration between 1975 and 1980 can be seen for other areas in Table 3.7.

We will now examine the specific spatial mobility in 1975–80 for each of the groups indicated in Appendix Table 3.2. For the members of a group living in each of the nine geographic divisions, we calculated the actual proportions remaining in the area during the period as well as the proportions going to each of the remaining divisions. This spatial mobility table for each group compared with that for all Americans shows some surprising results. Although the distinctive spatial distri-

[20]This procedure also ignores international migration into or out of the nation, differentials in fertility by group or by region within a group, and differentials in mortality. It is also unstandardized for age. Thus, it should not be interpreted as a possible future outcome—but as a technique of exploring the intrinsic ramifications of current trends. For a general discussion of Markov Chains, see D. J. Bartholomew, *Stochastic Models for Social Processes*, 2nd ed. (London: Wiley, 1973).

TABLE 3.7

Present and Expected Distribution
of the Population of the United States

Division	Percentage in Each Division	
	1980	Expected
New England	5%	3%
Mid Atlantic	16	7
East North Central	18	12
West North Central	8	7
South Atlantic	16	19
East South Central	7	8
West South Central	10	18
Mountain	5	8
Pacific	14	18
Total	100	100

NOTE: Distribution for 1980 is based on the population aged 5 and over who were residing in the United States in 1975. Expected distribution is based on a projection of 1975–80 net internal migration through a Markov Chain analysis (see text).

butions of most groups would decline over time if current migration patterns were to operate indefinitely, in a number of instances the index of dissimilarity (D) would be higher in the future than it is now. The indexes rise for the Irish, Swedes, Welsh, South Asians, and several residual groupings ("No response" and "All other"), and they do not change at all for English, Germans, French, and Americans. Under any circumstance, there is a high level of stability in the relative positions of the 25 groups considered, $r = .98$, although there is a general decline such that groups with indexes of dissimilarity from the remainder of the population of at least 17 tend to decline whereas those with lower indexes tend to rise (based on a regression equation where $a = 2.81$ and $b = .84$).

This is a surprising result since earlier we were inclined to interpret the magnitude of a group's unique spatial distribution as a function of length of residence in the nation. In a certain sense, this result is consistent with such a conclusion; to wit, in general the groups with spatial distributions most distinctive from the remainder of the nation's population are also the groups most likely to decline over time if everyone follows the observed 1975–80 patterns of change. However, if these patterns of change continue indefinitely, present-day differences would by no means be eliminated. This is, of course, implied by the correlation reported above between current levels of spatial distinctiveness and those projected into the future. If the ongoing patterns of migration were to eventually eliminate historically derived unique features of location for each group, there would be no correlation between 1980 spatial distributions for groups and their distributions in the future after the long-term shifts implied by contemporary migration patterns had a chance to work their way through.

Why is this the case and what does it mean for earlier interpretations? First of all, there is currently an important linkage between ethnicity and where people move. In general, groups that are disproportionately overrepresented or underrepresented in an area (compared with the rest of the nation's population) tend to have migration patterns which maintain these distinctive distributions. (In Appendix Table 3.2, we can compare the distributions for each group with that for the entire nation.) Poles, for example, compared with the entire population, had relatively larger proportions in the New England (9 versus 5 percent for the entire population), Mid Atlantic (32 versus 16 percent), and East North Central (33 versus 18 percent) divisions. Poles are below the national level in the remaining six divisions. The migration patterns for Poles during the 1975–80 span imply long-run declines for them in these areas (respectively, from 9 to 7 percent, 32 to 20 percent, and 33 to 24 percent) but the remainder of the population also declines so that there are still relatively more Poles in these areas than in the remainder of the country. Although the Polish proportions increase in all but one of the remaining areas, these proportions do not catch up to the increases for the remainder of the population. The net effect is that the Polish group still maintains a distinctive distribution.

Two different mechanisms could account for the maintenance of this distinctive distribution; either Poles have less propensity than others to leave the areas in which they are concentrated at present and/or they have a greater propensity than other groups to migrate *to* these areas from elsewhere in the nation. (The reader may wonder if the initial concentration of these groups would mathematically affect the long-term outcome, but the Markov model leads to the rather counterintuitive rejection of this as an influence in the long run.) An examination of the specific inmigration and outmigration rates in the Polish case discloses that both forces operate. Poles living in the Mid Atlantic and industrial Midwest divisions have a greater propensity to remain there than do other residents of these areas (albeit a slightly lower propensity to remain in New England), and in most areas they have a greater propensity for migrating to these locations than do other residents. This pattern is by no means unique to Poles. Americans of German ancestry are concentrated in both parts of the Midwest and slightly in excess of the national figure in the Mid Atlantic states. Their propensity to remain in the Midwest is greater than that of all residents of these areas, *and* their propensity to migrate to these areas from elsewhere is generally greater than that for other residents of the same locations. An analogous pattern is found for many other groups as well; Norwegians have an exceptional concentration in the West North Central states at present and their propensity to remain there is greater than average for all residents of that part of the Midwest; likewise, their propensity to migrate to it from elsewhere is also stronger. By contrast, in all but the Pacific states Norwegians have a greater propensity to leave than do other residents of those divisions.

On the other hand, the population reporting themselves as Russian in ancestry (reflecting Jewish patterns) have a rather distinctive pattern. They are heavily concentrated in the Mid Atlantic states in 1980 (41 percent of all Russians), and this figure would drop to 18 percent (compared with 7 percent for all Americans) if their current migration stream were to operate indefinitely. This would occur in a different way, however; the propensity of Russians to leave the Mid Atlantic states is greater than that for all residents of the area, but the propensity of Russians living elsewhere to migrate to these states is greater than that of other residents of the areas under comparison. As a consequence, the Russian percentage declines, but the group still maintains a higher proportion than does the national population as a whole. The behavior of Russians in the Pacific states is more in keeping with the general pattern observed above; Russians are slightly in excess of the national population in their concentration in the Pacific states. In turn, we find a lesser propensity for the group to leave and a stronger propensity for members of the group living elsewhere to enter. The Russian ancestry population, if the current migration patterns were to continue indefinitely, would eventually end up with 34 percent living in the Pacific.

There are a variety of possible explanations for the tendency of groups to maintain their distinctive regional concentrations, albeit in more cases than not there is something of a decline over time. There can be rural-urban differences in the propensities to outmigrate and some of the groups may well be relatively concentrated in those parts of the nation where they are also engaged in farming activities. The Norwegian data, for example, do not distinguish those living in Minneapolis–St. Paul from those living on farms. The age distribution is also not taken into account, and this is of potentially great importance insofar as age is related to both the propensity to migrate and the direction of migration. Aside from the agricultural issue, the groups differ on a wide variety of other skill levels and occupational features that could very well affect the propensity to leave; for example, service jobs and/or professional jobs might expand in an area at the same time as manufacturing jobs are declining. Chain migration factors may also play a role in terms of both the propensity to migrate to certain areas and the differentials in the propensity for groups to migrate into declining areas. Thus, possibly Norwegians living outside of the upper Midwest are more likely to have relatives, know others, or originally be from that area. Further, we should not rule out the possibility that some of the present-day concentrations are the product of such differential migration tendencies in earlier periods and hence the direction of the causal notions could be partly reversed. Moreover, there is the possibility that the groups' migration patterns may change over time, particularly as a function of generation in the United States. In such an event, projection of current migration patterns into the future may be even more inappropriate for "newer" groups than for the others. Finally, the 1975–80 period may be affected by especially idiosyncratic forces that are particularly misleading for a projection.[21]

In any case, ethnic and racial groups in the United States still maintain rather distinctive spatial distributions. Current patterns of internal migration are operating in the direction of moderately reducing some of the more distinctive geographic concentrations. But these current internal shifts, although of considerable consequence for the nation as a whole if they were to go on indefinitely, hardly work toward fully eliminating distinctive ethnic concentrations. The groups are generally leaving the same areas and generally increasing their representation in the Sunbelt. But this does not eliminate the concentrations because of several factors: Groups in the declining areas still vary in their propensity to leave; likewise, they differ in the propensity to enter these areas from elsewhere; and the destinations of the outmigrants from the geographic area appear to be affected by ethnic origin. As a consequence, current internal migration patterns indicate that at present there is little reason to expect the ethnic linkage to region to disappear even with massive internal population shifts.

Some International Comparisons

Although examples of ethnic isolation are still found in the United States and there is no evidence that they are currently disappearing, the observed levels are by no means uniquely high in this country. Indeed,

---

[21]Under any circumstances, it would be worth determining the reasons for the apparent contradiction between the results obtained here and those reported earlier with respect to the correlation between the historical patterns of arrival into the United States and spatially distinctive patterns of present-day location.

they are low compared with a number of nations. The situation for the numerically large groups in the United States, for example, is not comparable to that found in Canada for the French Canadian population. Persons of French ancestry (both single and mixed) amount to about 30 pecent of the nation's population, a figure in excess of that for even the British or Germans in the United States.[22] Nevertheless, despite their numbers, the spatial distribution of the French is striking in two different ways. First, 82 percent of Quebec's population is of French ethnicity, either exclusively or in some mixture. Second, 73 percent of all of Canada's French are concentrated in this one province. (The figure is even higher for those of single French ancestry, with 79 percent living in Quebec.)

Likewise, Yugoslavia experiences a level of spatial concentration unknown in the United States. The two largest ethnic groups, the Serbians and Croats, amount to 40 and 20 percent, respectively, of Yugoslavia's population. Some 74 percent of the Serbs live in Serbia, where they are 71 percent of the population; and 78 percent of the Croats live in Croatia, where they are 79 percent of the population. Concentration is as impressive for some of the smaller ethnic groups; for example, 95 percent of Macedonians in Yugoslavia are found in Macedonia, albeit they are only 69 percent of that area's population.[23]

This greater ethnic isolation and concentration could be due to a variety of factors. For example, the number of major political divisions in both Yugoslavia and Canada is far smaller than the 50 states found in this nation; the total population of the United States is roughly ten times the number in either of these nations; and there are significant historical forces operating in Canada to create and maintain the initial levels of isolation.[24] Likewise, the political structure of Yugoslavia operates to maintain these sharp regional differences.[25] But there are some fundamental differences even in very large nations; ethno-linguistic spa-

---

[22]Computed from data reported in Statistics Canada, *1981 Census of Canada, Population*, vol. 1: *Ethnic Origin* (Ottawa, Ontario: Statistics Canada, 1984), table 1. (The British are an even larger category in Canada.)

[23]Computed from 1971 census data reported in Paul A. Schoup, *The East European and Soviet Data Handbook: Political, Social and Developmental Indicators 1945–1975* (New York: Columbia University Press, 1981), tables C7 and C10.

[24]Stanley Lieberson, *Language and Ethnic Relations in Canada* (New York: Wiley, 1970b).

[25]George Klein and Patricia V. Klein, "United States and Yugoslavia: Divergent Approaches Toward Ethnicity," in Chester L. Hunt and Lewis Walker, eds., *Ethnic Dynamics: Patterns of Intergroup Relations in Various Societies* (Holmes Beach, FL: Learning Publications, 1979).

tial concentrations appear to be far more marked in India.[26] And the Soviet Union, despite a deliberate policy of moving ethnic Russians into other parts of the nation, has levels of concentration unmatched by major ethnic groups in the United States. For example, Belorussians constitute 79 percent of the population in Belorussia, Ukrainians 74 percent of the population in the Ukraine, Armenians 90 percent of the population in Armenia, Azerbaijani 78 percent of the population in Azerbaijan, and so on. In the massive Russian Soviet Federated Socialist Republic, Russian is the reported ethnicity for 83 percent of the population[27]

In short, the United States experiences levels of broad spatial isolation that are relatively modest compared with at least some other nations of the world. (This should not be confused with the issue of segregation within cities, which is discussed elsewhere in the monograph series.) Such a pattern is, no doubt, of importance as both a cause and an effect in the nature of the nation's ethnic and race relations. On the one hand, it reduces and minimizes the potential for separatist movements since the groups are not that isolated and the states are not that homogeneous.[28] Moreover, insofar as interaction occurs across ethnic lines—or there is at least contact between the groups—assimilation is encouraged. On the other hand, this relative heterogeneity reflects the fact that a variety of groups responded at the same time to the new economic opportunities developing in the nation. Of course, the great demographic role of immigrants and their descendants is due not merely to massive immigration but also to the demographic decimation experienced by the indigenous peoples of what is now the United States.

[26]See Stanley Lieberson and James F. O'Connor, "Language Diversity in a Nation and Its Regions," in Stanley Lieberson, ed., *Language Diversity and Language Contact* (Stanford, CA: Stanford University Press, 1981), p. 181.

[27]Computed from 1979 census data reported in Schoup, *East European and Soviet Data Handbook*, table C9.

[28]Stanley Lieberson, "Stratification and Ethnic Groups," *Sociological Inquiry* 40 (1970a): 172–81.

APPENDIX TABLE 3.1
Ethnic Distribution in Selected Urbanized Areas, 1980

Group	Percentage of Population with Specified Ancestry					
	Atlanta	Baltimore	Boston	Buffalo	Chicago	Cincinnati
English	27.0%	16.8%	18.9%	13.1%	9.5%	19.8%
German	11.5	26.1	7.3	28.7	20.0	39.4
Irish	16.6	17.4	29.8	17.7	14.5	19.3
French	3.4	3.0	7.5	4.6	3.0	4.1
Italian	1.5	5.0	16.9	15.0	7.1	3.0
Scottish	5.8	3.4	5.2	3.2	2.4	3.2
Polish	1.3	5.7	3.8	20.1	11.5	1.2
Dutch	1.9	1.8	.9	1.5	1.5	2.4
Swedish	.7	.8	2.0	.8	2.8	.4
Norwegian	.4	.5	.6	.4	1.2	.3
Russian	.8	2.4	3.8	2.1	2.5	1.3
Czech	.2	1.0	.2	.5	2.5	.3
Hungarian	.4	.6	.4	1.5	1.0	1.0
Welsh	.5	.6	.4	.8	.4	.8
Danish	.4	1.5	.3	.3	.5	.2
Portuguese	.0	.1	2.2	.1	.1	.0
Black	28.6	29.8	5.9	11.2	22.5	18.7
Mexican	.4	.1	.1	.2	5.5	.2
Puerto Rican	.0	.2	.8	.7	1.6	.0
Spanish—Other	.7	.5	1.3	.4	1.6	.2
American Indian	2.9	2.1	.7	1.0	1.1	2.6
American	6.6	3.2	3.3	2.0	2.1	5.0
United States	.1	.0	.1	.1	.1	.1
White/Caucasian	.4	.1	.2	.0	.0	.2
North American Other	.2	.3	3.0	1.0	.3	.1
Other SCE European	1.2	2.3	4.8	2.5	6.0	1.6
Other Northwestern European	.5	.3	.4	.3	.7	.5
Middle Eastern/North African	.3	.4	.8	.5	.5	.2
African, Caribbean, Pacific	.5	.7	1.2	.6	.5	.3
South Asian	.2	.3	.3	.3	.5	.2
Other Asian	.8	1.4	1.6	.3	2.0	.2
No Response	.1	6.1	7.0	3.7	4.8	7.2
All Other	.6	.7	1.2	.4	.8	.5

APPENDIX TABLE 3.1 *(continued)*

Group	Percentage of Population with Specified Ancestry					
	Cleveland	Dallas–Fort Worth	Denver	Detroit	Houston	Indianapolis
English	13.6%	26.6%	25.4%	16.3%	19.5%	24.4%
German	21.8	15.7	28.2	20.5	15.3	26.8
Irish	14.2	20.2	20.2	15.5	15.1	18.4
French	2.3	4.8	6.1	7.8	5.3	4.5
Italian	8.3	1.6	4.0	5.8	2.1	1.7
Scottish	3.0	5.9	6.1	4.6	4.6	4.3
Polish	8.6	.9	2.5	12.0	1.7	1.1
Dutch	1.4	2.5	3.2	1.9	1.8	2.8
Swedish	1.0	1.2	3.8	1.0	.9	.8
Norwegian	.3	.6	2.5	.4	.6	.5
Russian	3.1	.5	1.8	2.1	.6	.4
Czech	3.3	.7	1.1	.7	1.4	.3
Hungarian	5.4	.3	.7	2.0	.3	.3
Welsh	.9	.6	1.3	.6	.5	.7
Danish	.2	.3	1.3	.3	.3	.3
Portuguese	.1	.1	.1	.1	.1	.1
Black	20.3	16.1	5.4	23.1	20.1	19.0
Mexican	.2	8.3	8.0	1.0	14.4	.4
Puerto Rican	.6	.1	.2	.2	.2	.1
Spanish—Other	.5	1.5	5.3	.5	2.0	.4
American Indian	1.4	5.4	3.0	2.3	3.5	3.7
American	3.2	5.7	3.0	2.8	3.7	8.8
United States	.1	.3	.1	.1	.1	.1
White/Caucasian	.1	.3	.3	.1	.3	.3
North American Other	.4	.2	.6	1.2	.2	.3
Other SCE European	11.8	.9	2.6	4.6	1.1	1.3
Other Northwestern European	.4	.7	1.2	1.2	.5	.7
Middle Eastern/North African	.6	.3	.4	1.7	.5	.4
African, Caribbean, Pacific	.4	.4	.8	.5	.5	.4
South Asian	.2	.3	.2	.3	.4	.3
Other Asian	.5	.8	1.5	.7	1.7	.6
No Response	5.0	9.9	7.1	5.0	10.3	9.8
All Other	.5	.5	.9	.4	.4	.2

APPENDIX TABLE 3.1 *(continued)*

	Percentage of Population with Specified Ancestry					
Group	Kansas City	Los Angeles– Long Beach	Miami	Mil- waukee	Minneapolis– St. Paul	New Orleans
English	25.6%	17.7%	10.4%	10.1%	14.1%	12.7%
German	26.3	15.4	7.9	44.7	38.9	15.9
Irish	23.1	12.9	7.9	12.9	17.8	13.0
French	5.4	4.7	2.9	5.6	9.2	22.0
Italian	2.5	4.2	3.2	3.5	2.0	8.4
Scottish	6.1	4.2	2.3	2.0	3.2	2.2
Polish	1.5	2.3	2.6	15.8	5.9	.6
Dutch	3.3	2.1	.8	1.7	2.1	.9
Swedish	2.3	2.0	.6	2.3	14.4	.5
Norwegian	.7	1.4	.1	3.4	15.2	.5
Russian	.9	2.5	4.3	1.2	1.4	.6
Czech	.4	.6	.3	2.0	2.5	.2
Hungarian	.2	1.0	.9	1.4	.5	.2
Welsh	1.1	.7	.3	.6	.6	.2
Danish	.8	.7	.2	.9	2.4	.1
Portuguese	.0	.4	.2	.0	.1	.0
Black	16.1	10.5	17.5	13.2	2.7	35.7
Mexican	2.7	21.0	.7	1.7	.8	.6
Puerto Rican	.0	.4	2.1	.6	.1	.2
Spanish—Other	.5	4.7	29.5	.7	.5	4.3
American Indian	4.8	2.5	1.0	1.1	1.8	1.8
American	4.1	2.5	3.3	1.7	2.0	1.9
United States	.1	.1	.1	.0	.0	.0
White/Caucasian	.3	.2	.1	.0	.0	.3
North American Other	.2	.5	.4	.3	.6	.2
Other SCE European	1.7	3.0	3.4	4.9	4.2	1.0
Other Northwestern European	1.1	.8	.3	1.6	3.0	.4
Middle Eastern/North African	.3	1.0	.8	.2	.4	.3
African, Caribbean, Pacific	.5	1.0	2.5	.3	.5	.2
South Asian	.1	.3	.4	.1	.2	.1
Other Asian	.5	5.7	.5	.7	1.1	1.4
No Response	8.6	4.9	9.2	4.3	6.0	6.0
All Other	.8	1.0	2.2	.7	.6	.2

APPENDIX TABLE 3.1 *(continued)*

Group	Percentage of Population with Specified Ancestry					
	New York	Oklahoma City	Oxnard– Ventura	Phila- delphia	Pitts- burgh	Portland, OR
English	7.5%	27.2%	23.3%	13.5%	14.8%	27.8%
German	12.3	19.8	20.6	19.0	30.7	30.0
Irish	15.2	23.4	17.7	22.7	23.1	20.2
French	2.0	5.6	6.6	2.3	2.9	7.5
Italian	17.9	1.4	4.5	12.6	13.5	2.9
Scottish	2.0	5.2	4.5	3.3	5.7	7.4
Polish	6.4	.8	1.6	6.3	9.5	1.8
Dutch	1.2	3.6	2.9	1.4	1.6	3.7
Swedish	.8	1.1	2.1	.6	1.1	4.8
Norwegian	.6	.7	2.4	.2	.2	5.1
Russian	5.3	.3	2.2	4.8	3.4	1.1
Czech	.8	.7	.5	.3	1.6	.8
Hungarian	1.9	.2	.8	1.1	2.9	.4
Welsh	.2	.7	1.0	1.1	1.3	1.6
Danish	.3	.5	1.3	.1	.1	1.6
Portuguese	.5	.0	.4	.2	.0	.5
Black	17.7	10.5	2.4	23.2	9.3	3.3
Mexican	.2	1.9	20.0	.1	.2	1.2
Puerto Rican	5.2	.1	.1	1.2	.0	.1
Spanish—Other	6.1	.8	2.3	.9	.2	.9
American Indian	.7	9.8	3.5	.9	.8	3.1
American	3.1	7.6	3.4	2.8	2.8	4.3
United States	.2	.1	.0	.1	.1	.1
White/Caucasian	.1	.6	.3	.0	.0	.3
North American Other	.4	.4	.9	.3	.1	.9
Other SCE European	5.1	.7	2.2	3.3	10.9	2.8
Other Northwestern European	.5	.4	1.2	.4	.6	2.5
Middle Eastern/North African	.8	.7	.8	.2	.6	.4
African, Caribbean, Pacific	3.0	.9	.5	.7	.2	.7
South Asian	.6	.3	.0	.4	.2	.1
Other Asian	2.0	1.3	3.9	1.0	.3	2.3
No Response	5.4	12.3	5.5	5.6	5.3	8.8
All Other	1.5	.4	.8	1.1	.6	1.1

APPENDIX TABLE 3.1 *(continued)*

Group	Percentage of Population with Specified Ancestry					
	St. Louis	Salt Lake City	San Antonio	San Bernadino	San Diego	San Francisco–Oakland
English	17.1%	54.1%	15.0%	22.7%	23.4%	19.7%
German	36.4	14.8	15.7	20.5	20.9	16.4
Irish	21.3	10.8	11.6	16.6	17.9	15.9
French	7.4	4.5	3.8	6.2	6.0	5.2
Italian	4.4	1.6	1.4	3.7	4.8	7.3
Scottish	3.5	6.8	3.6	5.1	5.4	4.8
Polish	2.9	.6	1.8	1.7	2.7	1.7
Dutch	1.8	3.4	1.1	3.9	2.9	2.0
Swedish	.7	6.8	.7	2.3	2.6	2.5
Norwegian	.3	2.3	.5	1.3	2.0	1.6
Russian	1.4	.2	.5	1.0	1.5	2.2
Czech	1.2	.4	1.0	.8	.7	.6
Hungarian	.7	.1	.2	.8	.8	.6
Welsh	.6	2.6	.5	.9	.9	.7
Danish	.3	8.3	.5	1.1	.9	1.2
Portuguese	.1	.1	.1	.4	.7	2.5
Black	20.8	.8	7.5	7.0	5.9	12.5
Mexican	.4	3.0	45.4	18.0	13.8	6.1
Puerto Rican	.0	.5	.3	.2	.2	.6
Spanish—Other	.6	2.0	3.8	2.5	2.2	4.0
American Indian	3.4	2.0	2.1	4.7	3.4	2.3
American	3.5	2.9	2.0	4.0	2.6	2.0
United States	.1	.1	.0	.2	.1	.1
White/Caucasian	.2	.1	.3	.2	.2	.2
North American Other	.1	.2	.2	.7	.7	.4
Other SCE European	1.8	2.3	.9	2.0	2.7	3.2
Other Northwestern European	1.1	3.5	.5	1.2	1.0	1.3
Middle Eastern/North African	.3	.4	.3	.6	.4	.8
African, Caribbean, Pacific	.3	1.0	.4	.9	1.3	1.4
South Asian	.3	.1	.1	.1	.1	.4
Other Asian	.6	1.4	1.1	1.8	5.3	10.3
No Response	5.7	6.9	4.1	7.1	5.8	5.6
All Other	.6	.6	.4	.5	.9	1.1

APPENDIX TABLE 3.1 *(continued)*

	Percentage of Population with Specified Ancestry		
Group	San Jose	Seattle	Washington, DC
English	22.6%	28.0%	21.5%
German	19.3	24.8	17.4
Irish	16.6	19.1	16.3
French	5.9	7.6	4.1
Italian	7.1	2.9	4.1
Scottish	5.9	7.5	5.2
Polish	1.9	2.0	2.7
Dutch	2.4	3.4	1.7
Swedish	2.3	5.6	1.2
Norwegian	2.1	8.6	.8
Russian	1.4	1.2	3.0
Czech	.7	.9	.6
Hungarian	.7	.5	.7
Welsh	1.1	1.7	.9
Danish	1.3	1.6	.4
Portuguese	2.5	.2	.2
Black	3.5	4.3	29.7
Mexican	13.8	.9	.5
Puerto Rican	.5	.1	.2
Spanish—Other	3.5	1.1	2.2
American Indian	2.4	2.8	2.1
American	2.1	2.7	2.8
United States	.1	.1	.1
White/Caucasian	.2	.3	.2
North American Other	.6	1.0	.5
Other SCE European	2.3	3.0	2.8
Other Northwestern European	1.3	2.7	.7
Middle Eastern/North African	.9	.3	.9
African, Caribbean, Pacific	1.2	.8	1.7
South Asian	.6	.2	.8
Other Asian	8.0	4.5	2.5
No Response	6.6	8.2	5.3
All Other	.9	.7	1.0

NOTE: Individuals with multiple ancestries are counted more than once; thus, percentages in each area will add to more than 100.

APPENDIX TABLE 3.2

Projected Future Geographic Distribution of Ancestry Groups,
Based on Internal Migration Patterns, 1975–1980

Area	English 1980	English Future	German 1980	German Future	Irish 1980	Irish Future	French 1980	French Future
New England	6%	4%	2%	2%	7%	4%	15%	8%
Mid Atlantic	11	5	17	9	17	8	11	5
East North Central	16	10	27	18	18	11	19	13
West North Central	7	6	14	14	8	9	8	8
South Atlantic	20	21	12	14	15	17	10	11
East South Central	9	12	3	4	6	8	3	4
West South Central	10	17	7	14	11	21	14	25
Mountain	6	9	5	9	5	7	5	7
Pacific	14	16	13	17	13	16	14	17
D		10.3		19.9		7.9		15.9

Area	Italian 1980	Italian Future	Scottish 1980	Scottish Future	Polish 1980	Polish Future	Dutch 1980	Dutch Future
New England	13%	8%	7%	5%	9%	7%	2%	2%
Mid Atlantic	44	19	12	8	32	20	16	8
East North Central	14	12	16	10	33	24	25	17
West North Central	2	2	7	7	5	8	11	9
South Atlantic	8	10	19	20	8	14	13	15
East South Central	1	2	6	6	1	1	5	7
West South Central	3	9	10	17	2	6	9	17
Mountain	3	8	6	9	2	5	5	8
Pacific	11	29	17	18	7	16	15	17
D		30.1		5.2		30.6		8.2

APPENDIX TABLE 3.2 (continued)

Area	Swedish 1980	Swedish Future	Norwegian 1980	Norwegian Future	American Indian 1980	American Indian Future	American 1980	American Future
New England	6%	4%	2%	2%	3%	1%	4%	2%
Mid Atlantic	9	4	5	3	6	3	10	6
East North Central	20	11	19	15	15	10	17	11
West North Central	22	18	34	30	8	8	7	6
South Atlantic	7	7	4	5	15	12	23	26
East South Central	1	2	1	2	9	9	14	15
West South Central	4	8	3	8	20	8	13	20
Mountain	9	15	8	9	8	11	4	5
Pacific	22	31	24	26	16	17	9	9
D		32.6		35.6		16.0		16.9

Area	South Asian 1980	South Asian Future	Russian 1980	Russian Future	Czech 1980	Czech Future	Hungarian 1980	Hungarian Future
New England	4%	1%	8%	6%	3%	4%	5%	3%
Mid Atlantic	30	10	41	18	15	6	35	16
East North Central	18	19	14	10	30	17	30	20
West North Central	5	5	4	4	19	16	3	5
South Atlantic	13	27	12	18	7	8	10	13
East South Central	2	3	1	1	1	1	1	1
West South Central	7	14	2	4	11	23	3	5
Mountain	2	0	3	4	4	8	3	7
Pacific	18	21	15	34	10	15	12	30
D		21.0		31.0		21.2		29.2

APPENDIX TABLE 3.2 (continued)

Area	Welsh		Danish		Portuguese		Black	
	1980	Future	1980	Future	1980	Future	1980	Future
New England	3%	2%	3%	5%	40%	23%	2%	1%
Mid Atlantic	21	11	6	3	10	3	16	8
East North Central	20	13	16	10	2	3	17	15
West North Central	8	7	22	20	1	1	3	3
South Atlantic	12	12	6	9	4	6	29	30
East South Central	3	4	1	1	0	2	11	9
West South Central	6	14	3	6	1	3	13	19
Mountain	9	15	18	18	2	2	1	2
Pacific	18	22	24	28	40	57	8	14
D		16.1		35.2		59.3		18.7

Area	Mexican		Puerto Rican		Spanish–Other		No Response	
	1980	Future	1980	Future	1980	Future	1980	Future
New England	0%	1%	8%	17%	3%	1%	4%	2%
Mid Atlantic	1	.5	67	35	25	7	12	4
East North Central	7	4	10	6	6	3	18	10
West North Central	2	1	0	0	1	2	7	6
South Atlantic	1	1	6	16	19	23	20	21
East South Central	0	0	0	1	1	1	10	12
West South Central	34	39	1	2	10	15	13	25
Mountain	10	10	1	2	15	21	4	6
Pacific	44	44	7	22	20	25	12	14
D		50.3		45.8		25.4		14.2

APPENDIX TABLE 3.2 *(continued)*

Area	All Other	
	1980	Future
New England	7%	3%
Mid Atlantic	26	10
East North Central	14	8
West North Central	6	6
South Atlantic	16	24
East South Central	3	4
West South Central	6	8
Mountain	6	11
Pacific	18	25
D		18.6

NOTE: D = index of dissimilarity.

CULTURAL DIFFERENCES

THNIC and racial groups differed in cultural attributes at the time of their arrival in the United States. Many of these differences involved rather prominent characteristics: language, food, names, clothing, kinship structures, religion, and the like. While cultural values are less obvious than these material and organizational qualities, we can assume that the groups differed on this dimension as well. In this chapter we address two central questions. First, do the groups differ in cultural features at present? Second, if they do, are these differences linked to the historical positions observed among their ancestors in the heyday of immigration? While we can assume at least modest differences on many attributes, we are most interested in how much the historical past still influences ancestry groups in 1980.

A census is not the best source of information for answering these questions; one cannot obtain data on norms or nonmaterial culture.[1]

[1]Even for those dimensions of socioeconomic attainment to which the census is relatively well suited, the results are less than ideal. For example, in the area of education the census will tell us the number of years of schooling attained, but nothing about the *quality* of the schooling, the nature of the schools attended, let alone the subjects' scores on any standardized test. Except for special surveys, the census provides no direct evidence about mobility between parents and their children because information is not obtained from subjects about their parents' or their offspring's economic attainment—except where the two generations live in the same household. Fortunately, some superb studies exist dealing with ethnic factors in intergenerational mobility, and we can take advantage of

Moreover, some of the cultural attributes that are measured in the census would also require a generational cross-tabulation in order to draw meaningful conclusions—a situation not possible in 1980. For example, ethnic differences in the use of non-English tongues cannot be analyzed by generation in the 1980 census. Yet, in our estimation the generational factor is central to understanding the patterns of change with respect to the dominance of English as the mother tongue of people whose ancestors spoke different languages.[2]

Fortunately, three important cultural attributes lend themselves to analysis with census data. Immigrant fertility was covered as early as 1910 in the census and, moreover, rather substantial differences were found between the groups. Likewise, ethnic differences in nuptiality were observed many decades ago in the United States. For both of these variables, we can compare contemporary and past ethnic patterns to learn if there is continuity over time. In the case of educational attainment, again we can measure present-day differences and we also can ascertain whether the contemporary patterns have historical roots. Since all three attributes influence occupational and income attainment in varying degrees, these three cultural features of the groups are also highly relevant for evaluating a cultural interpretation of socioeconomic position.

Fertility

Historical Patterns

Fertility rates in the United States were far higher earlier in this century than they are at present. Native white women who had just completed their childbearing years in 1910 (ages 45–54) had borne 4,454 children per 1,000 ever-married women. Still, even by the standards of

---

their results: Peter M. Blau and Otis Dudley Duncan, *The American Occupational Structure* (New York: Wiley, 1967); Otis Dudley Duncan, David L. Featherman, and Beverly Duncan, *Socioeconomic Background and Achievement* (New York: Seminar Press, 1972); and David L. Featherman and Robert M. Hauser, *Opportunity and Change* (New York: Academic Press, 1978).

[2]In this regard, the reader is cautioned to exert great care before assuming that some of the recent migrant groups to the nation will not shift to English in the same ways as most earlier immigrants did. In order to draw such a conclusion, it is necessary to examine language behavior by generation of residence in the nation. For groups with a very large immigrant component, the presence of a large non-English mother tongue segment tells us nothing about intergenerational shifts over time. It is not that a shift to English is a certainty, but rather that we cannot draw the opposite conclusion when generation is not considered.

that time immigrant women were remarkably fertile. Although the rates varied widely among the nine immigrant groups under consideration, in all cases they exceeded the native white level.[3] Fertility ranged from 4,702 (per 1,000 women from England and Wales) to 7,314 per 1,000 women from Poland. The four new European groups all reported greater fertility than any of the five northwestern European groups (Austria-Hungary, with 5,910 births, was the lowest of the new groups compared with 5,385 for the highest of the old European groups). Although at first this may seem to reflect the effects of religion—new European groups are mostly Catholic and the older European groups are mostly Protestant—more is involved. Russians, who were largely not Catholic, reported 6,963 births per 1,000 women; women born in Ireland (and hence largely Roman Catholic, though 1910 data for Ireland did include Northern Ireland and thus some of these data refer to Protestants) reported 4,902 births per 1,000—a level also below that of the combined Scandinavian figure.

By 1940, fertility among immigrant women aged 45–54 was much lower; the average for 13 European groups was 3,298, ranging from a low of 2,217 (again, England and Wales) to a high of 4,710 (Italy). Compared with an average of 2,967 births to native white women, five of these 13 groups were lower: England and Wales, Scotland, the combined Scandinavian category, Germany, and Yiddish mother tongue women of Russian birth. The 1940 data are more refined for specific ethnic categories. For instance, in 1940 the Irish were from the Republic and therefore were almost entirely Catholic. Likewise, both Russia and Poland were subdivided into Yiddish and non-Yiddish mother tongue components in the 1940 tabulations.[4] In general, the southern-central-eastern (SCE) Europeans still experience higher fertility, but the gaps are not as sharp. Women aged 45–54 born in Eire had 3,098 births per 1,000, the highest level of any of the northwestern European groups and actually somewhat higher than the rate for women with Yiddish mother tongue from Russia (2,923) or Poland (3,021). But these are the only exceptions in the

[3]The 1910, 1940, and 1960 data are for women ever married; in 1980, the figures refer to all women, including those who were never married. The 1910 data are for the following nine groups: England and Wales, Scotland, Ireland, Norway-Sweden-Denmark-Iceland, Germany, Poland, Austria-Hungary, Russia, and Italy. U.S. Bureau of the Census, *Sixteenth Census of the United States: 1940, Population. Differential Fertility, 1940 and 1910. Women by Number of Children Ever Born* (Washington, DC: U.S.Government Printing Office, 1945) table 43.

[4]The 1940 data are based on all of the groups listed above (except for Poland, Austria-Hungary, and Russia). They also include Poland—Yiddish Mother Tongue, Poland—Other Mother Tongue, Czechoslovakia, Austria, Hungary, Russia—Yiddish Mother Tongue, and Russia—Other Mother Tongue. U.S. Bureau of the Census, *Differential Fertility: 1940 and 1910*, table 40).

1940 comparisons between five northwestern and eight SCE European groups. The new European groups still have higher fertility.

In fact, the variability between the European groups was actually greater in 1940 than in 1910. Although the standard deviation (SD) is 884 in 1910 and 767 in 1940, one has to keep in mind that the slightly lower SD in 1940 occurs with an arithmetic mean of 3,298 compared with 5,688 in 1910. The coefficient of relative variation (CRV) permits comparisons between SDs when the means of the poulations are quite different, by expressing SD as a percentage of the mean. CRV has risen from 15.5 percent in 1910 to 23 percent in 1940.[5] Until World War II, the immigrant groups differed considerably in their levels of fertility, with the rates almost always higher for SCE European groups. If we take into account that completed fertility declined substantially between 1910 and 1940, the relative variation was greater in 1940 since that mean shifted to a far greater degree than did the standard deviation.

Is there a continuity between these earlier immigrant results and present-day fertility in the United States of the later generations? Is the level of variation as great as it once was? Does the old-new distinction still operate? As we turn toward the current period, we must keep in mind that fertility that took place in the old country prior to migration cannot be distinguished from childbearing occurring after arrival in the United States. The data for immigrants range from women who arrived in the United States shortly after their own birth, to those who experienced part of their childbearing period here and part in their country of birth, as well as those who immigrated only at the end of their child-bearing years. Thus, comparisons between immigrants and the second generation are not as clear as we would like, let alone comparisons that move from a birthplace delineation (before 1980) to a system based on ancestry, as in the 1980 data. We can suggest general trends by comparing 1980 data with earlier patterns, even if the data are less than ideal.

Fertility in 1960

Immigrant fertility in 1960 can be compared with the second generation in that year and with immigrants 20 years earlier. There is again a continuity with the past, for the nine immigrant groups matched in both 1940 and 1960, rho is .64 ($P = .03$) between the fertility of women

[5]If only the same groups are matched in the two periods (this includes all but Austria-Hungary from the list in footnote 2 and includes the data for all of Poland and all of Russia in 1940), CRV increases from 16.5 percent in 1910 to 27 percent in 1940.

aged 45–54 in the two periods.[6] The average fertility for these immigrant groups has dropped from 3,407 to 1,992 per 1,000 ever-married women during this period (the 1940 figures here are slightly different from the earlier figures since they are now matched with 1960 data) and the SD declined even more rapidly (from 812 to 325) so that the CRV for the immigrant groups is 16 in 1960 compared with 24 in 1940. The old-new distinction is still relevant: On the whole, northwestern European groups tend to have lower fertility than do the groups from elsewhere in Europe, but there is a certain amount of overlap. The fertility of women born in Ireland is higher than that of four of the five SCE European groups (Italians are the only exception, and then only by a small number). In addition, women born in the United Kingdom have a fertility level identical to that of Russians and in excess of that for Austrians.

If we compare immigrants in 1960 with second-generation women aged 45–54, the relative positions of the immigrant groups tend to be repeated in the fertility levels occurring in the second generation as well (rho = .57, P = .06). The coefficient of relative variation is only 5 percent for the second generation compared with 16 percent for the immigrants—once again demonstrating the rapid narrowing of differences among these groups over a period of only one generation (the means are fairly similar, 1,992 versus 2,085, but the SD for the second generation is about a third of the immigrant level). The intergenerational comparison in 1960 indicates a decline in the differences between groups; indeed, the old and new groups have about the same average fertility.

Of course, cross-sectional comparisons between immigrants and the second generation can be misleading since the behavior of the immigrants in 1960 need not represent the behavior of the immigrant parents of second-generation women who were themselves aged 45–54 in 1960.[7] A somewhat better comparison can be obtained by examining the fertility of second-generation women aged 45–54 in 1960 and immigrant women aged 45–54 in 1940, and that comparison also fails to uncover a continuity among groups. There is no correlation between the relative positions (rho = .23, P = .28).

---

[6]The nine groups used for comparison are all of the European populations listed in the *1960 Census of Population. Subject Reports. Women by Number of Children Ever Born*, PC(2)-3A (Washington, DC: U.S. Government Printing Office, 1964) table 9, except that it was necessary to combine the data for Norway and Sweden in order to make it approximately comparable to the pooled data for Norway, Sweden, Denmark, and Iceland reported in 1940.

[7]Alma F. Taeuber and Karl E. Taeuber, "Recent Immigration and Studies of Ethnic Assimilation," *Demography* 4 (1967):798–808.

Fertility in 1980

The 1980 fertility data (Table 4.1) are different in several respects; they refer to American-born and foreign-born women of 16 specific ethnic ancestries (in turn divided into those of single and mixed origins) and are not limited to a specific generation of residence in the United States. Also, the data refer to children ever born to all women, regardless of whether or not they were ever married. (Since the overwhelming majority of women are married by the time they reach the end of the childbearing ages, the distinction is of modest significance for the fertility measure.) These factors militate against making much of comparisons with earlier periods, but intercohort analyses are appropriate for gauging trends and the number of ancestry groups (32, when including both single and mixed components of each group) permits more statistical analysis.

All indications are that the level of variation among white ethnic groups is relatively small and is getting smaller. CRV is 12 percent for the 32 groupings of women aged 65 and over in 1980; among the same

TABLE 4.1

Number of Children Ever Born per 1,000 Women,
by Age, Ethnic Origin, and Mix, for European-Ancestry Groups, 1980

Group	45–54 Years Old		65 Years Old and Over	
	Single	Mixed	Single	Mixed
English	2,857	2,966	2,327	2,126
German	2,959	3,047	2,189	2,109
Irish	3,142	3,059	2,339	2,300
French	3,192	3,092	2,482	2,139
Italian	2,565	2,902	2,375	1,966
Scottish	2,701	2,854	1,921	1,999
Polish	2,721	2,922	2,251	2,099
Dutch	3,249	3,099	2,684	2,640
Swedish	2,939	3,081	1,849	2,022
Norwegian	3,314	3,148	2,237	1,958
Russian	2,299	2,568	1,825	1,898
Czech	2,766	2,975	2,114	1,790
Hungarian	2,433	2,751	2,071	1,899
Welsh	2,972	2,819	1,962	1,969
Danish	3,073	3,150	2,229	2,248
Portuguese	2,748	2,978	2,783	2,545

32 groupings of women aged 45–54 in 1980, CRV is 8 percent—a low figure compared with almost all of the figures from earlier censuses. Moreover, a separate analysis of the pure and mixed components of these 16 ethnic groups indicates that the relative variation is declining for both the single- and mixed-ancestry components. The 16 mixed-origin groups, the subset of ethnics with the lowest relative variation in fertility, no doubt have more generations of residence in the United States than the single-origin members.

The distinction that was of such great significiance earlier in the century between northwestern and SCE European groups has essentially vanished by 1980. Although the differences are generally not significant, the northwestern European groups actually tend to have higher levels of fertility in 1980. In brief, by 1980 there are relatively small differences between the larger white ethnic groups with respect to their fertility—a situation radically different from the way it once was in the United States. In addition to this decline in the gaps between groups, the earlier old-new gap has disappeared, except in one circumstance where it has now actually reversed itself. Among single-ancestry women, aged 45–54 in 1980, those of Russian, Hungarian, and Italian origin have the lowest levels of completed fertility among those of unmixed origins. They are followed by one old group, the Scots, and then by the remaining three new European groups. The old groups have the nine highest rates of completed fertility. If anything, women of northwestern European origin now tend to have somewhat more children.

Finally, the fertility data enable us to determine whether differences exist between single- and mixed-ancestry components of each ethnic group. Insofar as the mixed-ancestry component of a given ancestry group is more likely to be of more generations' residence in the United States, this is a pertinent question since it provides further evidence about the degree to which the groups retain distinctive characteristics or become more assimilated. In terms of their relative fertility levels, the subsets of each ethnic group are rather similar. Among women aged 45–54, the coefficient of correlation is .87 between the mixed- and single-ancestry components of each of the 16 groups; among women aged 65 and over r is .79 (in both cases, $P < .005$). In terms of the levels of fertility, however, there do not appear to be consistent fertility differences between the mixed- and single-ancestry components of these ethnic groups. Among women who had just ended their childbearing years, there are no serious differences between the two components in terms of their levels of fertility. With respect to this behavioral characteristic, the mixed- and single-ancestry components of each ethnic group are reasonably similar.

Marriage

Historical Patterns

Historically, marriage rates among white immigrants in the United States differed from the host population. Immigrant women were less likely than native white women to remain single and the opposite held for immigrant men.[8] ("Single" refers to those people who have thus far never been married. Persons who were married, but are not at present, are classified as "divorced" or "widowed" but not "single." Hence the terms "never married" and "single" are used interchangeably here. Likewise, "ever married" includes those who are currently separated, widowed, or divorced—as well as those currently married.) Carpenter[9] interpreted these higher age-standardized rates among immigrant women as reflecting the "heavy excess of marriageable males among the foreign born [which] provides the females an unusually favorable opportunity for matrimony." Two additional factors probably contributed to this phenomenon. First there was a propensity for women from many groups to migrate here with their husbands or after their spouses were in the United States long enough to make a go of it—single women past the usual marital ages were less likely to come. Second, unmarried immigrant men often later brought a bride over from their homeland. In these cases, the migration process itself tended to select married women over single women more so that it favored married men over single men. Immigrant men, on the other hand, were more likely to remain single than were the native white men of native parentage, after taking into account their age distribution. Carpenter interpreted this as due to the sex ratios among immigrants which meant a relative scarcity of available females.

Although the influence of social mobility was not discussed in the case of immigrant men, it has certainly been applied to explain a striking marital pattern among the second generation. Among both men and women, the second generation in 1920 was far less likely to marry than were either immigrants of comparable age or native whites of native parentage.[10] This is particularly the case for the younger adult ages, with the gap narrowing in the somewhat older adult ages, suggesting some postponement in marriage for the second generation.

[8]Niles Carpenter, *Immigrants and Their Children: 1920*, Census Monograph 7 (Washington, DC: U.S. Government Printing Office, 1927).

[9]Ibid., p. 215.

[10]Ibid., table 100.

The explanation for this condition can only be conjectured. It may, however, be observed that the postponement or foregoing of marriage involves the deferment or avoidance of the financial obligations involved in marriage, more particularly in the support of children. It may be further pointed out that the second generation immigrants are particularly likely to seek relief from financial pressure in this way, for they are passing over from the social position and economic level of the foreign to the native group and could materially accelerate their progress by keeping themselves free, temporarily or permanently, from family burdens. In other words, to many of the children of the foreign born it seems to be of more importance to bridge the gap between the social and economic level in which they were born and that attained by the sons and daughters of the native Americans than it is to marry and have children. . . .

It is worth noting that the women as well as the men among the native born of mixed and foreign parentage display a disposition to delay or to avoid marriage. It may be indeed, that the daughters of the immigrants have a special motive for postponing marriage in that by waiting until they might have improved their economic status and broadened their social contacts they would widen the field from which they might choose their prospective husbands. It is very interesting to see the daughters of those women, who, among the white population, marry most frequently, go to the opposite extreme and marry most infrequently. Such a contrast betokens a veritable revolution among the women of the foreign population in their attitude toward marriage and the home and denotes a very rapid "Americanization," in this respect at least.[11]

Taking advantage of the 1950 census, which was the first to provide a breakdown of these second-generation groups by specific country of origin and age, Heer[12] was able to examine these matters in greater detail. He found lower percentages ever married for most of the second-generation groups, with the gaps being particularly wide (in absolute terms) at the younger ages. Heer was able to demonstrate that the differences between second-generation groups in the United States were somewhat correlated with the nuptiality patterns in Europe itself. For example, "residents of Ireland, like Americans of Irish descent, rank highest in their propensity to marry late or never to marry."[13] In terms of mobility, Heer found that the groups with the highest socioeconomic status (based on broad occupational categories) had greater percentages

---

[11]Carpenter, *Immigrants and Their Children*, p. 218.
[12]David M. Heer, "The Marital Status of Second-Generation Americans," *American Sociological Review* 26 (1961):233–41.
[13]Ibid., p. 237.

who were single. Likewise, because Roman Catholics at that time were less likely to practice birth control, religion influenced nuptiality as well. Predominantly Catholic groups were under more pressure to postpone marriage in order to reach a given level of socioeconomic achievement since it was more likely that marriage would not be accompanied by effective birth control.[14] Hence their percentage unmarried was necessarily higher than that for other groups with the same level of socioeconomic achievement.

Current Patterns

The 1980 census provides an opportunity to determine if an ethnic factor at present influences marital patterns among whites born in the United States. Unlike the problem confronting earlier investigators, the data are not restricted to the second-generation component of the population born in the United States, but are available for all generations. What are the ethnic differences in the propensity to get married?[15]

In 1980, there are still ethnic differences in the propensity to marry. Among groups of older men (aged 65 and over) of single ancestry, those with a substantial Roman Catholic component also tend to have higher percentages who never married.[16] Although the mean percentage single is higher for "Catholic ethnic groups" than for the others in seven of the eight comparisons (cross-tabulations by gender, single and mixed ancestry, and for those aged 65 and over and 25–34), this is the only instance where the gap between the set of groups is significant. Still, there is clearly a continuity with the past. For example, we determined the percentage who were single for various second-generation groups in 1930 (see Table 4.2).[17] These figures for the second generation in 1930 are still correlated with ethnic nuptiality levels reported in 1980. Among women the Spearman rank-order correlation between the 1930 data and the values for women aged 65 and over is .82 ($P < .0001$), and among

[14]Heer, "Marital Status," pp. 240–41.

[15]Given this analysis of nuptiality, the reader might wonder if a similar analysis of marital stability is possible. It cannot be done because the earlier data do not permit distinction between first and later marriages. Hence we cannot count as divorced those persons who were remarried at the time of the census.

[16]Ranking the seven "Catholic" groups and nine "non-Catholic" groups in a single array with respect to their percentage unmarried, the single-tailed probability of such a small overlap is .025. For a discussion of the procedure used to determine which groups have a relatively large Catholic component and which do not, see Chapter 7, pp. 232–35. The section also contains a caution about the procedures used.

[17]These data refer to the population aged 15 and over—standardized for age differences in each ethnic group, using the age- and sex-specific 1930 nuptiality rates for the native white of native parentage population.

TABLE 4.2

*Percentage Never Married, 1930 and 1980,
by Age and Gender, for European-Ancestry Groups*

	1930		1980			
	Second Generation		Women		Men	
Group	Women	Men	25–34 Years Old	65 Years Old and Over	25–34 Years Old	65 Years Old and Over
English	32%	37%	10%	6%	19%	4%
Scottish	36	40	12	9	21	5
Welsh	33	38	16	7	22	3
Irish	54	56	13	10	23	7
Norwegian	33	46	12	7	20	9
Swedish	36	44	12	9	22	6
Danish	30	38	10	4	21	6
Dutch	31	36	9	5	19	4
German	32	40	12	7	19	5
Polish	34	41	18	7	25	8
Czech	33	41	16	7	23	8
Hungarian	34	41	17	6	24	6
Russian	34	40	25	6	30	5
Italian	32	40	16	6	25	5
Portuguese	28	38	11	4	19	6

NOTES: Data for 1930 refer to second generation, aged 15 and over, classified by country of origin of parents and standardized by age (see text). The 1980 data refer to the ethnic ancestry response for all generations. French are excluded from this analysis because of the ambiguity involving two French categories in 1930 data.

men it is .78 (P = .0002). To be sure, there is some overlap here, but the continuity is found even among those who were not born in 1930— the population aged 25–34 in 1980. The rank-order correlations with second-generation 1930 rates are .57 (P = .01) and .50 (P = .03) for women and men, respectively. In short, in 1980 there are ethnic differences in the propensity to marry that can be traced back at least 50 years to patterns observed among the children of immigrants in the United States in 1930, although the differences and level of variation among the groups in 1980 is quite low.

In brief, white ethnic groups in the United States still differ from one another in their marital patterns in a systematic way that at least partly involves a continuity with immigrant and second-generation patterns observed many decades ago in the United States. A convergence may be operating for some of these characteristics because the gaps are relatively small, but the influence of the ethnic effect cannot yet be said to have entirely disappeared in contemporary marital and fertility patterns.[18] Indeed, in some respects the relative level of variation is rather substantial; the CRV for women aged 45–54 is 31 for the percentage single and 18 for the percentage marrying young.

Education: Current Patterns

Educational attainment is of great interest in the study of these ethnic and racial groups for three major reasons. It is one of three central variables in the study of socioeconomic attainment (along with occupation and income, both discussed in the next chapter). First, education is itself a source of prestige and is, additionally, a factor influencing entry into various occupational opportunities. Second, education is of interest simply because it was initially seen as a major institution through which the descendants of later immigrants would be "Americanized," that is, fit the model of appropriate behavior held by those who had arrived earlier and were in control of the social institutions. Finally, the immigrant groups initially differed greatly in their educational attainment at the time of arrival—in no small way reflecting the variation within Europe in the spread of literacy and universal education. As a consequence, these differences were noted quite early in the migration of different groups to the United States.

Median Years of Schooling

Let us first summarize the educational attainment of each group in terms of median years of schooling. The most impressive feature of educational attainment among the American-born components of each of 33 ethnic and racial groups in 1980 is the relatively low level of variation in median schooling that exists within each sex (reported in Table 4.3 and 4.4 for men and women, respectively). To be sure, some important differences do show up. Men of Russian origin (a group with a substantial Jewish component) have a median of 15.7 years of schooling. Since a college graduate has 16 years of schooling, this means that nearly half of this group are college graduates (18 percent are *only* col-

---

[18]Frances E. Kobrin and Calvin Goldscheider, in their study of Rhode Island, also observe ethnic differences in the age at marriage that are not fully explained by socioeconomic background factors. *The Ethnic Factor in Family Structure and Mobility* (Cambridge, MA: Ballinger, 1978), pp. 89–91.

lege graduates and 30 percent have gone beyond college). At the other extreme are Puerto Rican men, whose median years of schooling— 10.8—are nearly five years less than the median for Russian men. (These results for the Puerto Rican ethnic population are affected by the educational attainment of persons born in Puerto Rico who now live on the mainland.)

Still, the most striking feature of Table 4.3 is the relative uniformity of the medians. The arithmetic mean for the 33 groups of men is 12.8; almost all of the groups have medians that deviate by a relatively small amount from this figure. The CRV (5.8) is exceptionally small compared with the CRV values reported for other characteristics. It is slightly smaller (5.7) when the analysis is restricted to the 16 specific European groups, and even that value is due largely to the exceptional attainment of the Russian population. Without Russians, the 15 specific European groups have a CRV of 2.0, ranging about nine tenths of a year in their medians.

The relative uniformity of education—at least as measured by the median years of school—is even greater among women. CRV for all 33 groups of women is 3.9 compared with 5.8 for men. As before, women with the highest and lowest educational levels are, respectively, Russian (13.4 years) and Puerto Ricans (10.5 years). The relative educational positions of the different ethnic groups is largely the same in each sex. For the 33 groups, the Spearman rank-order correlation (rho) between the sexes is .98 ($P < .0001$).[19] As for men, the relative variation is even less among the 16 specific European-origin groups, CRV = 1.9 and is even less if the Russians are not included (CRV = 1.2).

All of the European groups have median levels of education that exceed nearly all of the major non-European populations under consideration. Among both men and women, the Portuguese median level of education, lowest of any of the 16 specific groups, exceeds the medians for blacks, Mexicans, Puerto Ricans, Other Spanish, American Indian, and South Asians (largely an Indian subcontinent population). The gaps are not great (see Tables 4.3 and 4.4), but they consistently favor the Europeans. The only major exception is the broad Other Asian category, which includes (among others) Chinese, Filipinos, Japanese, and Vietnamese. American-born men and women from this part of Asia exceed all but one of the specific European groups—the Russians. In some cases, the gaps in medians are extremely small, indeed showing up only with figures in greater detail than are presented in these tables. But it is very clear that the major European-origin groups in the United States

[19]The Spearman rank-order correlation between the sexes is basically the same when the ND indexes (see below) are computed for each group's educational distribution.

Educational Attainment, Men Born in the United States, Aged 25 and Over, 1980

Group	Median Years	High School 8 Years or Less	High School 1–3 Years	High School 4 Years	College 1–3 Years	College 4 Years	College 5 Years or More	ND
English	12.8	.14	.13	.30	.17	.13	.13	.14
German	12.7	.12	.12	.35	.17	.12	.12	.14
Irish	12.7	.13	.13	.33	.18	.12	.12	.12
French	12.7	.13	.13	.34	.18	.11	.11	.11
Italian	12.7	.11	.16	.34	.17	.11	.11	.11
Scottish	13.4	.09	.11	.28	.20	.15	.17	.26
Polish	12.8	.12	.13	.33	.17	.12	.14	.15
Dutch	12.6	.16	.14	.35	.16	.09	.09	.04
Swedish	13.0	.09	.10	.32	.20	.14	.16	.24
Norwegian	12.9	.12	.09	.31	.19	.14	.15	.21
Russian	15.7	.05	.07	.21	.18	.18	.30	.43
Czech	12.8	.13	.10	.33	.17	.13	.14	.17
Hungarian	12.8	.10	.12	.33	.16	.13	.15	.20
Welsh	13.4	.08	.10	.30	.21	.15	.17	.28
Danish	13.0	.09	.10	.31	.20	.15	.15	.24
Portuguese	12.5	.17	.16	.33	.18	.08	.08	.01
Black	12.0	.29	.21	.28	.14	.05	.04	−.19
Mexican	12.0	.31	.18	.25	.17	.05	.05	−.17
Puerto Rican	10.8	.37	.23	.23	.11	.03	.03	−.29
Spanish–Other	12.5	.20	.16	.29	.19	.08	.08	−.01
American Indian	12.3	.21	.18	.34	.16	.05	.05	−.08
American	12.2	.27	.18	.33	.11	.06	.05	−.15
United States	12.5	.21	.15	.28	.13	.11	.13	.04
White/Caucasian	12.7	.17	.15	.27	.18	.11	.13	.09
North American Other	13.1	.09	.11	.29	.18	.14	.19	.25
Other SCE European	12.7	.14	.13	.35	.17	.10	.11	.10
Other Northwestern European	13.3	.11	.09	.29	.18	.15	.19	.26
Middle Eastern/North African	13.8	.05	.10	.30	.19	.15	.22	.33
African, Caribbean, Pacific	12.6	.13	.16	.34	.19	.08	.09	.07
South Asian	12.5	.16	.14	.42	.07	.04	.16	.02
Other Asian	13.5	.07	.08	.32	.20	.16	.17	.29
No Response	12.3	.22	.17	.33	.14	.08	.07	−.07
All Other	12.9	.13	.12	.28	.17	.13	.17	.18

TABLE 4.4

Educational Attainment, Women Born in the United States, Aged 25 and Over, 1980

| | | Proportional Distribution | | | | | | |
| | | High School | | | College | | | |
Group	Median Years	8 Years or Less	1–3 Years	4 Years	1–3 Years	4 Years	5 Years or More	ND
English	12.6	.12	.15	.37	.18	.10	.07	.08
German	12.6	.11	.13	.42	.17	.09	.07	.07
Irish	12.6	.11	.16	.41	.18	.08	.06	.05
French	12.6	.11	.15	.41	.18	.08	.06	.05
Italian	12.5	.13	.16	.45	.14	.07	.06	.01
Scottish	12.8	.07	.12	.37	.22	.13	.10	.19
Polish	12.5	.14	.15	.41	.15	.08	.07	.03
Dutch	12.4	.16	.17	.41	.15	.07	.05	−.03
Swedish	12.8	.07	.10	.40	.22	.12	.08	.18
Norwegian	12.8	.09	.09	.40	.23	.12	.07	.16
Russian	13.4	.06	.07	.34	.20	.16	.17	.30
Czech	12.6	.13	.12	.41	.17	.09	.08	.07
Hungarian	12.6	.10	.13	.42	.16	.09	.09	.10
Welsh	12.9	.06	.10	.38	.22	.14	.10	.22
Danish	12.8	.07	.09	.41	.23	.12	.08	.19
Portuguese	12.4	.17	.18	.40	.16	.05	.04	−.06
Black	12.0	.25	.23	.29	.14	.05	.04	−.17
Mexican	11.4	.35	.19	.29	.12	.03	.03	−.27
Puerto Rican	10.5	.40	.20	.25	.10	.03	.02	−.33
Spanish–Other	12.3	.22	.17	.35	.16	.05	.05	−.09
American Indian	12.3	.18	.22	.38	.15	.04	.03	−.12
American	12.1	.23	.22	.37	.11	.05	.03	−.17
United States	12.3	.19	.21	.33	.13	.05	.06	−.06
White/Caucasian	12.4	.17	.19	.33	.16	.09	.07	−.02
North American Other	12.7	.11	.11	.40	.16	.09	.07	.12
Other SCE European	12.5	.13	.15	.41	.17	.10	.10	.04
Other Northwestern European	12.9	.09	.09	.36	.22	.14	.10	.19
Middle Eastern/North African	12.8	.07	.12	.40	.19	.13	.09	.17
African, Caribbean, Pacific	12.5	.15	.18	.35	.18	.07	.07	.01
South Asian	12.4	.20	.20	.27	.19	.04	.11	−.03
Other Asian	12.9	.09	.08	.36	.21	.13	.12	.22
No Response	12.3	.20	.19	.38	.13	.06	.04	−.11
	13.6	.13	.14	.39	.16	.09	.09	.07

are strikingly similar in their median years of school completed and that they generally enjoy an advantage over the leading non-European groups in the country, with one strong exception being those from Southeast Asia.[20]

Index of Net Difference

Despite these results, it would be erroneous to conclude that at present there is relatively little difference among European ethnic groups in their levels of educational attainment. The median is only one way of summarizing a distribution. And, like any summary measure, it simplifies more complex situations. The median tells us nothing about the distribution either below or above the 50th percentile. Therefore, in order to provide a fuller picture of the educational situation, each group's educational distribution is reported in columns 2–7 of Tables 4.3 and 4.4.

Even a cursory glance at these tables indicates how much variability within each educational category is concealed by the median measure. If we compare Portuguese and Danish women, for example, the percentage of Portuguese women with less than a high school education is more than twice the percentage for Danish women and likewise the Portuguese percentage with 1–3 years of high school is about double the Danish figure. On the other hand, the percentage of Danish women who are college graduates or postgraduates is, respectively, three times and double the Portuguese figures. By contrast, the difference in medians is less than half a year. Even a quick glance down the column for a given educational level in either table discloses a lot more variation by specific educational attainment than was found for the median.[21]

In order to summarize the educational attainment of each group in a way that is more sensitive to the total distribution, the index of Net Difference (ND) is provided in the last column of Tables 4.3 and 4.4.[22] ND compares each group's educational distribution with the educa-

[20]There are important educational differences within this broad category of "Other Asians" that will be covered in the monograph dealing with that population.

[21]The CRV for each of these educational categories is much higher than the CRV for the median, even when restricting the analysis to the 15 specific European-ancestry groups (again, Russians are excluded). CRVs for men range from 5.4 and 7.9 percent (among those who are high school graduates or with some college) to 20.3 and 22.9 percent (5 or more years of college or no more than an elementary school education). Among women, except for high school graduates, the CRV is even higher in all of the educational categories.

[22]For a more extensive description of the Index of Net Difference and the problems in using the median, see Stanley Lieberson, "Rank-Sum Comparisons Between Groups," in David Heise, ed., *Sociological Methodology 1976* (San Francisco: Jossey-Bass, 1975).

tional distribution for the total population aged 25 and over in 1980 regardless of gender or nativity. It ranges from $+1.0$ (if the least educated member of a given group exceeded the most educated member of the base population) to -1.0 (if the most educated member of a given group exceeded the least educated member of the base population).[23] Starting with all possible pairings between members of the group specified and the standard group, we can visualize three different outcomes: those in which the two people have an identical education, those in which the person from the group specified has the higher educational attainment, and those in which the person from the standard group has the higher educational level. ND gives the proportion of all cases in the second situation minus the proportion of all cases in the third. An ND of .19 for Danish women, for example, means that the percentage of Danish women whose education exceeds all women is 19 percentage points greater than the percentage of all women whose education exceeds women of Danish origin. These index values provide a summary of the educational attainment of each group that is more sensitive to the overall distribution. As such, it indicates that there is still considerable variation among the European ethnic groups in their educational attainment even if their medians are relatively similar. The CRV for the ND index is 46.0 percent for men compared with 2.0 percent for their median among 15 European groups; it is 93.7 percent for ND among women compared with 1.2 percent for the median.

Education: Historical Comparisons

This closer examination of the educational levels of European ethnic groups has indicated more diversity at present than is customarily recognized. How do the educational differences between the groups at present compare with earlier periods? Is the relative variation declining? Are past differences among the groups in their educational attainment still apparent among the American-born descendants? (In the next chapter we will consider what role these ethnic differences in education have in determining ethnic income and occupational attainment.) These questions are easier to ask than to answer. The 1980 census is, of

[23]Such extremes are impossible in view of the part-whole problem encountered by the use of the total population as a standard. Each group is included as part of the standard and therefore such extremes could not occur. The standard is used here merely as a base for measuring the relative position of each group vis-à-vis each other. It appears intellectually more defensible than taking any one group and using it as some sort of arbitrary standard. Although it would have been reasonable to take either the lowest or highest educational group as a standard against which to compare the others.

course, the first to provide ethnic ancestry data; moreover, data on the number of years of schooling were not obtained for adults until the 1940 census.[24] These two factors will limit all of the temporal analyses of socioeconomic change in this and the succeeding chapter. But beyond that, there is also the arbitrary nature of choosing an appropriate time for comparison.

As noted in Chapter 2, the European groups did not migrate to the United States at the same time; nor were the characteristics of a given ethnic group unchanging throughout time. Hence whatever starting period is selected can affect the comparison. For example, it is well known that the "old" European groups were generally more likely to farm in the United States than were those from SCE Europe.[25] But this is related to the different times of arrival of these groups in the United States, a factor that reflects two interrelated events: changing agricultural opportunities in the nation and shifts in the propensity for various subsets of a group to migrate to the United States. An examination in 1930 of the percentage living in rural areas shows a much more substantial old-new gap for those who had migrated before 1900 than those who had migrated in the preceding five years.[26]

There are limitations on the years for which data are available. But some choices exist and our general rule is to take as early a period as is available in the census during which there were sizable numbers of immigrants arriving from all parts of Europe. This means a reasonably good approximation for SCE European immigrant groups since the bulk of their migration occurred during a relatively narrow span of years, largely between 1880 and 1924. But it means a poorer approximation for those northwestern European groups who had arrived in sizable numbers over a much longer span. This is particularly a problem since it is almost certain that the characteristics of emigrants for a given ethnic group will change through the years. We will have to recognize this weakness as we proceed in the analyses of changes in socioeconomic positions. As for the American-born component, the same procedure is used; prior to 1980 we are confined to the second generation, and hence data for a given year—say, 1900—will tell us about a major segment of the American-born component of the newer groups but only about a much smaller component of the older groups.

Historically, there were vast differences in the expansion of education into different parts of Europe. The illiteracy figures for the 1890s,

---

[24]Stanley Lieberson, *A Piece of the Pie: Blacks and White Immigrants Since 1880* (Berkeley: University of California Press, 1980), p. 128.

[25]Well known at least to readers of Stanley Lieberson, *Ethnic Patterns in American Cities* (New York: Free Press, 1963a), p. 63.

[26]Ibid., table 12.

based largely on data for male army recruits in different European countries, indicate that illiteracy was far less frequent in northwestern Europe than elsewhere. It ranged from 1.1 per 1,000 population for the German Empire and Sweden and Norway to 170 for Ireland. By contrast, the figures for SCE Europeans ranged from a low of 238 for Austria to a high of 890 for Romania. Not only are the averages vastly different for the two subdivisions, 46 versus 560 per 1,000, but there is no overlap between the 11 northwestern European nations and the 9 elsewhere in Europe. These vast differences are also reflected in literacy rates of those who migrated to the United States. There is a Spearman rank-order correlation of .86 ($P < .0001$) between the level of illiteracy in Europe in the 1890s and the frequency of illiteracy among immigrants coming into the United States in 1910.[27]

In turn, are the educational levels among the immigrants to the United States still reflected in present-day ethnic levels of education? In correlating immigrant literacy data in 1910 with ancestry educational data in 1980, we have to be concerned about matching the categories. We are confident of a reasonably close match for 12 of these groups: Czech (Bohemian and Moravian in 1910), Dutch (Dutch and Flemish in 1910), English, French, German, Hungarian (Magyar in 1910), Irish, Italian (averaging between North Italian and South Italian in 1910), Polish, Russian (Hebrew in 1910), Scottish, and Welsh. For these 12 groups there is essentially no correlation between the levels of illiteracy reported by the immigrants in 1910 and either the 1980 ND index for educational attainment or their medians. For men, the respective rhos are $-.27$ ($P = .21$) and $-.17$ ($P = .30$); for women, they are $-.37$ ($P = .12$) between the levels for immigrants in 1910 and both measures of education in 1980 (the two are very closely correlated in terms of the rank positions of the groups).

There is additional evidence to support the conclusion that—at least for one significant period of migration to the United States—the present-day ethnic levels of educational attainment are unrelated to those found among the immigrants. Whereas we observed that northwestern European groups enjoyed a distinctive educational edge over the SCE European populations around the turn of the century, this gap has completely disappeared. By contrast, in 1980 there is no significant difference between old and new groups in their education. The Mann-Whitney test applied to both comparisons for each gender yields proba-

---

[27]Based on European illiteracy data and immigration data reproduced in Lieberson, *Ethnic Patterns*, tables 15 and 16. The match is less than perfect for the mixed ethnic-birthplace categories found in the two tables. But the correlation is so sizable for the 14 groups in which a rough match is possible that there is little reason to question the basic conclusion.

bilities far in excess of .05—indeed, the direction of the average difference is actually reversed in 1980 for men, albeit not significantly. Thus,
at present, although educational differences among ethnic groups remain in the United States, they are unrelated to the massive division
that once existed between European immigrants from northwestern and
SCE Europe.

When and how did these shifts occur? The 1950 census provides
educational attainment data for both the first and second generations
from ten different European origins as well as data for some other
groups. At that point, educational differences for the foreign-born were
still similar to the patterns observed decades earlier; the northwestern
European group with the lowest level of educational attainment still
exceeded the highest level for any of the new European groups. This was
the case for all immigrants in each sex, as well as for those aged 45 years
of age and over (Table 4.5, columns 1–4). Among the second generation
by 1950 (columns 5–8), however, the old-new gap had completely bro-
ken down. In all of the foreign-born comparisons between new and old,
the Mann-Whitney test points to significant differences; none are significant for the second-generation comparisons. Put another way, the correlation between the first and second generations with respect to the
ten groups' level of education is modest in 1950 once age is taken into
account.[28]

Another feature pointing to a decline by 1950 in ethnic differences
in education is disclosed when we compare CRVs obtained for the first
and second generations. For both genders, and in all possible age comparisons, the CRVs are considerably lower for the second generation,
indicating relatively more homogeneity. Among those aged 45 and over,
for example, CRV declines from 17 to 6 percent for men and 24 to 8
percent for women. To be sure, with such a small number of cases and
given the fact that the median is being used, all that we can conclude is
that the historical educational gaps between the European groups for the
second generation were certainly in decline by 1950.

Clearly, the shifts in the relative educational positions of the European ethnic groups are not to be explained by changes in the immigrants
arriving in the United States in later periods.[29] Rather these shifts in
educational attainment are to be seen primarily in the behavior of the
American-born components of each group. At the time of arrival in the

[28]Since these people were born at roughly the same period, these are not comparisons
between parents and offspring; rather they are intergenerational comparisons between persons of comparable age.

[29]This is because the relative impact of recent immigration on the entire population
of an ethnic group is going to be generally rather limited. The only exceptions, of course,
would be situations in which the ratio of recent to earlier migrants is relatively high.

TABLE 4.5

Median Years of Schooling, by Generation, Sex, and Age, 1950

	First Generation				Second Generation			
	Men		Women		Men		Women	
Group	All	45 Years and Over	All	45 Years and Over	All	45 Years and Over	All	45 Years and Over
Old								
England (and Wales)	9.0	8.8	9.2	8.7	10.7	8.9	11.4	9.6
Ireland	8.5	8.3	8.4	8.3	10.3	8.8	10.9	9.0
Norway	8.5	8.5	8.5	8.4	9.0	8.6	10.8	8.8
Sweden	8.5	8.5	8.5	8.5	10.6	8.8	11.7	9.0
Germany	8.7	8.6	.8.6	8.4	8.7	8.4	8.8	8.5
New								
Poland	6.5	5.5	5.4	4.3	10.2	8.2	10	8.1
Czechoslovakia	7.9	7.4	7.7	7.1	9.8	8.3	9.7	8.2
Austria	8.1	7.7	7.9	7.1	11.2	8.7	11.2	8.7
USSR	8.2	8.0	7.2	6.1	12.3	10.3	12.2	10.4
Italy	5.7	4.8	4.9	3.8	10.4	8.4	10.2	8.2
Other								
Mexico	3.7	2.9	3.9	2.7	7.6	3.5	7.6	3.2
CRV (European Group)	12%	17%	18%	24%	9%	6%	9%	8%

SOURCE: U.S. Bureau of the Census, 1950 Census of Population, vol. 4: Special Reports, pt. 3: Nativity and Parentage of the White Population (Washington, DC: U.S. Government Printing Office, 1954), table 20.

United States, there were substantial differences in the educational attainment of the immigrant groups. These differences reflect educational opportunities in their homelands, selective forces operating in the migration flows from each source, and possible cultural dispositions. It is impossible to sort these out with the data at hand; however, a good part of the variation must reflect differences in the educational opportunity structure in the Old World. Although obviously there are barriers to educational attainment in the United States, they are certainly not of the same magnitude as was found in Europe.

At any rate, the relative positions of the groups began to change among the American-born components. In 1960, the cohort of second-generation Russian men aged 75 and over (born in 1885 or earlier) did not particularly excel in education. Three other SCE European groups[30] and three of the five old groups (English, Irish, and Swedish second generations) had higher values. However, beginning with the cohort born in the United States between 1885 and 1895, the Russian men exceeded all of these groups. The educational levels reported in 1980 by the American-born members of these different ethnic groups show no trace of the gaps that existed among their immigrant ancestors.

In the area of education, differences still do exist between the groups—indeed, they are underestimated by those who use only the crudest ways of summarizing educational attainment—but these differences are unrelated to the relative positions observed among different immigrant groups at their time of arrival in the United States. Group differences are currently found in the educational levels of the American-born; in particular, a number of non-European groups are strikingly low in their years of schooling. The European groups are also far from homogeneous with respect to this characteristic; once education is measured with a more sensitive indicator than the median, it turns out that there is a fair amount of variation among them. But these differences among European groups are no longer to be understood in terms of any inheritance in position or disposition from their immigrant ancestors.

For all three of the measures described in this chapter—fertility, nuptiality, and education—we have found sharp declines in the differences among European-ancestry groups. For all three measures, once great differences among immigrants on these measures have declined to modest differences—although in the case of nuptiality the remaining gaps are correlated with earlier rankings. The once great divide between immigrants from northwestern Europe and those from SCE Europe has also completely disappeared on these three measures. For education at least, there remains an equally great divide between European-ancestry

[30]Lieberson, *A Piece of the Pie*, table 8.2.

groups and non-European minority groups. In the next chapter we examine whether similar changes have occurred on the two remaining socioeconomic variables considered—income and occupation.

It would be a mistake to assume that changes in nuptiality, fertility, and education completely reflect the changes which have occurred in all of the cultural attributes on which European groups initially differed at the time of their arrival in the United States. For one, there would be more incentive for these features to change than there would be for cultural features less closely and obviously linked to socioeconomic attainment. Nevertheless, the results are important because these are significant cultural features. And it is clear that, for the most part, only modest differences exist among white groups (a major exception being education for Russians). Moreover, the historic roots with earlier patterns are either nil or, at most, rather slight. However, there are still differences found between white groups. In the case of education, these differences become more apparent only when a more sensitive educational measure is employed. We must conclude that while differences do exist among white ethnic groups, they are relatively slight compared with either the differences that used to exist or the gaps currently found between these groups and those of non-European origin.

5

ECONOMIC ATTAINMENT

Occupations

ETHNIC and racial groups typically follow distinctive occupational
pursuits after their migration to the United States. A variety of
forces operate to generate these differences. *Timing of arrival* is
relevant for the occupations initially held, just as it is for location in
the country. In a dynamic economy, old occupational opportunities decline and new ones appear; therefore, groups that arrive at different periods encounter a distinctive set of occupational opportunities. At one
time, for example, the iron and steel industry was rapidly expanding in
the United States and hired very large numbers of unskilled immigrant
men; this would hardly be the case for present-day immigrants. The
occupational skills of the immigrants is another factor. For example,
almost three fourths of the 14,000 Ruthenians arriving in the country in
1905 reported themselves as either laborers or servants; by contrast,
well over half of the Japanese immigrants reported agricultural employment prior to emigration; the largest single category for Scots and Jews
was "industry."[1] Although hardly a precise term, it is more suggestive

[1] Based on data reported in Walter F. Willcox, *International Migrations*, vol. 1 (New
York: Gordon & Breach, 1969), pp. 450–59.

of skills than the "laborer, servant" category so frequently reported for a number of other groups—for example, Irish and Italians.

Other background factors also affect occupational chances. The immigrant differences in education discussed in Chapter 4 influence their potential for certain jobs after arrival. The immigrant groups also varied in their initial disposition toward remaining in the United States permanently; members of some immigrant groups viewed work in the United States as a temporary expedient in order to provide funds for those at home or to save a stake before returning to the Old World. Among other groups, migration was initially viewed as a permanent change. To be sure, many of the would-be sojourners never returned and became permanent residents, but certainly this initial disposition toward long-term residency would have affected the kinds of jobs taken. Certain activities make better sense as a "permanent" enterprise than as a quick source of income. *Location* also played a role in affecting occupational pursuits; the groups coming from different parts of the world naturally arrive at different points in the United States. As we saw in Chapter 3, the initial concentration of immigrants in certain areas of the country has long-lasting effects on the geographic distribution of ancestry groups. For the penniless and unsponsored, there is a propensity—at least initially—to remain near these points of entry. Hence the distinctive opportunities in such areas would affect the occupations pursued. A striking example, on this score, is the concentration of Asian immigrants on the West Coast and Hawaii. *Labor market discrimination* also affects the occupational composition of each group; an outcome that occurs under any type of queuing preference for some groups over others.[2]

The *distinctive cultural features* of each group—above and beyond the background factors that we normally associate with occupational attainment—are another set of factors. For example, in considering some of the occupational pursuits favored by the Irish (policemen and firemen), it is almost certain that they reflect the distinct advantage that an English-speaking immigrant group would hold over equally unskilled groups with different mother tongues. But that is a simple and relatively clear example; it is hard to avoid concluding that some of the distinctive occupational features of the groups reflect unique cultural features such as differences in their valuation of certain kinds of work. Finally, there were a number of *ethnic niches* created as members of a group hired later immigrants from the same homeland and thereby passed on the distinctive skills that they had gained in the United States to others in

---

[2]See Stanley Lieberson, *A Piece of the Pie: Blacks and White Immigrants Since 1880* (Berkeley: University of California Press, 1980), chap. 10.

the same group. This helps us to understand such phenomena as the ▽
relative concentration of Greeks, for example, in the restaurant business
or Italians in garbage collection.

Historical Comparisons

The 1900 census provides an extraordinary opportunity to compare
the occupational pursuits of both the immigrants and the second generation from 17 different nations. The data were never fully reported in
the series of volumes emanating from that census, but they were made
available for use by the Immigration Commission created by the Congress in 1907. The so-called Dillingham Commission published 42 volumes on immigrants and their descendants, one of which was almost
entirely devoted to the data on their occupations in the United States.[3]

Farming

There were vast differences between the immigrant groups in their
propensity to pursue agricultural activities. At one extreme, nearly half
of immigrant men from Norway and Denmark were employed in agriculture.[4] Bohemians (persons born in an area which later became part of
Czechoslovakia) were the only southern-central-eastern (SCE) European
group exceptionally active in agriculture (32 percent). Other groups were
the Swiss (38 percent), Swedes (30 percent), Germans (27 percent), and
French (22 percent). At the other extreme are a number of the SCE European immigrant groups: the least active being those men born in Hungary, Italy, Austria, Russia, and Poland. The Irish, English, and Scottish
were all more likely to farm than were these immigrants from new
sources, but they were distinctly less likely to do so than were those
referred to above from other parts of northwestern Europe. The pattern
is fairly similar for immigrant women. The exact rank order is somewhat different (rho = .80, $P < .0001$), but the old-new distinction holds
for women as well. Of course, this is expected since agricultural activities were often especially well suited for family operation. Among im-

---

[3]U.S. Senate, *Reports of the United States Immigration Commission: Occupations
of the First and Second Generations of Immigrants in the United States*, 61st Cong., 2nd
Sess., Document No. 282 (Washington, DC: U.S. Government Printing Office, 1911).
[4]Unless indicated to the contrary, the percentages in 1900 with different occupations
refer to those who do have an occupation and are so employed, rather than the total population of a given age.

migrants, the percentages in agriculture are considerably lower for women than men (compare columns 1 and 2 of Table 5.1, which give the data for 13 of these groups). The only interpretation we can give to this is a distortion in the data such that women on the farms were perhaps not counted as employed and hence not included, whereas women working elsewhere were included as working.[5]

For 13 of these immigrant groups, it is possible to match them with data for the American-born ethnic populations in 1980 (it was necessary to pool the English and Welsh in 1980 by arithmetic averaging and the Bohemians in 1900 were matched with the Czechs in 1980).[6] The decline of farming in the United States as an economic activity is mirrored in the data, which show much smaller percentages farming in 1980 than for immigrants in 1900 (see Table 5.1). At any rate, there is almost an exact correlation between the present-day ethnic participation in agriculture and the levels observed for immigrant groups 80 years earlier (Spearman rho = .96, $P < .0001$). Groups especially active in agriculture in 1900 are still especially active. Despite the inexact nature of the 1900 occupational data for women, there is also considerable continuity between 1900 and 1980 (rho = .86, $P < .0001$).

The occupational continuity for ethnic groups in agriculture also shows up in the coefficients of relative variation (CRV). (The CRV was introduced in the preceding chapter as a measure of the difference between standard deviations of two groups when the arithmetic means are quite different.) The CRV for 13 groups of American-born women in 1980 is 53 percent, not much of a decline from the CRV of 63 percent found among the immigrants from those 13 sources 80 years earlier. Likewise, the CRV for American-born men from these groups is 56 percent in 1980, high in itself and representing only a modest decline from the 62 percent among immigrant men in 1900. The persistence of ethnic differences in agriculture is explained by the fact that it is a declining activity. There is considerable movement out of farming; sons of farm-

[5]According to our source for these data (U.S. Senate, *Reports*, p. 5), the 1900 census employed the term "breadwinner" in its occupational data, meaning "everyone who is engaged in any kind of remunerative employment." However, the census occupational reports themselves refer to "gainful labor," which means "work upon which each person depends chiefly for support, or in which he is engaged ordinarily during the larger part of the time." By this latter meaning, it is probable that many women working on their family farms were not counted.

[6]The occupational delineations have changed greatly between 1900 and 1980, to say nothing of the many present-day occupations that were unknown at the beginning of this period. As a consequence, the comparisons over an 80-year span have to be viewed as only approximate, with the results subject to alternative interpretation. In particular, when there is no correlation between earlier and later periods, it is not certain whether this means that the categories have changed and/or there is no continuity for the groups in their concentration in the occupations specified.

TABLE 5.1

Percentage Employed in Agricultural and Service Occupations, Comparisons Between 1900 and 1980, by Gender

Group	Agriculture 1900 Men	1900 Women	1980 Men	1980 Women	Service 1900 Men	1900 Women	1980 Men	1980 Women
Bohemian	32%	10%	6%	2%	17%	35%	6%	13%
Danish	42	9	6	2	15	64	5	14
English and Welsh	18	5	4	1	11	40	6	12
French	22	5	3	1	21	46	7	15
German	27	9	5	1	17	55	6	14
Hungarian	3	1	1	0	25	54	6	12
Irish	14	3	3	1	30	70	7	15
Italian	6	4	1	0	42	20	9	14
Norwegian	50	14	8	2	13	64	5	15
Polish	11	4	2	1	31	34	7	13
Russian	10	2	1	0	10	18	4	7
Scottish	18	5	3	1	10	47	6	11
Swedish	30	4	5	1	17	76	6	14

NOTES: Agriculture refers to "agricultural pursuits" in 1900; "farming, forestry, fishing" in 1980. Service refers to "domestic and personal service" in 1900; "service" in 1980. Data are for foreign-born persons in the United States in 1900, classified by country of birth; native-born persons of specified ethnic origin in 1980. Bohemian refers to country of birth in 1900 and Czech ethnicity in 1980. Separate data for English and Welsh ancestry in 1980 are averaged to make comparable the combined English and Welsh data available for 1900.

ers are more likely to be white collar workers than farmers. But, more significantly, Davis[7] shows that there is almost no movement into farming among those of nonfarm origins. Thus, structurally, farming is an area which lends itself to the continuity of any earlier ethnic differences in concentration.

Professions

A very different pattern is found for the professional occupations. To be sure, the old European immigrant groups were more likely than the SCE Europeans to be in professional occupations.[8] But such old-new differences no longer exist in 1980 for either gender among the American-born components of the relevant ethnic groups.[9] As a matter of fact, in 1980 the old groups tend to have somewhat lower average percentages employed as professionals than do the new groups. This is a complete shift; unlike farming, the 1980 professional percentages of the ethnic groups in 1980 are uncorrelated with those among the immigrant groups in 1900 (the Spearman rank-order correlations are .03 and $-.06$ for men and women, respectively).

Under current census procedures, most of the occupations classified as "professional" require higher levels of formal education. Therefore, these results can be understood in terms of the educational changes described in the previous chapter. The reader will recall that a similar shift occurred between 1910 and 1980 with respect to education such that the earlier old-new distinction disappeared and, indeed, education in 1980 was uncorrelated with immigrant education in 1910. Given these educational developments during this period, the absence of a correlation between past and present is to be expected for a set of occupations dependent on education for achievement. This is exactly the case: For all 33 groups in 1980, the product-moment correlation between percentage employed as professionals and percentage with four or more years of college is .98 and .94 for men and women (in both cases, $P < .005$), respectively.[10]

[7]James A. Davis, "Up and Down Opportunity's Ladder," *Public Opinion* (1982): 11–51.

[8]The single-tailed probability of such differences between the five new and eight old European groups is .009 and .001 for men and women, respectively, based on the Mann-Whitney test.

[9]For the same 13 groups in 1980, $P = .36$ and .53 for men and women, respectively.

[10]If anything, the strength of this relationship is underestimated since the educational data refer to all persons over age 25, regardless of whether they had an occupation, whereas the occupational data refer to a more restricted population.

To a large degree, differences among ethnic groups in their participation in the professions can be understood in terms of differences in the group's educational attainment. This is indicated in Appendix Table 5.3, which compares the actual percentage in professional occupations with the level expected for each group after educational attainment is taken into account (this is also provided for other major occupational categories as well). We are struck by how close the fit is for just about all of the groups, even though the groups do differ in their actual percentage employed as professionals. (See Appendix Table 5.1 and discussion later in this chapter.)

Service Occupations

The absence of a historical linkage for the professional occupation category does not mean that the historical continuity found in farming is an anomaly—far from it. The broad 1900 census category "domestic and personal service" includes a rather diverse set of occupations, different for men and women in the relative importance of specific occupations within the category. For women, the five most important (in declining numbers) are servants and waiters, housekeepers and stewards, launderers and laundresses, nurses and midwives, boarding and lodging house keepers. For men, the numerically most important domestic and personal service jobs are laborers (not specified); servants and waiters; watchmen, policemen, firemen, soldiers, sailors, and marines; barbers and hairdressers.[11] Many other occupations are also included in this broad category. At any rate, this occupational category was extremely important in 1900, particularly for women. For the 13 immigrant groups, on the average just under half of the women were employed in these pursuits (mean of 48 percent, ranging from 18 to 76 percent). It was by no means a trivial pursuit for men as well, with an average of 20 percent in the same immigrant groups so employed (Table 5.1).

Despite the diversity within these categories, there is a correlation for both men and women with respect to the relative concentration of the different groups in the domestic and personal service occupations in 1900 and their concentration in what are called "service occupations" in 1980.[12] The present-day concentrations of white ethnic groups in the

---

[11]Based on data in E. P. Hutchinson, *Immigrants and Their Children: 1850–1950* (New York: Wiley, 1956), table 33.

[12]For men, Spearman rho is .74, $P < .01$; for women, rho = .56, $P = .02$.

service occupations (Table 5.1) reflect the relative concentrations observed among the immigrant ancestors 80 years earlier. This continuity is all the more impressive when one considers that the relative variation has declined substantially during this span.[13]

As we noted above, the major service and domestic occupations are rather different for each sex; accordingly, the relative concentration of women in this occupation is uncorrelated with the position of men from the same groups (for 1900, rho between the sexes is $-.02$; for 1980 it is .30, P is .17 in 1980). This gender difference is also reflected in the old-new distinction. Among women, in 1900 the old groups were more concentrated in these activities ($P = .005$, based on the Mann-Whitney test). This old-new gap remains in 1980, with the old ethnic groups still tending to pursue service and domestic occupations to a greater degree ($P = .047$). For men, the new and old groups do not differ in their propensity to pursue these occupations ($P = .42$), and the difference is not significant in 1900 ($P = .11$).

Specific Occupations

In addition to broad occupational differences between the groups in 1900, the specific occupations held by each of the immigrant groups, as well as their American-born offspring, were also distinctive.[14] More than a few of the ethnic stereotypes are based on these occupational characteristics. In 1900, the odds of a male Irish immigrant being employed as a policeman or fireman was more than four times greater than

[13]Comparability between 1900 and 1980 in the occupations included within the "domestic and personal service" category in the earlier period and the "service" occupations in 1980 is, of course, less than complete. Overall, it is our impression that the occupations are fairly similar in the two periods, albeit the relative numbers are not the same. However, except for nonrandom changes in the occupations included, any lack of comparability over time would work against finding the correlation observed over time. Our one concern pertains to "laborers (not specified)," which is included in this category in 1900 and is by far the single most important activity for men in this category. Computing the 1900–80 correlations without laborers in 1900, we find that the results for women are barely altered (rho = .54, $P = .03$) and rho for men does decline from .74 to .52 ($P = .04$). So, continuity over time in the service occupations is observed for both men and women even if the numerically important laborer category is excluded in 1900.

[14]A summary comparison between the overall occupational distributions in 1900 and 1980 is not feasible, even though it would be highly desirable, because the 1900 census used only five broad categories (trade and transportation, and manufacturing and mechanical pursuits, along with three already analyzed—agricultural pursuits, professional services, and domestic and personal service). By contrast, there is little overlap possible with the broad categories employed in the 1980 census. Consider, for example, the nine occupational categories shown in Appendix Table 5.1.

that for the remainder of the white male work force.[15] (To a moderate degree, two other English-speaking groups also exceed unity in this occupation (Scots, 1.4; English and Welsh, 1.3.) Except for German immigrants, all of the other groups indicated in Table 5.2 are low in this occupation. (A ratio of 1.0 would occur if the group showed no special propensity to be in the occupation; odds above 1.0 indicate a disproportionate concentration; below 1.0 indicates less than expected on the basis of work force size.)

More generally, for all of the groups and all of the occupations shown in Table 5.2, we see some of the groups concentrated and other groups underrepresented.[16] For example, the odds of immigrant German men being bakers in 1900 are 8.7 times greater than the odds for the rest of the white male work force, and their odds of being cabinetmakers are 6.7 times. (On the other hand, they are underrepresented as boatmen, fishermen, miners, and plumbers.) Italians have a strikingly high concentration as barbers and hairdressers and as hucksters and peddlers, and they are also disproportionately engaged as boot and shoe makers and repairers, tailors, miners, bakers, and fishermen. In other occupations, they are underrepresented. Russians have exceptionally high ratios for two of the occupations; 30 for tailors and 23 for hucksters and peddlers. There are other distinctive patterns exhibited in Table 5.2. All three Scandinavian groups, as well as Italians, are disproportionately employed as fisherman; Norwegians are especially concentrated as sailors; Hungarians as miners; and so on.

Some of these ethnic concentrations are relatively easy to explain in terms of Old World skills and backgrounds; others represent distinctive adaptations in the United States. Of course concentration or underrepresentation need not mean either a strong propensity for a job or an aversion to it since these figures reflect the wide variety of other forces discussed earlier, including discrimination, locational factors, queuing, background qualifications, and linkages that tend to persist once they are established. The question is whether any continuity exists over time

[15]Odds are determined by dividing one ratio by another. The odds ratio for Irish police, for example, is obtained by taking the ratio of police born in Ireland to all other white police and dividing it by the ratio of Irish-born breadwinners by all other white breadwinners (regardless of nativity). Thus, the odds ratio for Bohemian bakers of 3.0 means that the ratio of Bohemian-born to non-Bohemian bakers is three times the ratio of Bohemian to all other white breadwinners.

[16]These occupations were chosen with two criteria in mind: first, they appeared reasonably comparable to a census occupational category used in 1980; second, they are occupations in which at least one of the immigrant groups in 1900 was concentrated. There is no reason to believe that the concentrations in these occupations are typical for all occupations in 1900 or the changes through 1980 are representative of all changes.

TABLE 5.2

Odds Ratios in Specific Occupations, Immigrant Men, by Country of Birth, 1900

Occupation	Bohemia	Denmark	England and Wales	France	Germany	Hungary	Ireland	Italy	Norway	Poland	Russia	Scotland	Sweden
Bakers	3.0	1.2	.9	3.7	8.7	1.1	.8	1.6	.5	1.3	1.4	2.2	.8
Barbers and Hairdressers	.4	.6	.5	1.7	1.7	.4	.3	9.3	.3	.5	1.0	.4	.3
Boatmen and Sailors	.1	3.3	1.5	1.4	.7	.1	1.4	.6	7.1	.1	.7	2.2	3.8
Boot and Shoe Makers and Repairers	1.9	1.0	1.1	1.3	2.1	1.3	1.5	4.6	.9	1.6	2.7	.8	1.6
Cabinetmakers and Joiners	4.5	3.1	1.0	2.1	6.7	2.2	.3	.7	2.1	1.9	1.2	.9	5.2
Carpenters	1.0	1.5	1.1	.9	1.2	.2	.7	.3	1.9	.5	.5	1.9	2.0
Fishermen and Oystermen	.3	1.6	.3	1.1	.4	.0	.3	1.6	3.6	.2	.3	.5	2.3
Hucksters and Peddlers	.8	.4	.6	1.0	1.2	2.5	.8	7.9	.3	5.4	23.1	.3	.3
Miners and Quarrymen	.9	.5	4.4	2.3	.6	12.5	1.3	3.8	.5	3.1	1.6	3.0	1.7
Model and Pattern Makers	1.0	1.6	3.2	1.4	1.4	.3	.5	.2	.9	.2	.3	4.5	2.0
Plumbers and Gas and Steam Fitters	.5	.5	1.4	.5	.6	.3	1.7	.2	.4	.3	.7	2.4	.5
Tailors	9.4	1.2	.7	1.5	3.4	5.6	.7	3.9	1.2	6.6	30.2	1.0	2.9
Policemen, Firemen, Watchmen, etc.	.4	.8	1.3	.9	1.1	.3	4.3	.2	.6	.4	.3	1.4	.7

in ethnic concentrations in some of these occupations. On the one hand, there is a general leveling of ethnic differences; on the other hand, the patterns shown by immigrants in 1900 still have significant remnants among the American-born many generations later in 1980.

Comparing 1980 results (Table 5.3) with those found in 1900, we can readily observe a decline during the 80 years in each group's distinctive pattern of occupational concentration and avoidance. The odds ratios for Bohemians in 1900, for example, had ranged on one extreme from 9.4, 4.5, and 3.0 (tailors, cabinetmakers, and bakers, respectively) to 0.1 (boatmen and sailors), 0.3 (fishermen and oystermen), and 0.4 (both barbers and hairdressers and policemen-firemen-watchmen). But in 1980, the highest Bohemian ratio was only 1.7 (tailors) and the lowest was 0.4 (fishermen and oystermen). The average odds ratio for Bohemians in 1900 was 1.86 (a deviation from unity of .86) whereas it is .92 in 1980 (an average deviation of .08). For each of the 13 ethnic groups in the period between 1900 and 1980, without exception, the mean odds ratio has moved closer to 1.0 (see the bottom panel of Table 5.3).

This, of course, also means that ethnic variation within an occupation is also reduced. For example, the highest 1980 ratio for bakers is 2.4 (Italians), whereas in 1900 Germans had a ratio of 8.7, followed by 3.7 for the French and 3.0 for the Bohemians. In all but one occupational grouping—policemen, firemen, and watchmen—the average ethnic deviation from unity was greater in 1900 than in 1980 (bottom panel of Table 5.3). In general, then, there is a reduction of the distinctive ethnic occupational dispositions found in 1900 for immigrant men. This is to be expected under the normal assimilative processes. However, these early immigrant occupational patterns still have significant vestiges 80 years later in the occupational patterns of American-born ethnic descendants.

For some occupations, the concentration exhibited by American-born men in 1980 is correlated with the levels found 80 years earlier for immigrant men. Spearman rank-order correlations between the two periods for the 13 groups are .65 for barbers and hairdressers ($P < .01$), .83 for boatmen and sailors ($P < .001$), .61 for carpenters and joiners ($P = .01$), .74 for fishermen and oystermen ($P = .001$), .58 for miners and quarrymen ($P = .02$), and .77 for tailors ($P = .001$). In other words, the relative positions of ethnic groups in these occupations in 1980 is related to the relative position held by immigrants 80 years earlier, even though there is a general decline in the extreme ratios. To be sure, for other occupations there is no significant positive correlation and in the case of plumbers and gas fillers there is a significant negative correlation between the relative concentration of groups in 1900 and 1980. For three

TABLE 5.3

Odds Ratios in Specific Occupations, American-Born Men, by Ancestry, 1980

Occupation	Czechoslovakia	Denmark	England and Wales	France	Germany	Hungary	Ireland	Italy	Norway	Poland	Russia	Scotland	Sweden
Bakers	1.0	.6	.6	1.0	.8	1.1	.8	2.4	1.4	1.9	1.3	.8	1.7
Barbers and Hairdressers	.6	1.0	.7	1.0	.7	.7	.6	3.3	.9	.9	.8	.5	.6
Boatmen and Sailors	.6	2.0	1.0	2.8	.8	.7	1.0	.5	1.4	.4	.8	1.0	1.0
Boot and Shoe Makers and Repairers	1.1	1.9	.7	2.4	.4	.4	.9	2.2	.2	.8	.4	.6	.9
Cabinetmakers	1.1	.8	1.3	.6	1.0	.2	1.0	.8	1.3	.8	.9	1.1	1.7
Carpenters and Joiners	1.1	1.3	1.0	1.2	1.1	.7	1.0	1.0	1.2	.9	.4	.8	1.2
Fishermen and Oystermen	.4	1.8	1.3	2.3	.5	.0	.9	.7	2.1	.4	.4	1.4	1.1
Hucksters and Peddlers	1.2	.7	1.1	1.2	1.0	1.0	1.0	1.6	1.7	.8	2.2	1.3	.7
Miners and Quarrymen	.7	.2	1.1	.9	.6	1.4	.9	.4	.3	.6	.4	.6	.4
Model and Pattern Makers	.5	.0	1.0	1.8	1.5	1.1	.9	1.0	.9	2.0	.8	1.0	.5
Plumbers and Gas and Steam Fitters	1.2	1.0	.9	1.3	1.0	1.2	1.1	1.2	1.0	1.0	.4	.8	.9
Tailors	1.7	.2	.2	.3	.4	.6	.3	3.4	.6	1.6	2.7	.4	.3
Policemen, Firemen, Watchmen, etc.	.8	.9	.9	1.0	1.0	.9	1.4	1.4	.7	1.1	.7	.9	.9

Arithmetic Mean Odds Ratios, 1900 and 1980

	Czechoslovakia		Denmark		England and Wales		France		Germany		Hungary		Ireland	
	1900	1980	1900	1980	1900	1980	1900	1980	1900	1980	1900	1980	1900	1980
	1.9	0.9	1.3	0.9	1.4	0.9	1.5	1.4	2.3	0.8	2.1	0.9	1.1	0.9

	Italy		Norway		Poland		Russia		Scotland		Sweden	
	1900	1980	1900	1980	1900	1980	1900	1980	1900	1980	1900	1980
	2.7	1.5	1.6	1.1	1.7	0.9	4.9	1.0	1.7	0.8	1.9	0.9

Czech ancestry in 1980 is an approximation of Bohemian birthplace in 1900.

groups—Bohemians, Irish, and Russians—the relative concentrations in different occupations in 1980 are historically linked to the concentrations found in 1900 (Spearman rho is .56, .52, and .48, respectively ($P =$ .02, .03, .05). Although the correlations with 1900 are not statistically significant for the other groups, with only two exceptions they are also in a positive direction (one of the exceptions, the French, are nearly significant in the opposite direction).

In brief, some of the distinctive occupational patterns found among different immigrant groups many decades ago are still affecting their contemporary occupational patterns. When a group gains a foothold in an occupation that offers a relatively attractive set of opportunities, we can expect this advantage to be passed on to offspring. Thus, members of a given ethnic group will differ in their knowledge about a given job and the disposition to pursue it. However, occupations differ not only in the edge that inside knowledge and contacts give people, but also in their relative attractiveness and growth of the position through the years. Thus, there is no reason to expect ethnic continuity to be uniform for all occupations. The heritage of earlier decades had not disappeared by 1980; the early occupational concentrations by different ethnic groups has a definite impact—albeit muted—on the jobs currently held by different ethnic groups.

Occupational Distributions in 1980

Men

For each of 16 European ethnic groups, the occupational composition of each group in 1980 is compared with that of the remaining 15 groups, as well as with the distributions for some of the leading non-European groups in the nation. These results, obtained separately for American-born men and women, are summarized in Table 5.4. The indexes of dissimilarity, discussed in chapter 3, indicate the degree of similarity in the occupational composition between the group specified and the average for each of the remaining European groups or for the specific non-European populations. Excluding Russians for the moment, overall these white ethnic groups have relatively low average indexes of dissimilarity from the other specific white ethnic groups. The mean index of dissimilarity between the English and the 14 other groups is 6 (Table 5.4, column 4), ranging from a low of 3 (column 2) to a high of 10 (col-

TABLE 5.4

Index of Occupational Dissimilarity Between Specific Groups and the Average of 16 Major White Ethnic Groups, by Sex, 1980

	Men					Women				
				Excluding Russians					Excluding Russians	
Group	Average (1)	Minimum (2)	Maximum (3)	Average (4)	Maximum (5)	Average (6)	Minimum (7)	Maximum (8)	Average (9)	Maximum (10)
English	7	3	25	6	10	6	3	14	5	8
German	8	3	28	6	11	5	1	16	5	8
Irish	8	3	27	7	11	5	1	16	5	9
French	9	3	29	8	12	6	2	17	5	10
Italian	9	4	26	8	11	8	5	18	7	12
Scottish	10	2	18	9	18	7	2	14	7	14
Polish	9	4	27	8	11	6	3	16	5	9
Dutch	12	4	33	10	17	10	5	21	9	15
Swedish	8	3	22	7	14	5	2	13	5	11
Norwegian	9	4	24	8	15	6	2	14	5	11
Russian	25	18	35	NA	NA	15	8	21	NA	NA
Czech	8	3	25	6	12	6	2	15	5	11
Hungarian	8	4	22	7	14	6	3	13	6	12
Welsh	10	2	18	9	18	8	2	15	8	15
Danish	9	3	22	8	15	6	2	13	5	11
Portuguese	13	4	35	12	18	10	5	21	10	15
Black	35	23	52	32	37	29	19	39	26	33
Mexican	27	14	49	24	32	24	14	35	22	28
Puerto Rican	34	22	51	31	35	27	17	36	24	30
Spanish-Other	16	4	36	13	19	12	4	23	10	16
American Indian	24	12	45	21	28	17	7	27	15	21
South Asian	16	10	33	13	18	16	10	26	14	19
Other Asian	13	8	23	12	17	8	5	15	7	12

NOTES: Based on broad occupational categories; see text. Data refer to occupations in 1980 of persons born in the United States, aged 25 and over, who worked in 1979. NA. = not applicable.

umn 5).[17] The Czechs have a similarly low average index of dissimilarity. Even the Portuguese, a relatively recent group with the greatest dissimilarity from the remaining groups (if Russians are excluded), have an average index of occupational dissimilarity of only 12 from the remaining major white groups. These indexes of occupational dissimilarity are relatively low compared with either the dissimilarity of Russian-origin men from other groups of white men or compared with the dissimilarity between these white groups and some of the non-European groups.

The Russians are by far the white group with the highest average index of occupational dissimilarity from other groups of white men (25); the minimum index of 18 for Russians versus Scots and Welsh is actually higher than the maximum when the non-Russian European groups are compared with each other (see column 5). For many of the European ethnic groups—English, German, Irish, French, Italian, Polish, and Czech—their index of occupational dissimilarity from the Russian group is more than double their next highest index with the remaining European groups (column 3 versus column 5). In most other cases, the indexes are substantially higher with Russians than with any other group. The only exceptions are the Scots and Welsh; in both cases their indexes of occupational dissimilarity are 18, which is also about as high as they experience, but is not unique to their index with this group. The main source of these higher indexes experienced by Russians is easy to describe. Slightly more than one fourth of employed Russian-origin men are in the professional occupations (27 percent), but this broad category accounts for only 10 to 19 percent of men from the remaining 15 groups. This alone would contribute an index of from 4 to about 14 between Russian-origin men and the other groups (if the difference is divided by two and we assume proportionately equal contributions from all other occupations).

As noted earlier, the gap in professional occupations is accounted for in part by the exceptional levels of educational attainment among Russian-origin men. But there are differences in other occupational pursuits that contribute to their extraordinary position; Russians have the largest percentage of any group in the executive, administrative, and managerial occupations (23 percent versus 14 to 19 percent for the others); they had 16 percent employed in the sales occupations compared

---

[17]The lowest index values for men of English origin are with Germans and Czechs; the highest (excluding Russians) is with the Portuguese. The indexes of dissimilarity, when applied to occupational distributions, treat each occupational category as a nominal entity, as if the categories cannot even be ranked in terms of their distance from one another. See Stanley Lieberson, "Rank-Sum Comparisons Between Groups," in David Heise, ed., *Sociological Methodology 1976* (San Francisco: Jossey-Bass, 1975), and the literature cited therein. This is, of course, not true, but there is probably more to be lost than gained in ordering these broad and diverse classes.

with 8 to 11 percent for the remaining 15 groups. Given this concentration in these three broad occupational categories, obviously there must be compensatory areas where Russian-origin men are underrepresented. In that regard, 1 percent of Russian men are reported in the farming, forestry, and fishing occupations (compared with 1 to 8 percent for the others); 11 percent are in the precision production, craft, and repair occupations (compared with 18 to 24 percent for the other groups); and 9 percent are operators, fabricators, or laborers (well below the 14 to 24 percent reported for the other groups). In short, the concentration in professional occupations helps contribute to the rather distinctive occupational makeup for Russian men, but their concentration in other occupational groups also increases their occupational dissimilarity from other European ethnic groups.

The occupational situation for some of the leading non-European groups is not easily summarized. First of all, among the groups considered, blacks and Puerto Ricans in the United States have the highest average indexes of occupational dissimilarity from these European groups (an average of 35 and 34, respectively). Their lowest index of occupational dissimilarity from the 15 non-Russian European groups—23 and 22—is still higher than that for any of the non-Russian European groups from one another. Black and Puerto Rican men, in other words, are quite distinctive in their occupational patterns. American-born men of Mexican ancestry are not quite as distinctive; their average index is 27, two points higher than that for Russians. However, there is a small amount of overlap with the European patterns. The lowest Mexican indexes from European groups is 14 and 16 (men of Portuguese and Dutch origin, respectively), which is certainly high compared with the maximum indexes experienced by the 15 European groups from one another. But those values are not entirely outliers; there are at least a few pairings between the 15 groups that are at least as high as these (see the maximum figures in column 5, Table 5.4).

The average index for American Indians, Other Spanish, and South Asians (largely Asian Indians) from the European groups is lower than the levels attained by black, Puerto Rican, or Mexican men (24, 16, and 16, respectively). There is also overlap between some specific pairings with levels achieved among the pairings of European groups with one another, but they are still higher on the average than the index found among all but the Russian group. Other Asians (consisting largely of Chinese, Filipino, Japanese, Korean, and Vietnamese groups) have an average index of 13, which actually puts them at the same level as the Portuguese. So there is even more overlap with the European groups and indication that this grouping has a far less distinctive level of occupational dissimilarity compared with the minority groups discussed above.

Because this grouping includes a diverse set of specific ethnic groups, the results are not conclusive since the index of dissimilarity from whites for each of the groups could be substantially higher than the value reported for the pooled population.[18]

In summary, men in all but one of the major European ethnic groups tend to have relatively similar occupational distributions. Differences exist between this set of groups, but they are relatively modest compared with a substantially Jewish group or compared with the indexes between these groups and most of the major non-European populations in the United States. It is impossible to compare these values with those in an earlier period (see footnote 12), so we cannot decide if these similarities represent a shift over time. At present, however, it is clear that the European groups are much more similar to one another, and at the same time different in their occupational distribution than those reported by leading non-European groups in the country. It is also the case that Russian men differ on the average quite sharply from all of the other specific white groups that are examined in this study.

Women

Without exception, the average indexes of occupational dissimilarity are lower for women than for men in the 16 European-origin groups (compare columns 6 and 1, Table 5.4). Likewise, the difference between European and non-European women is less than the differences found among groups of men. These gender comparisons could mean that ethnic/racial effects are less for occupations held by women. In other words, the ethnic/racial effect is muted for women because they are already concentrated in certain occupations by virtue of the fact that they are women—gender differences in occupational distributions have a much stronger effect for women than do ethnic/racial effects. However, another possibility is that the broad categories used by the census do not distinguish women's occupations as well as men's, and hence the results are merely an artifact of the classification scheme.

Despite the somewhat lower levels of occupational dissimilarity, the patterns among women are basically similar to those reported above for men. For example, among women of European origin, the highest average index is found for Russians, just as it was for men. However, the average index for Russian women compared with the remaining Eu-

---

[18]This could occur if each of the ethnic groups had relatively distinctive occupational distributions, but if the combined distribution is not too different from that for each of the major white groups.

ropean-origin women is 15, as opposed to 25 for men. (The general drop-off for women is due to more than this group's influence, since averages drop in virtually all cases when the analysis excludes Russian-origin men and women; compare columns 4 and 9, Table 5.4.) Although non-European women also have lower dissimilarity indexes than do men of the same origin, their occupational distributions are still quite distinct from those found among the various European groups. The average indexes are 29 for black women, 27 for Puerto Ricans, and 24 for Mexicans—in all cases exceeding the Russian index by a relatively wide margin and well over double the next highest index for the white groups (10 for both Dutch and Portuguese women). The average index is 17 for American Indians and 16 for South Asians; both barely higher than that among Russians, albeit in excess of the Dutch and Portuguese averages. The index for women reporting Other Spanish origins (12) is lower than that for the Russians and not much higher than that for the Dutch and Portuguese; and the index for Other Asians (8) is below that for the latter two groups.

Overall, then, most of the non-European groups have occupational distributions that set them off from even the most distinctive European groups. However, there are some exceptions; as noted above, some of these non-European groups are less dissimilar than are the Russians, with an average index value not much different from several other European-origin groups. Still, the pattern for men is largely repeated here. With the exception of the Russians, the major European groups are much closer to one another in occupational composition than to major non-European groups in the country.[19]

Old-New Distinction

The major white ethnic groups are not only relatively similar to one another in their occupational composition, but there is also evidence that the old-new distinction has no bearing on the differences that do exist in the average indexes of occupational dissimilarity. For men, even if the Russian outlier is included, there is no significant difference between the groups ($P > .05$, based on the Mann-Whitney test); for women, a single-tailed test is just significant at the .05 level only when

---

[19]To be sure, the results are affected by the fact that the categories are so broad. An analysis of occupational dissimilarity based on a larger set of narrower occupational categories would yield generally higher indexes of dissimilarity. The reader should also keep in mind that the index of dissimilarity does not distinguish occupational categories by either their average rank or the closeness of one category to another (see Lieberson, "Rank-Sum Comparisons").

Russians are included, with northwestern European women reporting somewhat lower average indexes from the remaining women. The old-new distinction fails to generate a simple subdivision in the groups' relative proximity to one another's occupational patterns. Among English-origin men, to be sure, occupational distribution is closest to those of German origin and least like the Portuguese (Russians excluded). But that sort of pattern is not very common. German-origin men, for example, are closest to English and Irish, but their occupational distribution is also most dissimilar to distributions reported for two other old groups, the Scots and Welsh. A "new" group such as the Italians are more like the Irish and least like the Dutch and the Portuguese (the latter being a new group). English-origin women—whose indexes of occupational dissimilarity are only 3 compared with women from such old origins as German, Irish, and French—also have an index of 3 compared with Polish women. At the other extreme, their dissimilarity index is 8 with both Portuguese *and* Welsh women.

In brief, among both men and women in 1980 the major European-origin groups are generally much more similar to one another than to the non-Europeans in the broad set of occupations that they hold. Persons reporting Russian origins are the only exception among the 16 specific groups analyzed. On the other hand, the major non-European groups in the United States are generally far more different from these 15 groups of European origin than are the latter from one another. The broad occupational patterns of European groups are still far more similar to each other than they are to the patterns of the major non-European populations in the nation. Notwithstanding this majority-minority gap in the relative similarity of occupations, there are still differences between ethnic groups in their relative concentrations both in the broad occupational categories, such as farming and the services, and in some of the specific occupations discussed elsewhere in this chapter. Thus, there are still ethnic differences between the groups that are at least in part a function of long-standing historical patterns observed many decades ago. It is just that these differences within the white population are not as severe as those found when whites are compared with other segments of the society.

Income

It is difficult to overstate the importance of income in a study of ethnic and racial relations in the United States. Although there are many other material and symbolic dimensions of racial and ethnic competition and position, income is a central element both directly and indirectly. Probably the importance attached to many other societal attributes is at least partly due to their potential consequences for income— for example, the conflicts over education and occupation. Two central questions are: How do the leading white ethnic groups compare with respect to income? What is the position of the major non-European minorities compared with these white groups?

Comparisons of Current Income Distributions

Income is a complex subject to begin with, requiring a number of census questions. We can assume a certain degree of imprecision in the responses, even among subjects intending to give an accurate report. Such difficulties would not require any mention *if* one could assume that they were unrelated to ethnic or racial origin. But it is not certain that the errors and distortions are of equal magnitude for all of the groups. Of course, we have no knowledge about any differentials between groups in their disposition to give honest and full answers or in their confidence that such answers will not end up in the hands of the Internal Revenue Service.

We do know that these groups differ in specific occupations in ways that may affect the accuracy of some income figures. For example, the groups differ in their percentages in agriculture. Persons who are in a position to produce significant amounts of food for their own consumption as a side-product of their main activity (say, through a substantial garden) are probably not very likely to report this as income. Likewise, there are many other occupations which have such potentials for distortion. Owners of grocery stores can take food home for their own consumption without recording it as income (a practice that will lower reported income), or persons employing an automobile as a legitimate business expense (say, realtors or other salespeople) may be tempted to also use the car for personal purposes without separating the expenses involved. Insofar as ethnic differences in occupations on the average cancel each other out, there is no problem. But the groups do differ in specific occupations in ways that could possibly affect the reporting of income.

A few technical notes are necessary. The 1979 data are obtained for all American-born individuals aged 25 years and over in 1980, regardless of their participation in the labor force. Income in this study includes all income for each individual. Data are not pooled by family units, thereby avoiding some of the problems of analyzing mixed couples, let alone differences between groups in the percentage married and/or with both spouses working. We are simply interested in how different the groups are in the incomes of their members. Where family members received income jointly, appropriate amounts were apportioned among specific household members.[20] Finally, each group's gender-specific income distribution is described by computing its Index of Net Difference (ND) from the distribution of the entire U.S. population aged 25 and over of the same sex.[21]

The income distributions are summarized in Table 5.5. American-born men of Russian origin have an income far in excess of that found for any of the other groups shown in the table. The ND of .28 between Russian men and all men (presumably reflecting Jewish–non-Jewish differences) means that the income of Russians exceeds all men 28 percentage points more often than does the opposite inequality. Appendix Table 5.2 provides detailed data on the income distribution of each group. In the case of Russian men, for example, their percentage in the highest income category ($75,000 and over) is more than twice that for the next highest group (5 percent versus about 2 percent for Hungarians and Scots); their percentage in the second highest category (6) is about double that of the runners-up (Czechs, Danes, Hungarians, Swedes, and Welsh). Russian-origin men also have the largest percentage (27) of any group in the third highest income category.

Later in this chapter we will consider the influence of education and occupation on these income distributions. Hungarian men are the next highest group, albeit their ND of .18 is distinctly below the Russian level. In turn they are followed by the Danes, Poles, Swedes, and Welsh. At the bottom of the list of European groups are the Portuguese, who are slightly below the Dutch. As one might guess from these extremes on both the high and low end of the distribution, the old-new distinction does not operate with respect to distinguishing between the incomes earned by the groups. As a matter of fact, the mean ND index is slightly higher for the six SCE European groups than for the ten northwestern European ones.

At the other extreme, black and Puerto Rican men have ND indexes that are greatly below the level reported for all men: −.32 and −.31, respectively. To a lesser degree, American-born men of Mexican, Other Spanish, American Indian, and South Asian origin all have lower in-

---

[20]This is "Income 8"; see the description in U.S. Bureau of the Census, *Census of Population and Housing: 1980*, Public Use Microdata Samples, Technical Documentation (Washington, DC: U.S. Bureau of the Census, 1983e), pp. 91 and K-21.

[21]The standard is regardless of birthplace and is not adjusted for part-whole problems. It is viewed, then, more as a population for standardization purposes.

TABLE 5.5

Income Distribution of Ethnic Groups,
Indexes of Net Difference, by Sex, 1979

Group	Index of Net Difference	
	Men	Women
English	.07	.00
German	.11	.00
Irish	.07	.00
French	.08	−.01
Italian	.11	−.02
Scottish	.13	.06
Polish	.14	.02
Dutch	.05	−.05
Swedish	.14	.01
Norwegian	.10	.01
Russian	.28	.13
Czech	.13	.02
Hungarian	.18	.02
Welsh	.14	.05
Danish	.15	.01
Portuguese	.03	−.01
Black	−.32	.01
Mexican	−.14	−.12
Puerto Rican	−.31	−.10
Spanish–Other	−.07	−.07
American Indian	−.07	−.07
American	−.12	−.11
United States	.00	−.08
White/Caucasian	−.05	−.04
North American Other	.08	.02
Other SCE European	.17	.05
Other Northwestern European	.14	.04
Middle Eastern/North African	.16	.08
African, Caribbean, Pacific	−.11	.07
South Asian	.13	.21
Other Asian	−.06	.02
No Response	−.08	−.03
All Other	.04	−.01

NOTES: Based on 1979 income for all persons born in the United States, aged 25 and over, regardless of employment in 1979. Income of the total population of a given sex, regardless of birthplace, is used for comparison (see text for details).

comes than the level for all men. With the exception of American-born men from Southeast Asia ("Other Asians"), these major non-European groupings all have lower incomes than those experienced by men from any of the 16 specific origins shown in Table 5.5. Other Asian men would rank in the top of these European groups. Middle Eastern men also enjoy favorable earnings as well (their ND is .16 for those of American birth). Thus, in 1980, the distinction between European and non-European seems to be fairly strong in terms of the incomes that men report. (The sheer number of exceptions is affected by the pooling of all Southeast Asian men—if at least some of the major components had similarly high levels, specification of each of the groups would make it appear as if there are more exceptions.) Also, the socioeconomic level of American Indians is, by some criteria, badly overstated in these chapters. Namely, these results are based on all persons, regardless of race entry, who report some American Indian ancestral origin. The results are therefore greatly affected by whites (on the "racial" question) who report at least some American Indian ancestry on the ancestry question. Because they are relatively large in number compared with those who report themselves as American Indian on the racial question, results for the American Indian item is greatly affected by this white component.

Essentially, the results for women are not very dissimilar; the range of ND indexes is narrower even though they are computed against the distribution for all women. The groups maintain similar income ranks for both sexes (Spearman rho = .81, $P < .0001$, based on more detailed ND values than those shown in Table 5.5). As is the case for men, women of Russian origin have the highest ND level—.13—of any of the white groups, about double that of the second highest group, women of Scottish origin. In the case of women, however, four of the European groups have indexes lower than that for the average of all women (Dutch, Italian, French, and Portuguese). The old-new distinction is unrelated to the incomes of different groups of women, as was the case for men.

The pattern for women is somewhat different from the pattern for men. As with men, Mexicans, Puerto Ricans, Other Spanish, and American Indians occupy lower income positions than any of the specific European groups. However, there the similarity ends. Women in the Other Asian category exceed all of the European groups (their ND is .21 compared with .13 for Russian women). The ND for South Asian women, unlike that for South Asian men, is equal or higher than that found for most of the European groups. Finally, the income distribution of black women not only is more favorable than the Dutch (ND = .01 versus − .05), but is also comparable to—or slightly more favorable than—the levels reported for a number of other major white groups such as the English, German, Irish, French, Italian, Swedish, Norwegian, Danish, and Portuguese women. Thus, the color line is less sharply defined for women than for men. These differences among women reflect group differences in labor force participation as well as the income earned by women who are or are not in the labor force.

Historical Comparisons

Income data are difficult to obtain for early decades in this century—a surprising fact, considering the importance of income in the United States and, indeed, in most other societies. The census first asked an income question in 1940, but income was not tabulated by country of origin until the 1950 census. Information on housing costs—a characteristic that might be considered an approximate surrogate for income—is available for the foreign-born groups in 1930. We use both data sets to determine, as best as we can, if the relative income positions of the ethnic groups in 1980 can be traced back to those observed among immigrants decades earlier. A somewhat tenuous conclusion is necessary because the results are somewhat mixed—and we do not know if this means simple changes over time in the relative income positions of the groups *and/or* lack of comparability between the early and current income measures.

In 1930, among families headed by an immigrant, those of Russian birth have by far the highest rental costs and owned-home values (see Table 5.6). Thus, for the group in 1980 with the highest level of income, the housing cost data in 1930 suggests that the immigrants from Russia were highest in income in 1930 as well. The median value of homes owned by families headed by someone of Russian birth was $7,543 in 1930—far in excess of the groups in second and third place (Irish and Scots, respectively $6,203 and 5,933). Likewise, their median rental of $47 per month is well above—in relative terms for that period—the $36 spent by German, Irish, and French immigrant families. (In general, the groups' rank on the rental scale is repeated moderately well with respect to home value; Spearman rank-order correlation for the 16 groups is .54, $P = .02$). At the other extreme, the Portuguese in 1930 have the lowest housing costs of the 16 groups (for either variable). This is exactly the income situation in 1980 as well. However, despite this continuity over 50 years between these two extremes among the groups, for all 16 of the groups there is no significant rank-order correlation between either of the 1930 housing cost measures and the incomes of either women or men in 1980.[22]

Median income figures are available for the nine foreign-born groups in 1949 for all persons with income (no gender distinction is made). In order to estimate the behavior of immigrants in as early a time frame as possible, the data were computed for those aged 45 and over in

---

[22]The Spearman rho between 1930 rental costs and men's income in 1980 is .19 ($P = .24$); between rental costs and women's income it is .26 ($P = .17$); between house value and men's and women's income rho is, respectively, .31 ($P = .13$) and .35 ($P = .09$).

TABLE 5.6

Immigrant Housing Costs and Income, 1930 and 1949

| | 1930 | | |
Birthplace	Value of Owned Homes	Monthly Rentals	1949 Income
England	$5,559	$35.99	$1,966
Germany	5,460	36.02	1,941
Ireland	6,203	35.84	1,859
France	5,421	35.93	NA
Italy	5,752	27.33	2,248
Scotland	5,933	37.50	NA
Poland	5,703	27.23	2,213
Netherlands	4,978	31.80	NA
Sweden	5,025	34.70	1,728
Norway	4,229	32.68	1,641
Russia	7,543	47.16	2,513
Czechoslovakia	4,991	22.53	2,031
Hungary	5,800	33.78	NA
Wales	5,152	32.36	NA
Denmark	4,772	34.85	NA
Portugal	3,995	20.36	NA

NOTES: Housing costs refer to median rent or median value of nonfarm homes occupied or owned by foreign-born white families, classified by country of birth of head; 1949 income refers to median for all foreign-born persons of either sex, aged 45 and over, with income in that year. NA = not available.
SOURCES: U.S. Bureau of the Census, *Fifteenth Census of the United States: 1930, Population. Special Report on Foreign-Born White Families by Country of Birth of Head* (Washington, DC: U.S. Government Printing Office, 1933b), table 8. For Ireland, the figures for Northern Ireland and the Irish Free State were weighted by data reported in table 5. U.S. Bureau of the Census, *1950 Census of Population*, Vol. 4: *Special Reports*, pt. 3: *Nativity and Parentage of the White Population* (Washington, DC: U.S. Government Printing Office, 1954), table 20. Income data for England include Wales, but data for Ireland exclude Northern Ireland.

the 1950 census. Again, the Russian-born have the highest median income of all nine of the groups (Table 5.6). However, as before, the Spearman rank-order correlation between immigrant income in 1949 and the income of the ethnic groups in 1980 is not significant: with men's income in 1980 rho is .50 (P = .09); with women's income rho is .22 (P = .29).

In short, the results are somewhat mixed. The Russian and Portuguese immigrant income ranks in 1930 are identical to the positions occupied by the American-born members of these groups in 1980. However, there is no significant correlation between 1980 income and the situation in either 1930 or 1949. As a general rule, then, the relative income positions of the various white ethnic groups in 1980 cannot be predicted on the basis of immigrant incomes earlier in the century. Although we have no information on the income distribution of immigrants earlier in the century, it is difficult to believe that a pattern similar to that observed in 1980 occurred then, in particular since the old groups enjoy no advantage over the new in 1980. With several striking exceptions, then, we believe that the relative incomes of white ethnic groups in 1980 in general could not have been predicted on the basis of the incomes of the immigrant groups at the time of their arrival in the nation. None of the correlations between 1980 income and the immigrant figures for either 1930 or 1949 are significant.

It is possible that we did not find significant correlations between the relative positions of earlier immigrant groups and their descendants in 1980 because of problems in the comparability of the income data. These data are not fully comparable: Medians are used in some cases, and ND indexes in others; gender-specific data are compared with pooled data; individuals are compared with families; and direct and indirect measures of income are employed. Thus, conclusions based on such data are inexact to some extent. Another source of error is lack of complete correspondence between ethnic data and birthplace data.[23] These difficulties introduce errors which work against finding any association (assuming random errors); nevertheless, two of the Spearman correlations are almost significant anyway, and the signs for all of the remaining correlations are in the direction expected if continuity were to be found from earlier periods to the present time. So it is possible that the income patterns observed in 1980 for different European-origin groups were significantly evident among the immigrants before World War II, but are hidden because of changes in the data being used. Now that a sample of the 1940 census is available on tapes, it should be possible for researchers to resolve this issue.

Interrelations: Education and Occupation

It is widely recognized that various elements of socioeconomic achievement are interrelated. Therefore, a standard procedure in the analysis of achievement is to take into account earlier elements in the attainment chain to see how far such elements can account for chronologically later features. For example, since parental attainment affects the life chances of offspring, parental factors are often considered when

---

[23]Stanley Lieberson and Lawrence Santi, "The Use of Nativity Data to Estimate Ethnic Characteristics and Patterns," *Social Science Research* 14 (1985):31–56.

analyzing the attainment of the subjects under study. The basic census data are not conducive to intergenerational analyses of attainment, but there are studies on this topic which include information on ethnic and racial groups.[24] The question arises whether the ethnic and racial groups have distinctive rates of intergenerational mobility such that the offspring of some groups differ from the offspring of other groups in their mobility after parental backgrounds are taken into account. Studies have found that white national-origin and religious groups differ in socioeconomic attainment. Featherman[25] reports that "Jews, regardless of ethnic ancestry, attain higher levels of education, occupation and income than all other subgroups, while Roman Catholics of Italian and Mexican heritage achieve the lowest levels" (p. 207). However, if one controls for parental origins, the differences in occupational achievement are negligible. Featherman finds "no net effect of religio-ethnic affiliation remains during the ten year period [1957–67] after both social origins and prior achieved statuses are controlled. Thus there is no evidence of occupational and income discrimination on purely religious or ethnic grounds."[26]

There are differences in the educational attainment of religio-ethnic groups which cannot be accounted for by controlling for parental origins. Featherman finds that "net of social background, one's religio-ethnic origins have a direct impact on the completion of years of schooling." Yet in the transfer of educational attainment to occupational attainment there appear to be no differences among the white national-origin groups. In addressing this question, Neidert and Farley[27] use a cross-sectional model and find that in terms of occupational returns for educational investment white ethnic groups do not appear to differ. On the other hand, all of these studies on intergenerational mobility find that racial groups do continue to suffer discrimination.

Although the parental influence on attainment cannot be examined with the data available here, it is certainly possible to consider the interconnection of some of the main attainment elements for the respon-

[24]See, for example, Beverly Duncan and Otis Dudley Duncan, "Minorities and the Process of Stratification," *American Sociological Review* 33 (1968):356–64.

[25]David L. Featherman, "The Socioeconomic Achievement of White Religio-Ethnic Subgroups: Social and Psychological Explanations," *American Sociological Review* 36 (1971):207–22.

[26]Ibid., p. 207.

[27]Lisa J. Neidert and Reynolds Farley, "Assimilation in the United States: An Analysis of Ethnic and Generation Differences in Status and Achievement," *American Sociological Review* 50 (1985):840–50.

[28]See Stanley Lieberson, "A Reconsideration of the Income Differences Found Between Migrants and Northern-Born Blacks," *American Journal of Sociology* 83 (1978): 940–66.

dents themselves. The preceding chapter reported some differences between the groups with respect to their educational attainment,
particularly when the ND index was employed. Education is a powerful
influence on occupational attainment; certain levels are a formal (or at
least common) prerequisite for many occupations. In other ways, educational attainment appears to affect occupational opportunities by providing the skill and characteristics that affect the chances of employment and success in various pursuits. Also, it is reasonable to assume
that educational achievement is correlated with personality characteristics which are in turn favorable to attainment.[28] The ability to stay in
school, make normal progress, carry out assignments, get along with
peers and authorities, attend regularly, and the like, are all traits which
should be beneficial on the job market.

Given this general linkage between educational attainment and occupation, how far do ethnic and racial differences in educational attainment go in accounting for the observed occupational distributions? Using published census cross-tabulations of the occupations of men and
women aged 25 and over in 1980 by their education, we can ascertain
the occupational attainment that would be expected for each group
based on such rates applied to the relevant educational attainments of
the groups.[29]

The sequence usually assumed in the analysis of an individual's socioeconomic attainment is fairly clear: One obtains an education which
in turn affects occupation, and then the two influence income. This is
certainly a reasonable *chronological* sequence, but it should not be assumed that the *causal* sequence is necessarily of the same simple order.
In particular, it is hard to believe that people attending college are un-
mindful of the potential occupational and income rewards that may follow successful completion of their study. Accordingly, an analysis
which asks about the occupations or incomes of groups net of educational attainment is perfectly appropriate for some purposes. But we
have to recognize that ethnic racial differences in education are themselves in part the product of differences between groups in the pursuit
of income and occupational rewards.

A different view of socioeconomic attainment is one in which education (particularly after the required years of schooling), occupation,

[29]Derived from U.S. Bureau of the Census, *1980 Census of Population*, Vol. 2: *Subject Reports*, "Earnings by Occupation and Education," PC80-2-8B (Washington, DC: U.S.
Government Printing Office, 1984), table 2, which cross-tabulates years of schooling by
broad occupational categories for each sex in the recent experienced civilian labor force
with earnings in 1979. A part-whole problem exists in such standardization procedures
because the rates are based on the entire population (in this case including foreign-born as
well).

and income are joint and simultaneous pursuits. Now that is obviously a distortion, too; many people start college with only a vague occupational goal or switch to a new occupational goal which is far removed from what they would have anticipated. The truth, we suspect, lies somewhere between these two positions—but pursuit of this issue would take us far beyond the purview of this study. Although we have followed the conventional analysis here—and it is certainly valuable for examining the questions of whether the gap between groups remains after education is taken into account or whether education and occupation can account for income distributions—for some purposes the model is a genuine distortion of the pathways undertaken.

Jews, a group reporting remarkably high levels of education and enjoying very favorable occupational and income distributions, provide a nice example of this distortion. The normal propensity is to ask how much of their occupational or income distribution can be accounted for by their distinctively high educational attainment. But their distinctive educational attainment should not be viewed as occurring in a vacuum, that is, without a recognition on the part of Jewish individuals of the potential rewards of education. Yet this is precisely what often happens when investigators refer to the distinctive subcultural pursuit of education, as if the occupational and income rewards that follow are incidental to this.

Let us make our point with another perspective. Suppose that educational attainment in the society was inversely related to income and occupational attainment. Under such circumstances—admittedly counterfactual and therefore unknowable—would we assume that the traditional pursuit of education would lead Jews to achieve high levels and therefore exceptionally low income and undesirable occupations? The point is that this analysis assumes a conventional approach to the causal linkage between education, occupation, and income. Such a linkage is perfectly appropriate for the analysis which makes certain assumptions. But, for other problems, the operation of a more complicated set of causal linkages would be appropriate.

Occupational Patterns for Men

For men, the index of dissimilarity between the actual occupational distribution of each group and the distribution expected on the basis of their educational attainment is 6 for the average white ethnic group (see Table 5.7). (The gap would probably be even smaller if age distribution, region of residence, and parental background were also taken into account). Since the index for Swedish men is 6, a comparison between their actual and expected occupational distributions illustrates a fairly typical situation. Of the remaining 15 groups, 8 have indexes as low or lower than the Swedes and all but one of the remainder have indexes of dissimilarity of 7 or 8. The percentage of Swedish men employed in the executive, administrative, and managerial occupations is 18 rather than the 16 expected on the basis of education (the actual occupational distributions are shown in Appendix Table 5.1; the difference between these actual values and those expected on the basis of education are provided in Appendix Table 5.3). There is also a gap of 1 percentage point in excess of expected in some of the other occupational categories: professionals; technicians; sales; farming; and production, craft, and repair. On the other hand, their concentration in both the administrative support and service categories are 1 percentage point less than expected. The largest single difference for Swedish-origin men is the 4 percentage point gap (15 rather than the 19 expected) in the blue collar category of operators, fabricators, and laborers. So we can see that educational attainment, for most of the white groups, helps account for much of their occupational distribution, in the broad sense of the term.

Men of Russian origin are the European group whose occupational patterns are least accounted for by their educational attainment; their index is 14. This occurs even though the Russian educational distribution is strikingly different from the other groups of white men. Appendix Table 5.3 shows the sources of these differences. The percentage of Russian men employed in the executive, administrative, and managerial occupations exceeds the level expected by 4 percentage points, the largest gap among any of the white groups. The same gap occurs for professional occupations—again, the largest of any of the groups. In both of these areas, Russians have the highest expected level because of their educational position, but still exceed this expected level by the widest margin. Russian men have no special educational advantage over other groups in the sales category, reflecting the heterogeneity of positions within this category. However, the 16 percent of Russian men employed in this area by far exceed the 10 percent expected on the basis of educational level. Indeed, all of the other white groups have expected levels of about 9 or 10 percent and, in turn, differ by only 1 or 2 percentage points from that. Russians are also underrepresented at the bottom of the educational distribution. The educational distribution of Russian men gives them the lowest expectation among European groups in either of the major blue collar categories: production, craft, and repair or operators, fabricators, and laborers. But in both cases, they are way below expectations; in the first category, their gap is by far the largest in that direction, and they are tied with the Welsh group for the largest gap in the latter blue collar category.

TABLE 5.7

Indexes of Dissimilarity Between Actual and Expected Occupational Composition After Taking Ethnic Education Attainment into Account, Population Born in the United States, by Gender, 1980

Group	Occupational Dissimilarity	
	Men	Women
English	5	8
German	4	8
Irish	4	9
French	5	7
Italian	8	12
Scottish	7	9
Polish	5	11
Dutch	3	6
Swedish	6	7
Norwegian	8	6
Russian	14	13
Czech	6	11
Hungarian	7	11
Welsh	7	9
Danish	7	6
Portuguese	3	8
Black	18	12
Mexican	6	7
Puerto Rican	16	18
Spanish–Other	6	9
American Indian	6	3
American	4	5
United States	7	15
White/Caucasian	5	6
North American Other	5	9
Other SCE European	8	12
Other Northwestern European	7	7
Middle Eastern/North African	13	11
African, Caribbean, Pacific	12	7
South Asian	11	9
Other Asian	9	10
No Response	3	8
All Other	12	15

As for non-European groups, the occupational composition of black and Puerto Rican men deviates to a relatively large degree from the patterns expected on the basis of their educational levels (their indexes of dissimilarity are 18 and 16, respectively). The magnitude of these indexes means that their low status occupational distributions are generated by factors above and beyond what can be readily expected on the basis of their educational attainment. There are two important facts to keep in mind when examining the occupations of these groups in Appendix Tables 5.1 and 5.3; first, the importance of educational attainment shows up in the expected values for these groups based on the general linkage between education and occupation in the society; second, the differences between actual and expected occupational distributions of these groups are obtained after taking their low educational attainment into account. For example, only 6 percent of black men and 5 percent of Puerto Ricans are expected to be professionals. Their actual percentage is about the same as expected; so there is no reason to think that educational improvements would fail to be translated into professional jobs at a rate appropriate to that for all men in the United States. However, this is not the case for some occupations. For example, 6 percent of blacks and 7 percent of Puerto Ricans are in the executive, administrative, and managerial category; both are less than what would be expected with their educational distribution. This is also the case for sales occupations and farming, and both groups are substantially underrepresented in the production occupations compared with the figures expected on the basis of their educational attainment. On the other hand, Puerto Ricans—and blacks to a lesser degree—are overrepresented in the administrative support category and both have substantially higher representation in service jobs than would be expected on the basis of education, as well as in the operators, fabricators, and laborers category.

The index of dissimilarity for American Indians, Mexicans, and Other Spanish is 6 in all three cases—a relatively low index value even by white standards. Considering their educational distribution, American-born men of Mexican origin tend to be underrepresented in sales occupations and overrepresented in one of the blue collar categories, operators, fabricators and laborers. Other Spanish are especially overrepresented in service jobs, and men with at least some American Indian ancestry are in blue collar jobs to a greater degree than their educational composition would lead us to expect. The situation for these groups is not as severe as that for blacks and Puerto Ricans. The actual occupational distribution of these groups differs somewhat from expectations and these differences appear to be generally in a disadvantageous direction. In the case of the two Asian groups, their actual distribution deviates from the expected in ways that are reminiscent of both the European groups and other non-European groups. On the one hand, the South Asians are employed as professionals to a greater degree than would be expected on the basis of their education, and they hold operators, fabricators, and laborers jobs to a lesser degree than their education

would lead us to expect. On the other hand, this group is strongly overrepresented in the service sphere. Men whose ancestry is from other
parts of Asia, largely Southeast Asians, are relatively more concentrated
in technical and agricultural jobs than would otherwise be expected, and
are especially underrepresented in the operators, fabricators, and laborers category. A rather large percentage are employed as professionals—
17—which is in excess of all but three of the white groups specified
(Russians, Scots, and Welsh). But this figure is relatively easily understood when the educational levels of Southeast-Asian men is taken into
account (this leads to an expectation of 16 percent professional).

In summary, all of the white groups' occupational distributions are
affected by more than their educational distribution, with Russians
being particularly noteworthy. For the most part, however, these deviations from the occupational distribution expected on the basis of education are modest in magnitude, albeit generally meaning a greater concentration in the white collar occupational pursuits, particularly those
that might offer income and/or status advantages. Other unmeasured
factors might help account for some of these differences—for example,
parental background, region of birth and residence, differences in age
distribution of the groups, and so forth—as well as the possibility of
generally minor cultural and normative differences between white ethnic groups in this domain. Several non-European groups—Mexicans,
Other Spanish, and American Indians—have only modest differences
from the occupational patterns that would occur based solely on their
educational composition. The differences are generally to their disadvantage, but clearly up to now the conversion of education to occupation has largely followed the general societal pattern. Among the two
broad categories of Asian men, the actual and expected occupational
patterns are somewhat higher than those found for white groups, other
than Russians. The deviations from the expected patterns are mixed, in
some cases meaning concentration in more attractive occupations and
in other cases in less attractive ones.

The position of black and Puerto Rican men, by contrast, is strikingly different. First, the occupations of these men differ to the greatest
degree from those expected on the basis of their education. Second, the
deviations from expectations would greatly overrepresent them in what
are considered the less attractive occupational categories. Given their
generally low educational levels and a poor pattern of educational conversion, the combination for men from these two groups is extremely
damaging, as inspection of their occupational distribution in Appendix
Table 5.1 indicates. This is not an entirely surprising finding given the
long history of active discrimination against these groups in American
society.

Occupational Patterns for Women

The role of education in accounting for occupational patterns among women, as measured by these indexes of dissimilarity, is somewhat different (Table 5.7). Compared with men, the actual occupational distributions of women are generally more dissimilar from the distribution expected on the basis of their educational composition and the gender-specific linkage between these two attributes (compare the two columns of Table 5.7). The existence of these higher indexes of dissimilarity means that other factors besides education are relatively more important in affecting the occupations held by women than those held by men. The data set used in this model to take education into account—the education-by-occupation cross-tabulation for all women in the experienced labor force—is applied to the educational attainment of all women in each ethnic/racial group, regardless of whether the latter are working. If the applicability of the educational cross-tabulation with occupation is more distorted for women by such factors as marital status and spouse's occupation, this in turn could generate higher indexes of dissimilarity for women.[30]

Once again, blacks and Puerto Ricans are notable for their disadvantaged position. Puerto Rican women have an exceptionally high index of dissimilarity; black women are less distinct, but still have a relatively high level. The occupations held by women from both of these groups deviate from the expected in a more unfavorable way than is the case for women from other groups under consideration (see Appendix Table 5.3). As is the case for men from these groups, Mexican, Other Spanish, and American Indian women do not have such sharp differences between their actual and expected occupational distributions. In the case of women, we uncovered an old-new difference in certain occupational concentrations. Women of northwestern European origin show a stronger attachment to service jobs than do women of SCE European origin. By contrast, the latter have a stronger attachment to white collar office work (occupations listed as administrative support, including clerical) than do women from the old European sources. This takes a little effort to understand; for the reasons given in footnote 30, all of these white groups are below the percentage expected in service jobs and all

---

[30]Differentials in labor force participation by educational level will help explain, for both men and women, results where virtually all of the groups appear to be overrepresented or underrepresented in a given occupation. If, for example, women (or men to a lesser degree) with higher levels of educational attainment are especially likely to work, this would lead to an apparent overrepresentation of all women (or men) in the professions or other activities drawing heavily on highly educated people. In addition, the rates are based on the entire population of the specified age and sex; hence occupational differences between foreign-born and the native population will also help generate one-sided sets of signs.

exceed the percentage expected in the lesser white collar positions. However, the deviations are of greater magnitude for one set of groups than for the other. Among the ten old European groups of women, the deviations from expected service employment range from 1 to 4 percentage points; among the six new groups, the deviations range from 4 (in only one case) to 6 percentage points (Mann-Whitney U Test, $P < .001$). The results are quite similar for administrative support occupations, but in the opposite direction, with virtually no overlap between old and new in the magnitude of their deviations from the expected levels based on education (Mann-Whitney U Test is again $P < .001$).

A complete investigation as to the causes of this surprising old-new difference in these broad occupational categories is not possible here. But we did try to determine if these differences in 1980 have historical roots, examining the data for 15 groups of immigrant women in 1900.[31] Based on the Mann-Whitney test, the nine old groups have significantly larger percentages employed in the domestic and personal service occupations than do immigrants from six new groups ($P < .01$) The range is quite substantial, since this was a generally important category for immigrant women in that period; the four groups with the lowest percentage so employed are those born in the new sources of Russia (18 percent), Italy (20 percent), Poland (34 percent), and Bohemia (35 percent). At the other extreme are some of the northwestern European sources; 76 percent of Swedish-born women are so employed, followed by 70 percent of Irish-born women, and 64 percent of Danish- and Norwegian-born women. The reason for this historical situation, let alone its continuity for 80 years, would carry us far afield. Certainly, we would have to examine the specific occupational components of the diverse set of occupations included under these rubrics. However, it may well reflect the greater disposition of northwestern European women to accept such employment in homes and the more favorable disposition of Americans to employ immigrant women from northwestern European sources as domestics and as servants.[32]

On the other hand, no historical roots are associated with the 1980 old-new gap in the lesser white collar positions. For both first and second generations in 1980, there is no significant difference between old and new women in their employment as clerks and copyists in 1900. Locational factors may be operating here to generate the contemporary old-new gap. Namely, many opportunities for lesser white collar employment exist in the larger metropolitan areas generally, particularly in the Northeast and parts of the Midwest, where major corporate headquarters are found, as well as insurance companies, banking and finance,

---

[31]U.S. Senate, *Reports*, table 11B.
[32]See Lieberson, *A Piece of the Pie*, p. 310, for relevant differences among men.

gnificant employers of lesser clerical workers. These admin-
actions are concentrated in areas where SCE European
lisproportionately represented. Hence their employment op-
a this area may exceed those for the old stock whites in the
___, this surprising finding calls for future study.

In summary, the general conclusions made about the role of education in accounting for the occupations held by men seem to operate here
as well for women. There are some exceptions, to be sure. And, for the
reasons indicated above, a more complex model is particularly needed
here for women. We are impressed by some important old-new differences that are linked to the occupations held by women. These differences probably reflect the role of location in one case and historical
roots in the other.

Interrelations: Income, Education, and Occupation

Finally, the issue arises as to how far these ethnic/racial differences
in education and occupation can account for the group differences in
income. The expected income distribution is determined for the groups
based on their existing occupational and educational characteristics applied to the income distributions for all American-born persons of the
same sex (aged 25 and over) who have the same combined occupation
and education. This yields an income distribution for each group which
is what would be expected if members of that group had the same incomes as do all men (or women) with comparable education and occupation. This standardization procedure also includes education-specific
rates for those not working. The results are shown in Table 5.8.

There are several striking features in the data for men. All 16 of the
specific European-origin groups have higher income distributions than
would be expected on the basis of the combined influence of their education and occupations. (A positive ND index means that the actual
income distribution is above the level expected; a negative value means
that the actual is below the level expected.) The situation for the non-
European groups is largely in a negative direction. Blacks and Puerto
Ricans have especially high negative ND indexes—which means that
their incomes are well below the level expected on the basis of their
educational and labor force positions. Mexicans, Other Spanish, American Indians, Africans, and South Asians also have lower incomes than
are expected on the basis of their education and occupational attainments. Among non-Europeans, American-born men of Southeast Asian
origin (the "Other Asian" category) enjoy incomes slightly in excess of
the expected levels, and this is also the case for men of Middle Eastern
ancestry. (Again, there is evidence that the incomes of Southeast Asians

TABLE 5.8

Index of Net Difference Between Actual Income and Expected Level
Based on Occupation and Education, American-Born, 1980

Group	Men	Women
English	.02	.00
German	.05	−.01
Irish	.03	−.01
French	.03	−.02
Italian	.04	−.03
Scottish	.04	.03
Polish	.06	−.01
Dutch	.03	−.02
Swedish	.05	−.02
Norwegian	.03	−.02
Russian	.10	.03
Czech	.06	.00
Hungarian	.08	−.01
Welsh	.03	.02
Danish	.05	−.02
Portuguese	.02	−.02
Black	−.19	.05
Mexican	−.07	−.10
Puerto Rican	−.16	−.01
Spanish–Other	−.06	−.06
American Indian	−.04	−.08
American	−.04	−.04
United States	.01	−.01
White/Caucasian	−.06	.01
North American Other	.06	.01
Other SCE European	.03	.00
Other Northwestern European	.04	.00
Middle Eastern, North African	.03	.01
African, Caribbean, Pacific	−.11	.04
South Asian	−.10	−.01
Other Asian	.02	.09
No Response	−.03	.02
All Other	−.02	.01

are not limited by the same forces that appear to handicap most of the leading non-European groups in the country.) Incomes are lower than expected among men giving no response, or vague and unusable responses, or simply selecting American. Among the European groups, Russians have an exceptionally favorable income distribution (ND = .10), which suggests that incomes of Jews are in excess of the combined effects of their initially favorable educational and occupational levels. Hungarian- and Polish-origin men also exceed their expected levels by a somewhat wider margin than do a number of the other groups.

The situation for women is radically different. Overall, the gaps between their actual and expected income levels are not as wide as those for men. Moreover, the various groups have different patterns. Of the 16 specific groups of European origin, 11 have negative ND indexes, meaning their incomes are actually below the levels obtained by all women of comparable education and labor force position. Black women have higher income levels than are expected, and "Other Asian" women have the widest excess income over what would be expected solely on the basis of occupation and education.

Some specific comparisons help illustrate the impact of these differences in more concrete terms. The actual ND between men from the lowest and highest income groups (black and Russian, respectively) is .54—a strikingly high figure. This means that if all black and Russian men in the United States were paired together in 1980, Russians would have the higher incomes 54 percentage points more often than would blacks have the higher incomes. (In 19 percent of all such comparisons, blacks would have the higher income; in 73 percent, Russians would have the higher income; and in the remainder, blacks and Russians would be in the same income category.) Comparing the income standardized for each group's education and occupational distributions, Russians would be expected to exceed blacks by 30 percentage points. Thus, a substantial income gap between these groups exists solely because of their differences in occupation and education. But on top of this, another 24 percentage points exist above and beyond those factors.

Russians are an exceptionally high income group for whites generally. Russian men enjoy an ND of .22 and .26, respectively, in comparison with Irish and Portuguese men (NDs of .15 and .18 would exist if only occupation and education were operating). However, these groups still enjoy substantial NDs over black men—a good part due to factors other than occupation and education. For Irish men, ND over blacks is .38, with the expected ND being .18. Similarly, Portuguese men have an actual ND of .35 versus blacks, whereas it would be .15 if only education and occupation were operating. To be sure, in all of these cases these gaps may in part reflect certain technical factors; for example, differences within each broad occupational category are not taken into account, as well as age, parental factors, and so on. Still, differences of this sort seem to underlie a pattern that we have found elsewhere in this chapter. Namely, there are important white ethnic differences still present in various socioeconomic dimensions, but they are modest compared with the gaps found between whites and most of the nonwhite groups in the nation.

In summary, even after taking occupation and education into account, there are substantial income gaps for most non-European men that remain unaccounted for. This operates above and beyond the various forces that themselves lead non-Europeans to have different occupations than do Europeans with comparable levels of education. White men, of different ethnic origins, for the most part enjoy somewhat higher levels of income than is found in the society as a whole for men of comparable occupation and education. In effect, there is an important color line operating such that whites generally have moderately higher incomes and non-Europeans generally significantly lower incomes than the rates for the entire population of American-born men. (These gains and losses are asymmetrical because the overall rates used for the standardization are influenced by the substantial white proportion of the population. Hence a sizable deficit for the numerically smaller non-European population translates into only a moderate gain for the much larger white population.) This pattern is not found among women in these groups; their income distributions tend to differ less from expectations. In effect, there is less of an ethnic/racial effect operating on women's incomes, net of education and occupation. This gender gap has been observed earlier in this chapter for other socioeconomic features as well. We cannot be certain as to what accounts for these differences between the actual and expected income distributions for each group. But the results are certainly consistent with an interpretation that there are discriminatory forces affecting the ability of non-Europeans to convert their existing occupations and educations into the same incomes as do whites, albeit there are smaller differences among whites in this as well.

Summary

In this chapter we have shown that although there are some signs ○ of continuity in ethnic concentrations in certain occupations from earlier in the century, for the most part socioeconomic inequalities among white ethnic groups are both relatively minor and unrelated to patterns of ethnic inequality found earlier in the century. The once major differences among specific white groups as well as the old-new distinction in occupation and income are largely gone. The differences which do continue for these groups are interesting but, except for Russians, are rather subtle.

The patterns for blacks and Puerto Ricans show both continuing discrimination and/or an inability to translate education into occupation and income at the same level as the rest of the population. The division between whites and nonwhites remains strong, even as the division that once existed between whites has largely disappeared.   ◌

APPENDIX TABLE 5.1

Ethnic Occupational Composition, Population Born in the United States, by Gender, 1980

	Executive, Administrative, Managerial	Professional Specialty	Technicians and Related Support	Sales	Administrative Support, Including Clerical	Service	Farming, Forestry, Fishing	Precision Production, Craft, Repair	Operators, Fabricators, Laborers
MEN									
English	16%	15%	3%	10%	6%	6%	4%	21%	18%
German	16	13	3	10	6	6	5	22	19
Irish	16	13	3	10	7	7	3	22	19
French	15	12	3	10	6	7	3	24	19
Italian	17	13	3	11	8	9	1	21	17
Scottish	19	18	4	11	7	6	3	18	14
Polish	15	15	3	9	8	7	2	22	20
Dutch	14	11	3	9	6	7	5	24	23
Swedish	18	16	4	10	6	6	5	21	15
Norwegian	17	15	4	10	5	5	8	19	16
Russian	23	27	3	16	6	4	1	11	9
Czech	17	15	3	10	7	6	6	21	16
Hungarian	17	16	3	11	8	6	1	20	18
Welsh	19	19	4	11	6	6	3	19	14
Danish	18	15	4	11	6	5	6	20	15
Portuguese	14	10	3	8	6	10	5	22	24
Black	6	6	2	3	8	15	4	17	38
Mexican	8	6	2	5	7	10	7	25	32
Puerto Rican	7	5	2	5	10	17	2	18	34
Spanish—Other	12	10	3	8	7	12	3	22	23
American Indian	9	7	2	7	5	8	4	29	29
American	10	7	2	8	5	7	6	27	28
United States	16	13	3	12	5	7	5	22	19
White/Caucasian	13	14	3	10	5	6	5	22	21
North American Other	14	12	4	9	7	8	2	25	20
Other SCE European	18	20	4	11	7	6	2	18	16
Other Northwestern European	18	18	4	10	6	5	7	19	14
Middle Eastern/North African	19	19	4	19	6	6	1	14	11
African, Caribbean, Pacific	10	10	4	6	9	13	3	19	27
South Asian	11	15	2	9	5	15	2	24	18
Other Asian	16	17	6	9	9	8	6	17	12
No Response	12	9	2	9	6	7	5	25	25
All Other	16	19	3	15	6	6	3	17	14

WOMEN

	9%	19%	3%	11%	31%	13%	1%	2%	10%
English	9	19	3	11	31	13	1	2	10
German	9	18	3	10	32	14	1	2	10
Irish	9	17	3	11	33	15	1	2	10
French	9	16	3	11	32	15	0	2	10
Italian	8	15	3	12	36	14	1	2	9
Scottish	10	22	3	10	33	11	1	2	6
Polish	8	18	3	11	34	13	2	2	11
Dutch	8	14	3	10	30	17	1	2	13
Swedish	9	20	3	11	33	14	2	2	7
Norwegian	9	19	3	10	32	15	1	1	7
Russian	12	29	3	12	31	7	0	2	4
Czech	9	19	3	10	34	13	2	2	7
Hungarian	9	21	3	10	34	12	0	2	8
Welsh	11	24	3	10	32	11	1	2	7
Danish	10	20	3	10	32	14	2	2	7
Portuguese	8	13	4	11	32	14	1	2	16
Black	5	13	3	5	22	31	1	2	18
Mexican	5	9	2	8	28	23	3	3	18
Puerto Rican	5	10	2	5	28	14	0	4	31
Spanish–Other	8	14	3	9	32	19	1	3	12
American Indian	7	10	3	11	28	20	1	3	16
American	7	10	3	12	27	18	2	3	19
United States	11	16	2	15	29	14	0	2	11
White/Caucasian	8	16	3	12	28	16	1	3	14
North American Other	8	17	3	10	34	15	0	1	11
Other SCE European	10	22	3	11	33	11	1	2	8
Other Northwestern European	9	23	4	10	30	13	2	2	7
Middle Eastern/North African	14	20	3	12	31	12	1	0	7
African, Caribbean, Pacific	9	13	4	9	27	23	0	2	11
South Aisan	7	19	0	6	30	19	2	2	17
Other Asian	11	17	4	10	35	12	1	3	7
No Response	8	11	3	11	30	16	1	3	16
All Other	10	19	2	14	34	11	1	2	6

NOTE: Data in 1980 are for persons aged 25 and over, who had worked in 1979.

APPENDIX TABLE 5.2

Income Distribution of Ethnic Groups, by Sex, 1979

Group	Under $2,000	$2,000–2,999	$3,000–3,999	$4,000–4,999	$5,000–5,999	$6,000–7,499	$7,500–9,999	$10,000–11,999	$12,000–14,999	$15,000–19,999	$20,000–24,999	$25,000–49,999	$50,000–74,999	$75,000 and over
MEN														
English	.05	.02	.03	.03	.03	.05	.08	.07	.10	.17	.14	.18	.02	.02
German	.04	.02	.02	.03	.03	.04	.07	.07	.11	.19	.15	.19	.02	.01
Irish	.04	.02	.03	.03	.03	.05	.08	.07	.10	.18	.15	.18	.02	.01
French	.04	.02	.03	.03	.03	.04	.08	.07	.11	.19	.15	.18	.02	.01
Italian	.04	.02	.03	.03	.03	.04	.07	.07	.11	.20	.16	.19	.02	.01
Scottish	.03	.02	.03	.03	.03	.05	.07	.07	.10	.17	.14	.21	.03	.02
Polish	.04	.02	.02	.03	.03	.04	.07	.07	.10	.20	.17	.20	.02	.02
Dutch	.04	.02	.03	.03	.03	.05	.08	.06	.11	.18	.14	.17	.02	.01
Swedish	.04	.02	.02	.03	.03	.04	.07	.07	.11	.18	.15	.21	.03	.01
Norwegian	.04	.02	.03	.03	.02	.04	.07	.06	.10	.18	.15	.20	.02	.01
Russian	.03	.01	.02	.02	.02	.03	.06	.05	.08	.15	.14	.27	.06	.05
Czech	.04	.02	.02	.03	.03	.04	.07	.06	.10	.19	.17	.20	.02	.01
Hungarian	.04	.01	.02	.02	.03	.04	.06	.06	.09	.18	.17	.22	.03	.02
Welsh	.03	.02	.02	.03	.03	.04	.08	.07	.10	.17	.14	.21	.03	.02
Danish	.04	.02	.02	.03	.03	.05	.07	.06	.10	.18	.16	.21	.03	.02
Portuguese	.05	.02	.03	.03	.03	.05	.08	.09	.11	.19	.15	.15	.01	.01
Black	.14	.07	.06	.05	.04	.07	.11	.08	.10	.13	.08	.05	.00	.00
Mexican	.09	.03	.04	.04	.04	.07	.11	.09	.12	.18	.12	.08	.01	.00
Puerto Rican	.13	.05	.05	.04	.04	.07	.12	.11	.13	.13	.06	.04	.00	.00
Spanish—Other	.07	.03	.04	.04	.03	.06	.09	.08	.11	.17	.13	.12	.01	.01
American Indian	.07	.04	.04	.04	.04	.06	.09	.09	.11	.18	.13	.12	.01	.00
American	.07	.04	.05	.05	.04	.06	.10	.08	.11	.16	.11	.11	.01	.01
United States	.07	.03	.03	.03	.04	.06	.09	.08	.11	.15	.13	.16	.03	.02
White/Caucasian	.08	.03	.04	.04	.03	.06	.09	.08	.10	.15	.13	.13	.02	.02
North American	.04	.02	.02	.03	.03	.04	.08	.07	.12	.20	.16	.15	.02	.01
Other SCE European	.04	.02	.02	.03	.03	.04	.07	.06	.09	.18	.16	.22	.03	.01
Other Northwestern European	.03	.02	.02	.03	.03	.04	.07	.06	.10	.17	.15	.21	.03	.02
Middle Eastern/North African	.05	.02	.02	.02	.02	.04	.08	.05	.09	.16	.14	.23	.05	.02
African, Caribbean, Pacific	.10	.03	.03	.04	.04	.06	.10	.07	.12	.18	.12	.10	.01	.00
South Asian	.10	.00	.04	.06	.00	.04	.07	.06	.19	.22	.10	.09	.01	.01
Other Asian	.04	.02	.01	.02	.02	.04	.07	.07	.11	.19	.17	.20	.02	.02
No Response	.09	.04	.04	.04	.05	.05	.10	.08	.11	.16	.12	.12	.01	.01
All Other	.06	.03	.03	.04	.03	.05	.09	.07	.09	.14	.13	.18	.03	.02

APPENDIX TABLE 5.2 *(continued)*

WOMEN

English	.34	.08	.07	.06	.05	.06	.07	.10	.06	.07	.02	.06	.02	.02	.00	.00
German	.34	.07	.07	.06	.05	.06	.07	.10	.07	.07	.02	.06	.02	.01	.00	.00
Irish	.34	.08	.07	.06	.05	.06	.07	.10	.07	.07	.02	.06	.01	.01	.00	.00
French	.34	.07	.07	.06	.05	.06	.07	.10	.07	.07	.02	.06	.01	.01	.00	.00
Italian	.36	.07	.07	.05	.05	.06	.06	.09	.07	.06	.02	.06	.02	.02	.00	.00
Scottish	.31	.07	.07	.06	.05	.06	.07	.10	.07	.07	.03	.07	.03	.01	.00	.00
Polish	.34	.07	.08	.06	.05	.06	.08	.09	.06	.08	.03	.07	.03	.02	.00	.00
Dutch	.36	.09	.07	.06	.05	.06	.07	.09	.07	.06	.02	.05	.02	.01	.00	.00
Swedish	.34	.07	.07	.06	.05	.06	.07	.09	.07	.08	.03	.06	.02	.02	.00	.00
Norwegian	.34	.08	.07	.06	.05	.05	.07	.09	.07	.07	.02	.07	.05	.04	.00	.00
Russian	.29	.06	.06	.05	.04	.05	.06	.09	.07	.09	.05	.09	.03	.01	.00	.00
Czech	.33	.08	.07	.05	.05	.06	.07	.09	.07	.08	.03	.07	.03	.02	.00	.00
Hungarian	.34	.07	.05	.06	.05	.06	.06	.10	.07	.07	.03	.07	.03	.02	.00	.00
Welsh	.31	.07	.07	.06	.05	.06	.07	.09	.07	.08	.02	.07	.02	.02	.00	.00
Danish	.34	.07	.07	.06	.05	.07	.07	.09	.07	.08	.02	.07	.02	.02	.00	.00
Portuguese	.34	.07	.07	.07	.05	.06	.08	.11	.07	.07	.02	.05	.02	.01	.00	.00
Black	.28	.12	.09	.06	.06	.06	.08	.10	.06	.06	.02	.05	.01	.01	.00	.00
Mexican	.42	.07	.06	.06	.05	.05	.08	.09	.06	.03	.01	.03	.01	.00	.00	.00
Puerto Rican	.35	.08	.10	.09	.08	.08	.09	.09	.05	.02	.01	.02	.01	.01	.00	.00
Spanish—Other	.38	.08	.07	.06	.05	.05	.07	.10	.06	.04	.01	.04	.01	.01	.00	.00
American Indian	.37	.08	.07	.06	.05	.05	.08	.10	.06	.06	.01	.04	.01	.01	.00	.00
American	.39	.10	.08	.06	.05	.05	.07	.09	.05	.03	.01	.03	.01	.01	.00	.00
United States	.38	.10	.07	.05	.05	.05	.07	.08	.05	.03	.03	.03	.03	.02	.00	.00
White/Caucasian	.35	.09	.07	.05	.05	.06	.08	.09	.06	.04	.02	.04	.02	.02	.00	.00
North American	.32	.07	.08	.07	.05	.06	.07	.11	.07	.06	.02	.06	.02	.02	.00	.00
Other SCE European	.33	.07	.06	.06	.05	.05	.07	.09	.07	.08	.03	.08	.03	.02	.00	.00
Other Northwestern European	.33	.07	.07	.05	.05	.05	.07	.10	.07	.07	.03	.07	.02	.02	.00	.00
Middle Eastern/North African	.32	.06	.06	.05	.05	.07	.08	.09	.07	.08	.04	.08	.03	.03	.00	.00
Africa, Caribbean, Pacific	.28	.08	.08	.07	.05	.08	.08	.11	.08	.07	.02	.07	.02	.01	.00	.00
South Asian	.28	.11	.07	.06	.04	.11	.02	.16	.06	.05	.01	.05	.01	.02	.00	.01
Other Asian	.24	.05	.05	.04	.04	.07	.12	.10	.10	.11	.05	.11	.05	.03	.00	.00
No Response	.34	.09	.07	.06	.05	.05	.06	.10	.06	.05	.02	.05	.02	.01	.00	.00
All Other	.33	.08	.08	.06	.06	.06	.07	.09	.06	.06	.02	.06	.02	.02	.00	.00

NOTE: Data are for for all persons born in the United States, aged 25 and over in 1980, regardless of work status in 1979.

APPENDIX TABLE 5.3

Actual Occupational Composition Minus Expected After Taking Into Account Ethnic Educational Attainment, Population Born in the United States, by Gender, 1980

	Executive, Administrative, Managerial	Professional Specialty	Technicians and Related Support	Sales	Administrative Support, Including Clerical	Service	Farming, Forestry, Fishing	Precision Production, Craft, Repair	Operators, Fabricators, Laborers
MEN									
English	.02	.01	.00	.01	.00	-.02	.00	-.00	-.03
German	.01	.01	.00	.00	.00	-.02	.01	.00	-.02
Irish	.02	.01	.00	.01	.00	.00	-.01	.00	-.03
French	.01	.01	.00	.01	.00	-.01	-.01	.02	-.03
Italian	.03	.01	-.00	.02	.01	.01	-.03	-.01	-.05
Scottish	.03	.02	.00	.01	.00	-.01	.00	-.01	-.04
Polish	.01	.02	.00	.00	.01	-.01	-.02	.01	-.01
Dutch	.01	.01	.00	-.00	.00	-.01	.00	.01	-.01
Swedish	.02	.02	.01	.00	-.01	-.02	.01	.00	-.04
Norwegian	.01	.01	.01	.01	-.01	-.02	.04	-.01	-.04
Russian	.04	.04	.00	.06	.00	-.02	-.02	-.05	-.05
Czech	.02	.01	.00	.00	.00	-.02	-.02	.01	-.05
Hungarian	.02	.02	.00	.01	.01	-.01	-.03	.00	-.02
Welsh	.02	.03	.01	.02	.01	-.01	-.01	.00	-.04
Danish	.02	.00	.00	.02	-.01	.02	.03	-.00	-.04
Portuguese	.01	.00	.00	.00	.00	.01	.00	-.02	-.01
Black	-.04	.00	.00	-.04	.03	.06	-.02	-.08	.10
Mexican	-.03	-.01	.00	-.03	.01	.00	.01	.01	.03
Puerto Rican	-.02	.00	-.00	-.02	.05	.07	-.04	-.07	.04
Spanish—Other	.00	.01	.00	-.01	.01	.04	-.02	-.01	-.02
American Indian	-.02	.	-.00	-.01	-.01	-.01	-.01	.04	.02
American	-.01	.00	.00	.01	-.01	-.02	-.00	.02	.00
United States	.03	.01	-.00	.03	-.01	-.01	-.00	.00	-.05
White/Caucasian	.01	.02	.01	.02	-.01	-.02	.01	.01	-.01
North American Other	.01	.01	.00	.01	.00	.00	-.02	.03	-.03
Other SCE European	.02	.04	.01	.00	.00	-.01	-.02	-.02	-.03
Other Northwestern European	.02	.01	.01	.01	-.01	-.02	.03	.00	-.04
Middle Eastern/North African	.02	.01	.01	.00	.00	.00	.00	-.05	-.06
African, Caribbean, Pacific	-.04	.00	.01	.09	.02	.05	-.02	-.04	.04
South Asian	-.01	.02	-.01	-.03	-.01	.07	-.03	.01	-.06
Other Asian	.00	.01	.02	.01	.02	.01	.02	-.02	-.06
No Response	.00	.00	.00	-.01	.00	-.01	.00	.01	-.01
All Other	.01	.04	.00	.06	.00	-.01	-.01	-.04	-.06

APPENDIX TABLE 5.3 (continued)

WOMEN

English	.01	.03	.00	.01	.02	−.04	.00	−.04
German	.01	.03	.00	.01	.02	−.03	.01	−.04
Irish	.01	.03	.00	.01	.03	−.03	.00	−.05
French	.01	.03	.00	.01	.02	−.03	.00	−.04
Italian	.01	.03	.00	.02	.06	−.05	−.01	−.06
Scottish	.02	.03	.00	.01	.03	−.04	.00	−.05
Polish	.01	.04	.01	.01	.05	−.06	.00	−.04
Dutch	.01	.03	.00	.01	.01	−.03	.01	−.03
Swedish	.01	.03	.00	.01	.02	−.02	.01	−.05
Norwegian	.01	.03	.00	.04	.01	−.01	.01	−.05
Russian	.03	.04	.00	.01	.03	−.06	−.01	−.05
Czech	.01	.04	.00	.01	.04	−.04	−.01	−.07
Hungarian	.01	.05	.00	.01	.05	−.05	.00	−.06
Welsh	.02	.05	.00	.01	.02	−.04	−.01	−.04
Danish	.01	.03	.00	.01	.01	−.01	.01	−.04
Portuguese	.01	.02	.01	.01	.03	−.06	.00	−.01
Black	−.02	.03	.01	−.05	−.02	.08	.00	−.02
Mexican	−.01	.01	.00	−.01	.04	−.02	.02	−.03
Puerto Rican	.00	.03	.00	−.04	.07	−.13	−.01	.07
Spanish—Other	.01	.03	.00	−.01	.05	−.02	.00	−.05
American Indian	.01	.01	.01	.01	.01	−.01	.00	−.02
American	.00	.01	.00	.02	.01	−.04	.00	−.00
United States	.03	.03	−.01	.05	.03	−.07	−.01	−.06
White/Caucasian	.00	.02	.00	.02	.01	−.04	.00	−.02
North American Other	.00	.03	.01	.00	.05	−.03	−.01	−.04
Other SCE European	.02	.05	.00	.01	.04	−.05	.00	−.06
Other Northwestern European	−.00	.04	.00	.01	.01	−.02	.01	−.05
Middle Eastern/North African	.05	.02	.00	.02	.01	−.04	−.02	−.05
African, Caribbean, Pacific	.02	−.00	.01	.00	−.01	.04	−.01	−.04
South Asian	.00	.04	−.03	−.04	.04	−.02	−.01	.00
Other Asian	.02	−.03	.01	.01	.06	−.03	.00	−.04
No Response	.01	.02	.00	.02	.03	−.05	.00	−.02
All Other	.02	.03	−.01	.05	.06	−.06	.00	−.08

NOTES: Actual occupational data are for persons aged 25 and over who had worked in 1979. Standardization is based on a gender-specific education-by-occupation cross-tabulation for all persons of these ages applied to educational distribution of groups, regardless of labor force status.

6

INTERMARRIAGE

<small>ο</small> I<small>NTERMARRIAGE</small> has been a long-standing topic of interest for sociologists because it can be understood as both an indicator of the degree of assimilation of ethnic and racial groups and an agent itself of further assimilation for the couples who intermarry and for the next
<small>σ</small> generation.

> Intermarriage for individuals means either the crossing of ethnic taboo lines and/or the demise of such prohibitions. Moreover, the group rates reflect not only the complex interplay of attractions and antipathies, but also the status afforded to each ethnicity, the nature and frequency of their contact, the strength of social pressures, and the structure of ethnic cleavages in the society. Theoretically, it is impossible to visualize a full assimilative process if ethnicity is still seriously affecting the choice of mates.[1]

<small>υ</small> Intermarriage—for whatever reason that it occurs—has consequences both for the individuals involved and for the future viability and nature
<small>ο</small> of the ethnic groups themselves. For the individuals involved, intermarriage functions to create more ethnic heterogeneity in their social networks and may possibly lead to a diminution or dilution of ethnic identity. For the individual children of intermarriage the determination of

[1]Stanley Lieberson and Mary C. Waters, "Ethnic Mixtures in the United States," *Sociology and Social Research* 70 (1985):43–52.

ethnic identity becomes a question and a decision in a way that does not exist for the children of an ethnically homogeneous marriage.

The consequences of intermarriage for the ethnic group have received considerable attention in the sociological literature. On that score, a landmark empirical and theoretical study of intermarriage and its consequences is Adams's classic pre–World War II study of Hawaii.[2] Also extremely influential is Gordon's position of intermarriage as the indicator of structural assimilation[3]—the type of assimilation that he argued could lead to the complete assimilation of the ethnic group into the dominant society. An ethnically homogeneous marriage creates a family that can pass on to children the values and cultural forms of that particular ethnic group.

As we might expect, the topic of ethnic intermarriage has attracted considerable interest.[4] For an overview of the extensive research literature, see Heer;[5] he discusses the causes and consequences of intermarriage, the types and quality of data available, and the major studies on this topic. However, the availability of 1979 and 1980 census data greatly enhances the opportunities for determining the actual rates of interethnic marriage, particularly for white groups.[6] Several studies have utilized these data thus far,[7] but the census data are extraordinary and

[2]Romanzo Adams, *Interracial Marriage in Hawaii* (New York: Macmillan, 1937).

[3]Milton M. Gordon, *Assimilation in American Life: The Role of Race, Religion, and National Origins* (New York: Oxford University Press, 1964).

[4]For example, Andrew M. Greeley, *Ethnicity in the United States* (New York: Wiley, 1974); Harold J. Abramson, *Ethnic Diversity in Catholic America* (New York: Wiley, 1973); Milton M. Gordon, *Assimilation in American Life: The Role of Race, Religion, and National Origins* (New York: Oxford University Press, 1964); Richard D. Alba, *Italian Americans: Into the Twilight of Ethnicity* (Englewood Cliffs, NJ: Prentice Hall, 1986); Richard D. Alba and Mitchell B. Chamlin, "A Preliminary Examination of Ethnic Identification Among Whites," *American Sociological Review* 48 (1983):240–47; Richard D. Alba, "Interethnic and Interracial Marriage in the 1980 Census." Paper presented at the meetings of the American Sociological Association, Washington, DC, 1985; Teresa Labov and Jerry A. Jacobs, "Intermarriage in Hawaii, 1950–1983." Paper presented at the Annual Meetings of the Population Association of America, Boston, 1985.

[5]David M. Heer, "Intermarriage" in Stephan Thernstrom, ed., *Harvard Encyclopedia of America Ethnic Groups* (Cambridge, MA: Belknap Press, 1980), pp. 513–21.

[6]This is less the case for blacks and to a certain degree for some other nonwhite groups because in many states it is possible to obtain data from marriage records—which are a superior source of information. Studies of white ethnic intermarriage, on the other hand, have been obliged to use less than ideal data sources, often with relatively small numbers and/or restricted to a particular locale. The only exceptions, to our knowledge, are analyses based on much smaller sample surveys of the nation's population, such as the General Social Survey of the National Opinion Research Center.

[7]Richard D. Alba and Reid M. Golden, "Patterns of Ethnic Marriage in the United States," *Social Forces* 65 (1986):202–23; Alba, "Interethnic and Interracial Marriage" and *Italian Americans: Into the Twilight of Ethnicity* (Englewood Cliffs, NJ: Prentice-Hall, 1986); Stanley Lieberson and Mary C. Waters, "Ethnic Mixtures in the United States," *Sociology and Social Research* 70 (1985):43–52.

have not received the extensive analysis that they deserve. Indeed, they merit a full monograph.

Our concern with intermarriage in this chapter and the next is limited to four important issues: (1) We consider the rates of outmarriage for ethnic and racial groups in the United States in 1980 and the trends over time; (2) we also consider one of the consequences of intermarriage through an analysis of the marital behavior of mixed-ancestry individuals who themselves are the product of intermarriages somewhere in previous generations; (3) in those cases of intermarriage, we determine who marries whom; (4) finally, we ascertain what causes groups to differ in their outmarriage and what is responsible for the changes over time. We consider those causes of intermarriage which are most amenable to examination with census and survey data—the effect of structural forces such as composition and segregation on the availability of marriage partners and the effect of education on the level of ingroup marriages. In addition, the marriage patterns are examined to see if they are affected by the social rankings of the groups and/or their religious affiliation. This chapter will be concerned primarily with the first two issues while the next chapter will the address the last two.

An Overview of Intermarriage

Whether or not intermarriage takes place can be broadly defined as dependent on four factors:

1. The existence of formal legal proscriptions against intermarriage or the existence of strongly held ethnic taboo lines. There are no legal prohibitions in the United States at present, though not very long ago various states had laws forbidding intermarriages between blacks and whites. Those laws have since been declared unconstitutional.

2. The relative availability of partners from within and without the group. The structural determinants of this factor have had a lot of attention from sociologists and are most importantly influenced by (a) group size (referred to in this chapter and the next as composition), (b) the distribution of these groups geographically throughout the country, and (c) the degree of segregation or contact that the groups have with one another in a particular location.

3. Informal attitudes and opinions about intermarriage. These operate to some unknown degree for white ethnic groups in the United States. They include parental advice against intermar-

riage in general, as well as against intermarriage with persons belonging to specific groups; the attitudes an individual holds toward outgroup members; and the attitudes outgroups have toward the potential bride or groom.

4. The degree of overlap between ethnic membership and nonethnic characteristics. This affects intermarriage even when persons are indifferent about the ethnic or racial origins of a potential mate. Since social class affects marital choice, mating will be nonrandom with respect to ethnicity and race to the extent that class and ethnic boundaries overlap. Some marriages which occur because of class endogamy will appear to be due to ethnic endogamy. The perceived social status of a particular ethnic group will also affect the degree of intermarriage and this in turn is partly a consequence of the social class origins of members of that group.

High rates of intermarriage are a necessary condition—albeit an insufficient one—for assimilation. Given the fact that the family is such a central force in the socialization process generally, the impact of intermarriage on the maintenance of the group into the future is self-evident. A homogeneous nuclear family, along with a homogeneous extended family, is more able and likely to pass on to offspring the ethnic feelings, identification, culture, and values that will help perpetuate the group. To be sure, other forces affect ethnic identification: peers, the nature of the residential area, attitudes of outsiders, and the like—to say nothing of the macrosocietal factors such as discrimination and official rules governing ethnic identity. The latter may profoundly affect the outcome of intermarriages. In the case of marriages between blacks and whites, for example, the offspring have been unambiguously labeled black. Nevertheless, if a group experiences high level of intermarriage, this can be viewed as a potentially important factor working against the long-run maintenance of the group as a separate entity.

Whatever the disposition toward mates of a given group, clearly the ethnic composition of the population will modify and affect the actual marital choices observed. If a group is numerically important in a given area, many ingroup marriages will occur even if all members are totally indifferent toward the ethnic origin of their mate. But even if they are not indifferent, the manifestation of their antipathies and preferences will be modified and affected by the actual composition of eligible mates. Put another way, in a society where most men have dark hair, the vast majority of women will marry dark-haired men even if they have a strong preference for blond men. Finally, insofar as ethnic groups differ in social, economic, and geographic characteristics which affect the marriage market, these, too, will play a role in the marital patterns observed for a given group. This is because these characteristics will modify and affect both the ability of members to pursue their marital choices and the disposition of others toward the group. These last two features—composition and the socioeconomic characteristics that are relevant for marital choice of each ethnic group—represent what might well be called the structural factors affecting intermarriage, as distinct from the dispositions of the marrying population themselves.

The above factors can help explain the existence of intermarriage, trends in those rates over time, and differences between groups. However, there are also broad societal forces to consider. For one, the nature of the courtship process itself will have a significant bearing on intermarriage. The shift to marital choices based on romantic love or other individualized decisions will undercut the direct impact of the family on the marital decision made by young adults. The preferences of parents and family are not unknown to people of courtship age, but in the aggregate they are less of a determinant than they would be in the context where parental and familial approval was critical—to say nothing of cultures in which arranged marriages are practiced. Related to this, of course, is the entrance of persons into the labor market prior to marriage, the frequent movement out of the family home, spatial mobility, and other factors which undercut the ability of the family to supervise an offspring's premarital choices. Of course, this does not totally negate the family influence since the socialization process will have occurred prior to this stage. The very minimal levels of intermarriage found between some segments of the American population, as we will see later in the chapter, means that we should not underestimate the potential influence of childhood socialization and other factors in minimizing intermarriage even with the presence of romantic love and other individualized decision-making criteria for the choice of spouses.

Another general social process is the importance of ethnic and racial matters in the society generally and with respect to members of a specific ancestry group. There is reason to think that *white* groups in the United States find their European ancestry to be of decreasing significance to them. This is a process to be expected given that the groups are of an increasing number of generations' residence in the United States and hence, given the assimilative process, they are increasingly similar to other whites with different European heritages. (This does not mean the absence of any differences between white ethnic groups, but it does mean a *decline* in such gaps.) From this perspective, intermarriage can be viewed as both affected by general assimilative process and potentially moving it further along. Of course, the latter possibility depends on what happens to the offspring of mixed couples—a matter that we will see actually has many possibilities.

Also, it is reasonable to assume that members of a given ethnic/ racial group are by no means uniform in their dispositions toward inmarriage and likewise that they vary in attitudes toward specific outgroups. As a consequence, a full model would consider not merely the average disposition of each group and its changes over time, but the dispersion around that average as well. Under any circumstance, in light of all of these other variables discussed above, there is no reason to assume that a group's general level of outmarriage—or its level with respect to specific other groups—is simply a function of the joint disposition of the group toward others coupled with the disposition of others toward the group. These dispositions will be radically affected by the various forces influencing contact and attractiveness net of the person's ethnic/racial origin. Indeed, we are essentially modeling intermarriage as a multivariate probabilistic process in which the ethnic/racial disposition of each person is but one independent variable. This means that there are persons who choose mates from groups toward which they have a fairly strong antipathy and there are others who inmarry even though they are indifferent about selecting an ingroup spouse.[8]

It is not possible to test an elaborate model of intermarriage with census data. The issues are probably too complicated for any study to examine the entire range of variables we have outlined above. For example, the average contact members of a given group—say, X—have with potential mates from groups X, Y, Z, and so on, is extremely difficult to ascertain. It would mean (1) evaluating all sorts of social contexts in terms of their potential influence on choice of mate and (2) determining the ethnic/racial makeup in each situation for each member of group X. For example, the workplace is no doubt a source of contact with potential mates. But members of group X differ in the job that they have and—even for those holding the same job—they differ in the specific ethnic/racial makeup of their specific coworkers. Even in that context, given the high levels of divorce and remarriage, it is not easy to determine who the potential mates are in each specific context. We could analyze the same problem for other features of the contact variable. How important is the ethnic/racial makeup of an individual's immediate neighborhood as opposed to the city or metropolitan area in which the person resides? Relative to both work and residence, how important is the ethnic/racial makeup of one's friends of the same sex or how important is the makeup of the educational institution that many attend at the time when marital choices are beginning to be made?

---

[8]To be sure, in some cases the antipathy may be so powerful as to minimize the impact of the other factors.

Defining Intermarriage

Since intermarriage—by definition—means a marriage across specified group lines, the statistical results are affected by how the groups are
classified and delineated. As is often the case in the United States,
blacks provide the most extreme example. We consider the marriage
between two blacks as an ingroup marriage, but a little reflection will
show that this is only because social processes have superimposed a
broader category on a set of detailed categories (the latter being a set of
specific ethnic groups of Africa). Indeed, generally these ethnic roots are
lost. Were these tribal delineations relevant—and therefore likely to affect choice of mate—then many *ingroup* marriages would be *outgroup*
marriages. So, too, in the case of white groups, the distinction between
an inmarriage and an outmarriage is a function of what the society and
the populations themselves determine to be separate groups. For example, if Sicilians and northern Italians are considered separate groups,
spouses belonging to these different groups are intermarried; if both are
viewed as Italians, such a marriage is an ingroup marriage. This is resolved—in what is inevitably a somewhat arbitrary way since the
boundaries are dynamic and shifting—by using the delineations indicated in the tables and discussed in Chapter 1.

A separate problem occurs even after the categories are delineated;
namely, inmarriage and intermarriage are sometimes best viewed not as
absolute categories in which a couple either are or are not intermarried.
Rather, instead of seeing this as a simple dichotomy it is more correct
to say that these are polar types on a continuum. To be sure, in many
instances a dichotomy does describe the situation, when marriages occur between single-ancestry persons: If the husband's ancestry is G, either the wife is a G (and there is homogamy) or the wife is not a G (and
there is intermarriage). Likewise, some cases involving multiple ancestry cause no problem: If husband is of mixed BD origins, and wife is
either a G or reports some set of mixed origins that includes neither B
nor D, clearly an intermarriage has occurred. A decision is also not ambiguous when both mates report the same mixture—for example, if a
BD is married to another BD.

This model does not always fit, however, in cases involving one or
more spouses of mixed ethnic or racial origins. The group lines are by
no means automatically known and, therefore, it is not always clear
whether a given couple is homogamous or heterogeneous with respect
to ethnic ancestry. The difficulty lies in situations where a mixed person (say, a BD) is married to someone who shares some but not all of
the same origins (say, the mate is a B or a DF), In such cases, where
there is partial overlap, how should marriages by classified? The substantive issue, then, of what *is* an intermarriage must obviously be dealt

with before one can approach the technical matter of measuring the number of intermarriages.

The answer is not universal for all societies and may even change in a society over time or vary for different groups. It hinges on the way in which persons of mixed ethnic and/or racial origins are classified by the society. In many cases, such persons are classified as belonging to one of the groups to which their parents belonged. This is largely the case for persons of mixed black-white origins in the United States at present. The society generally labels such persons as black. Because of this delineation, a marriage between someone of mixed black-white origins and someone who reports being white is generally considered an intermarriage; a marriage between a mixed black-white person and a black person who reports no white ancestry is an inmarriage. This is not inevitably so—a wide variety of other outcomes are possible. For instance, American Indians currently have more latitude than blacks in American society in their self-definitions. There is a propensity in at least some quarters of the American Indian population to want to exclude as "American Indian" those who report themselves as "white" in answer to the "racial" question, but report mixed Indian-white origins in the ethnic question. Snipp[9] argues that the group reporting an American Indian ethnic ancestry "includes *bona fide* members of the Indian population, along with persons who . . . have nothing in common with the . . . characteristics . . . typical of persons ordinarily considered as American Indians." He goes on to state a preference for the race data in analyzing many problems. At any rate, persons responding white on the "race" question and Indian on the ancestry item may be labeled as white or as Indian, depending on other behavioral characteristics and, in turn, the nature of such a person's marriage will be classified accordingly.

A totally different outcome for persons of mixed origins is to place them into a new category which is separate from either of their ancestral groups. This is the case for the "Coloured" population of South Africa and for the situation in Southeast Asia where the term "Eurasian" was used to describe persons of mixed origin. When that process operates, then someone of mixed origins is outmarrying when choosing a spouse of unmixed origin from either of the root groups.

Finally, the most complex and imprecise circumstance of all is one which we believe characterizes the situation for an increasing segment of whites in the United States. Namely, in varying degrees, someone who is part X and part Y in origins has a variety of routes to take in identification: declaring oneself and/or being labeled by others as an XY,

[9]C. Matthew Snipp, "Who Are American Indians? Some Observations About the Perils and Pitfalls of Data for Race and Ethnicity," *Population Research and Policy Review* 5 (1986):237–52.

an X, or a Y.[10] (This ignores complete distortions, a matter dealt with in Chapter 8.) But until further information is obtained on this phenomena, persons of mixed white origins are viewed simply as persons with mixed origins of the groups specified. Accordingly, the most realistic and appropriate step is to examine the marital patterns of mixed white persons without employing a simple dichotomy such that *all* their marriages are either purely and simply in marriages or outmarriages. Rather, if there is a partial ancestral overlap with their spouse, this will be viewed as an intragroup marriage to some degree. In essence, for someone of mixed XY ancestry, can focus on the X and determine if the mate shares a common X ancestry; likewise, we can focus on the Y and ask, separately, if the mate of an XY shares a common Y ancestry. Since marital patterns tell us a great deal about the ethnic taboos and delineations operating within the society, it ought to be possible to draw some conclusions about the meaning of ethnic mixing in the United States through an examination of the marital patterns of mixed-ancestry indiviuals.[11]

For some of the analyses of this population we combine in each ethnic category persons who are of single unmixed ancestry with those of mixed ancestry who share the origin in part. Where the subgroups are pooled, we define an inmarriage for a given ethnic group—say, X—as situations in which a woman, who is partly or entirely X, is married to a man who is partly or entirely X. An outmarriage, *from the perspective of group X*, occurs when a woman, who is partly or entirely X, is married to a man for whom no X ancestry is reported.[12] In other cases,

---

[10]This is not to rule out the possibility that even the root groups will differ in the way they categorize someone with a given ancestral mix; for example, a person who is part Jewish might be classified as "Jewish" by non-Jews and "Non-Jewish" by Jews.

[11]A fascinating issue, but one that we cannot fully address here, are the social forces operating to determine the delineation system used in a given societal context. See, however, William Petersen, "The Classification of Subnations in Hawaii: An Essay in the Sociology of Knowledge," *American Sociological Review* 34 (1969):863–77.

[12]The operationalization of inmarriage is strictly in the context of the group specified. Thus, if an AB woman (one who is part A and part B in ancestry) is married to a BC man (one who is part B and part C), the marriage will count as an intermarriage when we analyze the behavior of group A women, but will also be an ingroup marriage when the behavior of group B women is considered. The situation is somewhat different in those parts of the analysis where single and mixed members of a given group are analyzed separately, but the problem still applies to the latter segment.

The truncation problem discussed in Chapter 2 is relevant here since we know only about those ethnic origins recorded by the Census Bureau. Hence the truncation of ethnic ancestry responses can only work toward concealing ingroup marriages. (On this score, however, we would expect underestimation to be less than might otherwise be the case because we would anticipate that spouses with a common ethnic ancestry would tend to emphasize that ancestry and hence it would appear early in their listings.) Nevertheless, it is the case that inmarriage from the perspective of an individual spouse is not the same as inmarriage from the perspective of a given specific ancestry of the spouse.

where special analysis is made separately of single- and mixed-ancestry women, we describe exactly what the criteria are for marital determination.

There are a few other technical matters to mention at this point. In all cases, the data refer only to those women who are in their first marriage. In all but one situation, there is no restriction on the number of marriages for their husbands. (The section on mixed-ancestry marriages is confined to husbands who are also in their first marriage.) In all circumstances, the analysis is confined to marriages in which both partners are American-born.

Finally, the information obtained from the census inevitably refers to the *prevalence* rather than the *incidence* of intermarriage. Census data on marriage have certain inherent disadvantages because they refer to the prevalence of *surviving* marital combinations rather than the incidence of marriages to a population "at risk" during a specified period of time. In other words, we know only about the different husband-wife combinations of those who are still married at the time of the census. Except for the legal limits linked to age, we do not know when the people were married and we do not know about all those marriages that were dissolved prior to the census. This is a special problem if various marital combinations differ in either the age at which they occur or the length of time before dissolution. Of particular concern here are any differentials between mixed and homogeneous couples in their divorce rates, differentials between different sets of intermarriage combinations, or differences in the likelihood of one spouse dying.

General Patterns of Intermarriage

Current rates of inmarriage vary widely among ethnic groups in the United States (Table 6.1, column 1). The highest level is for blacks: 99 percent of American-born black women in their first marriage have mates who are also black. At the other extreme, less than 10 percent of either Welsh- or Danish-ancestry women are married to men of the same origin. The inmarriage rates for Mexicans, Puerto Ricans, and women who declare themselves American are distinctly lower than those for blacks—but still quite high. Of the three largest white groups, about half of the English- and German-ancestry women report husbands who are partly or wholly of the same origin. The inmarriage rate for Irish women is somewhat lower: 40 percent of those in their first marriage have a husband who is at least partly Irish.

A "high" or "low" rate of intermarriage is, of course, a relative matter, depending on the nature of the comparison. Certainly one of the best methods is to compare the observed level with what would be expected under the conditions of random mating in the population. *If it were the case that everyone selected a mate without regard to ethnicity or race, and* if all other social conditions affecting marital choice were indentical for these groups (such as geographic location, social class, education, and religion), a simple result would occur. Namely, inmarriage for women of each ancestry would be strictly a function of the ethnic composition of relevant men (in this case the ethnic composition of men married to all women in their first marriage). For example, since about 5 percent of women in their first marriage have a husband who reports at least some Italian ancestry (Table 6.1, column 2), we would expect 5 percent of women in each group to be married to Italian men. This means that if mates were chosen by chance we would expect 5 percent of Italian women to be inmarried (and then, of course, we would expect 95 percent of Italian women to be married to non-Italians). In turn, since about 25 percent of husbands have at least some German ethnic ancestry, we would expect to find 25 percent of German women as well as women of other origins to have German husbands. If ethnicity did not affect choice of mate either directly or indirectly, the mates chosen by a group of women would be strictly a function of the ethnic composition of husbands and would not indicate any differences in the propensity toward inmarriages. However, because German is a common ancestry, 25 percent of German-ancestry women would have endogamous marriages whereas only 5 percent of Italian women would have endogamous marriages if marriages occurred under this random model.[13]

In reality, 39.5 percent of Italian women marry men who are at least partly Italian and 48.6 percent of German women marry men who report at least some German ancestry. In other words, Italian women and German women marry their co-ethnics much more than they would based on a simple random choice model. For statistical purposes, these differences in intermarriage are best described as the ratio of in:out marriages. In the case of Italian women, where 39.5 percent marry within the group (part or whole) and 60.5 percent marry out, this means that the ratio of in:out marriages (column 3) for Italian women is .65 (39.5/60.5). Column 3 restates the information provided in column 1 in terms of the

[13]Since marriage markets are affected by local population conditions rather than simply the national composition, this indicates why one expects a group's level of intermarriage to vary in different subareas of a nation as a function of their ethnic composition. Figures in column 2 sum to more than 1.0 because those men reporting more than one origin are counted more than once even though the appropriate denominator is the total number of men.

TABLE 6.1

Intermarriage Rates, American-Born Women in Their First Marriage, 1980

Group	Women Inmarried (1)	All Husbands (2)	In:Out Ratio Group (3)	In:Out Ratio Others (4)	Odds Ratios (col 3)/(col 4) (5)
English	56.1%	24.7%	1.289	1.67	7.7
German	48.6	24.5	.944	.205	4.6
Irish	39.5	17.9	.653	.145	4.5
French	21.4	5.4	.273	.045	6.0
Italian	39.5	5.2	.652	.034	19.0
Scottish	21.2	5.1	.269	.045	6.0
Polish	29.8	3.7	.424	.027	15.5
Dutch	19.3	3.0	.239	.025	9.5
Swedish	13.2	2.1	.152	.019	8.1
Norwegian	22.0	1.7	.282	.013	20.9
Russian	39.8	1.7	.661	.011	61.4
Czech	17.7	1.0	.215	.008	26.8
Hungarian	12.2	.8	.139	.007	18.9
Welsh	6.9	.9	.075	.009	8.4
Danish	9.0	.8	.100	.007	14.2
Portuguese	29.2	.3	.413	.002	180.3
Black	98.7	7.4	74.414	.002	32,998
Mexican	76.0	1.7	3.175	.004	742.7
Puerto Rican	78.7	.4	3.699	.001	3,468
Spanish—Other	43.4	.8	.766	.004	174.6
American Indian	26.4	2.8	.359	.022	16.4
American	79.0	5.3	3.765	.010	365.4

odds for women of a given ethnic ancestry marrying a man of the same or different ancestry. In the case of non-Italian women, for example, the ratio of Italian:non-Italian husbands is .03 (column 4), far less than the comparable ratio of .65 we saw for Italian women. Dividing the ratio for Italian women by the ratio for non-Italian women, we see in column 5 that the odds that an Italian woman will marry an Italian man are 19 times greater than the odds that a non-Italian woman will marry an Italian man.

A value of 1.0 would occur if women in a group were selecting ethnic compatriots at exactly the level that all other women marry men of such an origin. A level in excess of 1.0 means that the inmarriage ratio exceeds what would occur under chance factors. (A level under 1.0 would occur only if there was an aversion to marrying ethnic compatriots.) These calculations provide added information about the levels of intermarriage initially observed in Table 6.1, column 1. For example, an equal percentage of Italian and Irish women are married to men who belong to their respective groups. But 17.9 percent of men are partly or wholly of Irish origin (column 2), whereas only 5.2 percent are of Italian origin. As a consequence, the inmarriage ratio is much higher for Italians than for Irish (19.0 versus 4.5) when these compositional factors are taken into account (see column 5). Because the percentage of Russian and Norwegian husbands of first-married women is identical (column 2), one would expect, on the basis of composition alone, to find the women in each group to be equally as likely to marry ethnic compatriots. Some 22 percent of Norwegian women are married to Norwegian men, far in excess of the 1.7 percent of men who are of Norwegian ancestry. The endogamy is far greater for Russian women, of whom 39.8 percent are married to ethnic compatriots. The ratio is 20.9 and 61.4 for Norwegians and Russians, respectively (column 5).

The most striking difference in overall inmarriage rates evident in Table 6.1 is that for blacks. For black women in their first marriage, the ratio of black to nonblack husbands is 33,000 times greater than the ratio of black to nonblack husbands among other women in the United States. Differences between white groups in their inmarriage rates are small by comparison, although there is an important source of variation. Among whites in general, groups of northwestern European origin have the lowest rates. Although the three largest ethnic groups all have relatively high levels of inmarriage, analysis of column 5 indicates that their ingroup propensities (4.5 for Irish, 4.6 for Germans, and 7.7 for English) are *relatively* moderate compared with any other group (except for Scottish and French women). Besides the five mentioned above, the ratio for Dutch, Swedes, and Welsh are also below 10.0; the highest ratios are 14.2 and 20.9 for Danes and Norwegians, respectively. The SCE European groups are generally more recent to the United States, and hence the American-born components examined here are closer to the immigrant generation and are also less likely to be of mixed ancestry (a factor to be considered in the next chapter). For these newer groups, the odds of selecting a compatriot husband generally yield higher ratios than those for the rest of the population. They range from 15.5 for Poles, 19.0 for Italians, 18.9 for Hungarians, 26.8 for Czechs, 61.4 for Russians, and 180.3 for Portuguese. Thus, except for Norwegians, all of the northwestern European groups have lower inmarriage ratios than do any of the specific SCE European populations.

Hispanic and Asian groups in the United States tend to have higher odds ratios of in:out marriage than do any of these European groups. Values of 742.7, 3468, and 174.6 are obtained for, respectively, Mexicans, Puerto Ricans, and Other Spanish; the values are likewise high for Asian groups. The ratio for American Indians is relatively low—16.4— but these are individuals who answer American Indian on the ancestry question—not necessarily on the race question. Therefore, this ratio is in effect heavily weighted by women of mixed ethnic ancestry who answered "white" not "American Indian" on the race question. Accordingly, the odds ratio for a more restricted definition of "American Indian" would probably be higher than this. Finally, women who report themselves as "American" or "United States" or "White/Caucasian" tend to have high inmarriage ratios.

Trends in Intermarriage Rates

It is natural to ask about trends over time in the intermarriage rates. Because ethnic data in the 1980 census are novel and hence cannot be compared with earlier periods, differences between age cohorts in 1980 provide the only indicator of shifts in intermarriage. We run into the same problems with such a procedure as was noted earlier, although there are special forms that this problem takes with intermarriage.[14] To minimize the problem of using age cohort data to infer longitudinal changes we exclude women who were not in their first marriage and the foreign-born[15] If there are any differences between young and old women of German ancestry, say, in their outmarriage rates, we at least know that it is not due to outmarriage differentials between those in first versus later marriages. To be sure, this adjustment hardly eliminates all problems with this procedure—especially since we do not know about differential survivorships of exogamous versus endogamous marriages.

For the most part, the cohorts examined in Table 6.2 indicate that the propensity toward ingroup marriages declines with age after changes in composition are taken into account. (Shifts in the sheer percentages of each group intermarrying, without taking into account changes between cohorts in composition, also generate rather similar conclusions.)[16] In general, white groups that initially had relatively strong propensities toward inmarriage experience substantial declines in each successive age cohort (after composition is taken into account). This

[14]Stanley Lieberson, "The Price-Zubrzycki Measure of Ethnic Intermarriage," *Eugenics Quarterly* 13 (1966):92–100.

[15]The marriages of the foreign-born were excluded throughout this analysis to avoid problems with this procedure. It is difficult to talk about choice of mate for this population, except for those who arrived in the United States at a very young age. Adult immigrants may have been married prior to arrival here or may have returned to the homeland for a mate or were engaged to someone who they later brought over. Charles A. Price and J. Zubrzycki, "The Use of Intermarriage Statistics as an Index of Assimilation," *Population Studies* 16 (1962):58–69.

[16]See Lieberson and Waters, "Ethnic Mixtures," table 2.

TABLE 6.2

Intermarriage Rates, American-Born Women in Their First Marriage, 1980, by Age

	Odds Ratios by Age					
Group	65 Years and Over	55–64 Years Old	45–54 Years Old	35–44 Years Old	25–34 Years Old	Under 25 Years Old
English	9.5	8.1	7.7	7.8	6.1	9.2
German	6.7	5.2	4.7	4.4	3.9	4.7
Irish	6.5	5.3	5.0	4.4	3.6	3.8
French	6.9	6.8	7.1	5.6	5.0	6.4
Italian	1,137.4	52.6	31.5	14.8	8.2	7.5
Scottish	6.0	6.3	5.6	5.9	5.4	6.2
Polish	65.6	37.8	20.4	11.3	7.2	8.2
Dutch	11.6	10.2	9.9	9.8	8.3	8.2
Swedish	16.3	12.2	8.7	8.0	5.3	5.6
Norwegian	37.0	30.0	24.3	21.7	13.8	17.3
Russian	141.5	74.2	79.6	61.4	34.0	38.9
Czech	122.4	48.6	32.4	17.7	11.2	15.6
Hungarian	64.7	43.3	18.7	10.7	10.4	8.2
Welsh	11.2	8.7	8.2	7.6	8.9	2.9
Danish	28.0	16.8	14.1	10.2	10.4	19.9
Portuguese		641.1	243.7	131.5	72.6	87.9
Black	79,495.5	115,659.9	92,902.2	57,029.6	19,131.3	8,601.6
Mexican	7,165.1	5,204.6	2,815.6	928.5	386.4	213.5
Puerto Rican		20,669.7	11,476.8	5,161.9	1,622.6	1,197.9
Spanish—Other	599.9	401.5	318.1	171.1	107.3	82.3
American Indian	39.9	30.9	19.2	16.7	12.3	9.3
American	245.2	347.7	462.6	449.4	412.6	242.8

NOTE: Data are not shown for Portuguese and Puerto Rican women 65 years of age and over because there are fewer than 100 women in the age cohort.

change is least pronounced for groups with initially lower levels of in-marriage (generally, groups from northern or western Europe), but nevertheless the general pattern holds for all groups. Indeed, the correlation between intermarriage ratios in the youngest and oldest age cohorts is not especially close (r is .60 for the 16 individual European groups shown in Table 6.2 for both periods).[17] Thus, not only are levels of in-group marriage declining, but also the relative positions of the groups are in flux.

[17]Moreover, inspection of the scatter diagram discloses that this correlation is largely generated by one outlier. Without Russians, the correlation for the remaining 14 groups is .33 between the levels in the youngest and oldest cohorts.

Let us consider the pattern among Italian women. The odds ratio for elderly Italian women (aged 65 and over in 1980) is 137.4. This means that the arithmetic ratio of Italian to non-Italian husbands is 137 times greater for Italian women than it is for all other women (meaning those without any Italian origin). In similar fashion, albeit less spectacularly, the ratio for Polish inmarriages—compared with the propensity of other women to marry Polish men—is 65.6 among the oldest cohort of women. These ratios are down to 7.5 and 8.2 respectively, in the youngest cohort. The change for Hungarians parallels that of Poles; and other European groups with relatively high inmarriage propensities in the older ages also show sharp declines during this span (for example, Norwegians, Russians, Czechs, and Danes).

There has been an overall increase in outmarriages for all of the groups, both European and non-European. Except for the Scots, every group has a lower inmarriage ratio in their youngest cohort than in their oldest. This occurs despite the possibility (to be considered later) that ingroup marriages are specially overestimated in the youngest cohort. In general, the levels of inmarriage for groups of non-European origin are higher than those for groups of European ancestry. In the oldest cohort, for example, the European groups have inmarriage ratios that range from 6.0 to 141.5; in the youngest, these run from 3.8 to 38.9 (Portuguese decline from 641.1 to 87.9 in the more limited age range available for them). By contrast, blacks, Mexicans, and Puerto Ricans have much higher levels in all periods. The other Spanish category is also higher than all of the European groups, with the exception of Portuguese in the youngest cohort. (American Indians are a difficult group to compare because their ratios can easily be misinterpreted as unusually low for a nonwhite group. Their ratio ranges from 39.9 for the oldest cohort to 9.3 for the youngest—ratios closer to the European groups than to the non-European groups.)

Interpreting the Youngest Age Cohort

There is a curious quirk to the general pattern of an increase in outmarriages with progressively younger ages. On the one hand, in most cases the inmarriage ratio declines in progressively younger cohorts. Comparing the oldest cohort (those aged 65 and over) with the next oldest (aged 55–64) in 1980, we see a decline in the ratio for all but five groups. Likewise, in all but five cases there is a decline between the latter and the 45-to-54-year-old cohort. And there are even fewer exceptions to this general decline in marital homogamy when the next two intercohort comparisons are made. The levels for the youngest cohort (under age 25) in 1980 are rather surprising under the circumstances; in half of the cases, composition-adjusted intermarriage has increased over the 25-to-34-year-old cohort.

This finding is somewhat puzzling and we can only speculate as to the reasons for it. One possibility, of course, is that the data are misleading since it is impossible to take into account differentials in marital dissolution with prevalence data of this nature. The distinctive and massive reversal in the youngest age cohort leads us to reject this as a sufficient interpretation. Another possibility is simply that there is a true reversal in the propensity toward increasing outmarriage (after taking composition into account). We are also inclined to reject this hypothesis—although we recognize that future longitudinal data could support such a conclusion. Another possibility is that the intermarrying propensities of the cohort are not reflected in these data since so many in the very youngest age cohort are still unmarried. This could be true if mixed marriages occur at somewhat older ages, and/or if the propensity for misreporting of ethnic origin in the direction of family homogeneity occurs most strongly for the less educated who presumably marry at earlier ages. Later in this chapter, rather convincing evidence will be presented to support the latter interpretation.

This curiosity about the youngest cohort should not sidetrack us from several important summary statements that can be made about Table 6.2, subject to the technical cautions listed earlier. The overall trend is toward declining ingroup marriage for white groups in the United States (and to a less dramatic degree, for other groups as well). Because the groups with the relatively strongest propensities toward inmarriage are the ones with the sharpest declines with progressively younger cohorts, the gaps among the groups in the younger cohorts (ages 25–34 is probably the best comparison to make) have narrowed considerably. Nevertheless, the fact is that all of the ratios are well in excess of the level that would occur if choice of mate was related to ethnic origin (in which case the ratio would be 1.0). And it is still the case that the highest ratios among the white groups are reported mainly by the new European groups (although these levels are much lower than they used to be). The actual changes between age cohorts, without taking composition into account, are shown in Appendix Table 6.1. The interested reader can trace specific groups over time and find some striking changes in the post–World War II period for some of the SCE European groups.[18]

[18]See Lieberson and Waters, "Ethnic Mixtures," p. 46.

Marriages Among Whites of Mixed Origins

Since intermarriage is increasing between white ethnic groups, it means that each new cohort consists of an ever-larger segment of persons who are of mixed ethnic origin.[19] As a consequence, the behavior of mixed-ancestry persons is of considerable importance for understanding current and future trends. A model of intermarriage in which everyone has a single ancestry is progressively inadequate for describing the actual martial pattern among whites in the United States. We therefore move away from the "classic" intermarriage question in which persons with a single known ethnic ancestry—say, Irish or German or Polish—marry someone with either the same single ethnic ancestry or a single different ancestry. Instead, the basic question for persons of mixed origin is whether their choice of mate reflects the following possible outcomes: a pattern that falls somewhere between those ancestors who have a single ancestry, a pattern in the direction of unmixed persons with one of the common ancestries, or a pattern quite distinctive from that found among unmixed persons of either ancestry. In effect, we are asking how strong is an ethnic group's hold on persons of mixed origins?

As noted at the outset of this chapter, the consequences of intermarriage are not necessarily uniform for all groups within a nation, let alone for all nations. One outcome, not uncommon in the world of race and ethnic relations, is for a new hybrid group to form; witness the Coloured in South Africa or the Eurasian offspring of white-Asian parentage in various Asian colonies Another possibility is for the existing ethnic distinctions to disappear and for a new grouping to form; such is the case for the merging of a wide variety of groups leading to an "English" population in present-day England or the formation in the New World of "Mexican" or "Puerto Rican" ethnic populations from diverse ancestral groups that have significantly declined as distinctive entities.[20] Another outcome is for the mixed offspring to be classified more or less as members of only one of the ancestral populations. This is essentially the case for black-white mixes in the United States.

Finally, a variety of other outcomes are possible, and these are especially relevant for white persons of mixed ethnic origin in the United States or in other settings where there is not a rigid boundary operating. One is that the offspring of an XY mixture function somewhere in the range between the way single-ancestry Xs and single-ancestry Ys function, in which case, persons reporting mixed XY ancestry have mates

[19]Part of this section is drawn from Lieberson and Waters, "Ethnic Mixtures."
[20]Stanley Lieberson, 1985b, "Unhyphenated Whites."

with an ethnic distribution that falls somewhere between the distributions reported by persons of single X ancestry and persons of single Y
ancestry. Then one could consider not only if their choice falls within
the range between the two groups, but if it is closer to one than the
other (but not as extreme as would the offspring of black-white matings). Another possibility is that the mixed offspring of XY marriages
behave in a manner totally unrelated to that of either Xs or Ys, perhaps
showing no particular ethnic affinity for either group when it comes to
choice of mate. If, additionally, the offspring of XY marriages had a very
strong affinity for other XY offspring, this outcome could lead to the
development of a new ethnic population.

These different possibilities help us to understand why various
interpretations exist about both the meaning of intermarriage for an individual and the consequences of a relatively high rate of ethnic intermarriage for a group. Presumably, intermarried persons in the aggregate
are more assimilated on other variables than are those who are not. For
instance, Johnson[21] argues that intermarriage directly affects the social
networks of both husband and wife, as well as the extended family—
making these networks ethnically heterogeneous. Abramson[22] also
found evidence that the religious behavior of husbands and wives
changes and becomes less distinctively ethnic with intermarriage, leading him to conclude that exogamy does lead in part to the lessening of
distinct cultural forms. Cohen[23] argues that a number of empirical studies support the hypothesis of a close association between intermarriage
and the assimilation of ethnic groups.

Thus, we can describe high intermarriage rates as an indicator of
assimilation. But while we can assert that intermarriage is more of an
act of assimilation than nonintermarriage, it is another matter to assume that there is a decline of ethnic identity for the offspring of intermarried parents. The existence of intermarried parents does not necessarily describe the assimilation of the offspring. We are able to address
this question here by looking at the marital choices not simply of persons with a single white ethnic ancestry, but rather at the choices
among persons who are themselves of mixed ancestry. To what degree
do such people leave the ethnic fold(s) of their parents? In the context
of the issue raised here, do individuals with mixed ancestry continue to
show patterns of ethnic affinity in their own marriage behavior?

[21]Colleen Leahy Johnson, *Growing Up and Growing Old in Italian American Families* (New Brunswick, NJ: Rutgers University Press, 1985).

[22]Harold J. Abramson, "Interethnic Marriage Among Catholic Americans and
Changes in Religious Behavior," *Social Analysis* 32 (1971):31–44.

[23]Steven M. Cohen, "Socioeconomic Determinants of Intraethnic Marriage and
Friendship," *Social Forces* 55 (1977):997–1010.

Mixed-Ancestry Marriages

The analysis is confined to a single cohort, those aged 25–34 in 1980.[24] Columns 1 and 2 of Table 6.3 show that in all but two groups the mixed-ancestry component has lower inmarriage rates than does the single-ancestry one. Among Norwegians, for example, 24 percent of single-ancestry women are married to men who are either partly or entirely of Norwegian origin; by contrast, only 15 percent of women with part Norwegian ancestry are married to men who are at least partly Norwegian. The relative "hold" of each group on the mixed and unmixed segments is shown in columns 7 and 8, which give the in:out ratios of women of single and mixed ancestry. The inmarrying propensities for women of mixed ancestry are, in all cases, well above 1.0 (the value that would occur if the propensity to marry men of the ancestry specified was no different from that operating for all other women). Not only are the mixed-ancestry ratios lower than the single-ancestry ratios, but the intergroup differences among the women with mixed ancestries are smaller. For the first nine groups, compare the striking uniformity in column 8 with the variation in column 7.

Even though women of mixed ancestry are less likely to marry endogamously than women of single ancestry and are more like each other in terms of their inmarriage rates, this does not mean that they share nothing with their single-ancestry compatriots. There is a close correlation between the positions of the unmixed and mixed members of the groups with respect to the propensity to outmarry, albeit the levels are generally lower for the latter (r is .94 for the 16 European groups shown in Table 6.3). If a group's single-ancestry members have relatively low rates of intermarriage, the mixed-ancestry members will have relatively low rates as well.

Not only is a group's "hold" lower for women of mixed origins, but the nature of their ingroup marriages are also radically different. For those of single ancestry, inmarriages tend to occur most often with mates who are also of single ancestry; when mixed-ancestry women inmarry, more frequently their husbands are of mixed ancestry. This pattern is strikingly uniform. For all of the groups in Table 6.3, we see that the percentage of single-ancestry women who marry a man with the same single ancestry (column 3) is considerably greater than the per-

[24]The rates of inmarriage and outmarriage for both mixed and unmixed persons of a given ancestry are affected by age (Lieberson and Waters, "Ethnic Mixtures," table 3). Since the groups differ in the relative age distributions of their unmixed and mixed components, the best procedure is to look at a specific age category. Because of special problems with those under age 25, this is the youngest cohort for which we can obtain data that permit a relatively unproblematic analysis.

TABLE 6.3

Ingroup Marriages, Women of Single and Mixed Origins, Aged 25–34, 1980

Group	Ancestry of Women		Women of Single Ancestry		Women of Mixed Ancestry		In:Out Ratio of Women by Ancestry	
	Single (1)	Mixed (2)	Single-Ancestry Husband (3)	Mixed-Ancestry Husband (4)	Single-Ancestry Husband (5)	Mixed-Ancestry Husband (6)	Single (7)	Mixed (8)
English	64%	42%	55%	8%	10%	32%	10.0	4.1
German	51	44	36	15	11	33	4.6	3.6
Irish	38	35	25	13	6	29	4.0	3.5
French	30	16	22	8	3	13	8.9	4.0
Italian	33	20	26	7	10	10	11.0	5.5
Scottish	13	19	8	5	1	18	3.7	5.6
Polish	25	17	18	7	5	12	9.5	5.8
Dutch	28	14	23	5	2	12	15.0	6.6
Swedish	9	10	6	3	2	8	4.9	5.4
Norwegian	24	15	17	7	4	11	19.0	11.0
Russian	39	25	28	11	8	18	50.0	26.0
Czech	13	7	11	2	2	5	17.0	8.4
Hungarian	10	7	8	2	1	6	14.0	9.1
Welsh	8	7	6	2	1	6	10.0	8.6
Danish	8	7	6	2	2	5	12.0	10.0
Portuguese	28	9	23	5	4	5	129.0	35.0
Black	99	92	98	1	24	68	25,698.0	3,205.0
Mexican	77	28	75	2	14	15	507.0	61.0
Puerto Rican	80	33	78	2	21	13	2,198.0	278.0
Spanish—Other	56	14	53	3	3	10	213.0	27.0
American Indian	39	22	34	4	3	19	22.0	27.0
American	81	NA	81	NA	NA	NA	413.0	NA

NOTE: NA = not applicable

centage of such women who marry a mixed-ancestry man with a common origin (column 4). The opposite pattern holds for women of mixed origins (compare columns 5 and 6). Consider women of German origin; 36 percent of the unmixed marry men of unmixed German origin and 15 percent marry men of part German ancestry. Among women of part German origin, however, only 11 percent are married to men of unmixed German origin and 33 percent have mates who are of mixed German origin. Columns 5 through 8 or Table 6.3 show that the same pattern holds for all of the groups.

A similar result is obtained for outmarriages. Compared with compatriots of mixed ancestry, single-ancestry women who outmarry into a given group are far more likely to marry single-ancestry men. Mixed-ancestry women from the same group are relatively more likely to outmarry men of a given ancestry who are of mixed origins. This pattern is remarkably widespread, and the complete set of data cross-tabulating spouses by single and mixed origins is given in Appendix Table 6.2. We have summarized the patterns for several groups in Table 6.4, which indicates the propensity to marry mixed- and single-ancestry men of three different groups. Germans and Poles are included because they represent major old and new European groups; Scots are included because they are an exceptional group whose single-ancestry men and women have lower inmarriage rates than do the mixed components in each gender.

The results are strikingly uniform. Consider outmarriages with German-ancestry men: The unmixed members of each European group are more likely to marry a single-ancestry German man and, on the other hand, mixed women are more likely to intermarry men of part German origin (Table 6.4, columns 1 and 2). The pattern is largely duplicated for intermarriages with Scottish-origin men as well. (Very small numbers are involved in all three of these cases as well as in two of the three exceptions for Polish men.)[25] The only serious exception is mixed women of English origin, who marry single-ancestry Poles somewhat more frequently than do their unmixed compatriots.

Women of English origin provide a good illustration of the general outmarriage pattern viewed from the perspective of the wives. Among

[25]In these exceptions, the number of outmarriages with Scottish-origin men are 14 single-ancestry women of Czech origin, 7 single-ancestry women of Hungarian origin, 3 single-ancestry women of Portuguese origin, and 15 women of mixed Portuguese origin. Likewise, in the case of marriages with Polish men, two of the three exceptions to this general pattern are rather minor: the percentage of single-origin Czech women who marry single-origin Poles is just slightly less than the percentage for mixed-origin women who mate with such men; and the figures for Portuguese women are based on trivial numbers, four and nine outmarriages for unmixed- and multiple-ancestry Portuguese women.

TABLE 6.4

Intermarriages, Women of Single and Mixed Origins, Aged 25–34, 1980

Wife's Ancestry	Percent of Women Married to Husbands with Ancestry					
	German		Scottish		Polish	
	Single	Mixed	Single	Mixed	Single	Mixed
English						
Single	8.78%	6.84%	7.20%	2.40%	1.01%	0.59%
Mixed	8.38	28.31	0.59	7.99	1.34	3.16
German						
Single	35.63	15.33	1.03	2.87	2.20	1.62
Mixed	11.41	32.85	0.64	6.42	1.66	3.86
Irish						
Single	14.20	10.31	1.43	3.05	2.28	1.35
Mixed	9.18	27.99	0.70	8.52	1.76	3.27
French						
Single	12.68	8.64	1.73	2.18	2.62	1.22
Mixed	9.29	26.78	0.49	6.55	1.61	3.46
Italian						
Single	8.20	12.22	0.76	2.57	4.26	4.29
Mixed	7.31	25.23	0.37	5.10	3.04	5.55
Scottish						
Single	16.63	8.52	8.32	4.87	1.22	0.61
Mixed	8.29	25.88	1.35	17.61	1.05	2.88
Polish						
Single	12.05	12.46	0.92	2.83	18.22	6.75
Mixed	8.24	26.05	0.45	4.76	5.13	11.69
Dutch						
Single	16.69	11.52	0.89	2.51	2.07	1.62
Mixed	9.32	28.31	0.74	5.90	1.04	2.82
Swedish						
Single	21.37	12.95	1.56	3.43	2.65	1.72
Mixed	9.59	30.34	0.54	7.25	1.62	3.42
Norwegian						
Single	19.31	15.58	0.93	2.65	1.40	1.25
Mixed	13.15	31.72	0.08	6.08	0.90	3.86
Russian						
Single	7.28	10.28	0.32	2.22	6.96	6.96
Mixed	6.32	21.17	0.29	4.31	3.35	12.84

those of unmixed ancestry, slightly more marry single- than mixed-ancestry German men (8.8 and 6.8 percent, respectively). Among women of mixed ancestry, by contrast, only 8.4 percent are married to German men of single ancestry, but 28.3 percent are married to men of part German origin. In similar fashion, 7.2 percent of single-ancestry

TABLE 6.4 *(continued)*

Wife's Ancestry	Percent of Women Married to Husbands with Ancestry					
	German		Scottish		Polish	
	Single	Mixed	Single	Mixed	Single	Mixed
zech						
Single	20.00	15.88	0.29	3.82	3.82	2.35
Mixed	10.98	30.49	0.72	5.49	3.90	4.62
ungarian						
Single	16.25	10.42	0.00	2.92	9.17	4.58
Mixed	9.59	25.12	0.17	5.29	3.14	7.11
elsh						
Single	15.28	9.03	6.94	4.86	2.08	1.39
Mixed	8.29	30.86	0.43	10.14	1.00	2.71
anish						
Single	17.93	10.33	1.63	2.72	1..09	0.00
Mixed	10.34	28.10	1.55	6.03	0.34	2.76
rtuguese						
Single	6.75	8.59	0.00	1.84	0.00	2.45
Mixed	4.64	21.13	1.03	6.70	0.52	4.12
ack						
Single	0.05	0.09	0.00	0.01	0.01	0.01
Mixed	0.00	1.44	0.00	0.72	0.24	0.00
exican						
Single	1.98	3.85	0.27	0.37	0.27	0.42
Mixed	5.75	20.35	0.00	5.31	0.88	3.54
erto Rican						
Single	2.06	5.68	0.00	0.62	0.41	0.41
Mixed	7.94	11.11	0.00	1.59	1.59	1.59
anish—Other						
Single	3.37	5.39	0.34	0.67	1.01	0.00
Mixed	5.51	20.80	0.00	5.76	1.00	1.50
nerican Indian						
ingle	11.03	5.98	0.82	1.44	0.52	0.31
Mixed	2.19	1.47	0.18	0.49	0.39	0.25

English women marry single-ancestry Scottish men, a figure in excess of the percentage for mixed-ancestry English women (0.6), but 2.4 percent of the single-ancestry English are married to mixed-origin Scottish men whereas 8.0 percent of mixed origin English women have such husbands. Marriages with men of Polish origin also show a similar differential, albeit not as dramatic. Single-ancestry English women are more likely to marry single-ancestry Polish men than mixed-origin Polish men (1.0 versus 0.6 percent), but the propensity is in the opposite direction for mixed-ancestry women of part English origin (1.3 and 3.2 percent marry, respectively, Polish men of single and mixed origin).[26]

It could be that persons of mixed origin have parents who intermarried (and hence in the aggregate may be less strongly attached to their groups) and/or are the descendants of more distant ancestors who intermarried. In addition, insofar as there is a generational linkage between unmixed- and mixed-origin persons—such that the former are generationally closer to the immigrant generation (see Chapter 2), the ethnic ties could be stronger for the unmixed members of the group. On the other hand, persons of mixed origin—say, persons of ancestries AB—are pulled to marry not only an A but also a B. As a consequence, this could lead to weaker inmarriage rates when an AB is choosing a mate of either origin. It is also possible that unmixed members of a group have more contact with potential mates from their own group—whether this involves residential segregation, associational activities, or other forces influencing choice of mate. Another possibility is that reporting of single versus mixed ancestry varies systematically across households.

In short, persons of mixed origin differ from their unmixed compatriots with respect to both inmarriages and outmarriages. Women reporting only one ancestry are more likely to marry within the group, although those of mixed origin also chose ingroup men far in excess of the rate that would occur under chance circumstances (if ethnic origin was not affecting choice of mate and was uncorrelated with other social attributes that affect such choices). Inmarriages for the two subsets also differ in another important way—namely, the single-ancestry members are relatively more likely to pick other single-ancestry mates; mixed-origin women are relatively more likely to marry other mixed-origin members of the group.

[26]Obviously, differences in the respective numbers of single-and mixed-ancestry men of a given origin affect the potential rates of outmarriage for women, but these can be viewed as more or less the same for all sets of women and hence composition does not have to be adjusted. For example, there are more mixed- than single-ancestry German men married to women in this cohort and, moreover, a smaller proportion of the former are inmarried. As a consequence, the opportunity for non-German women to marry a man of German mixed origin is greater than the opportunity to marry a man of single German ancestry. But the relative numbers apply to all women even if, say, more of the mixed are outmarried than the single-ancestry women of a given origin. To be sure, an iterative adjustment of the sort used in log-linear analyses would lead to some changes not taken into account in this way, but the magnitude of these differences shown in Table 6.4 are far beyond the adjustments likely if we could apply such an iteration to the complex situation here where spouses appear more than once. (Moreover, we see that the same pattern holds for women of Scottish and Swedish origins, situations where the unmixed women have higher outmarriage rates than those of mixed origin.)

Mixed- Versus Single-Ancestry Combinations

Distortions or reporting errors could be partly responsible for the patterns reported here. For example, if couples who are both of mixed origin tend to distort their responses in order to claim a common ancestry, this will exaggerate the number of inmarriages between mates of mixed origin. Another possibility is that an inmarriage between mixed- and single-ancestry mates leads to de-emphasis of the unshared origin in the mixed person and hence the marriage is reported between two single-ancestry spouses. On the other hand, this pattern may reflect true events, rather than merely distortions. Perhaps there are differences in the contact levels such that residential patterns and other factors affecting residential propinquity strongly favor mixed persons meeting other mixed persons with a common ancestry and likewise such factors favor unmixed persons meeting other unmixed members of the group. To be sure, these data could reflect both true differences in marital propensities and artificial distortions; short of intensive field work, we have no easy way of ascertaining the existence and extent of such distortions. However, we do know that such distortions in reported ethnic origin operate—at least in the sense of the inconsistency found in the 1971–72 Current Population Survey study (cited in Chapter 2).

A second issue pertains to those single-ancestry women who do outmarry, since they are especially likely to report a mate who is also of unmixed origin. As we noted earlier, this occurs not only among outmarriages with certain groups, but among virtually all types of outmarriages. This result is also open to several different interpretations. Again, it is likely that it reflects an enumeration problem such that some respondents simplify both their own and their mate's ethnic origins. If it is not an artifact of the data (or entirely so), there are several possible interpretations. Such an intermarriage pattern could also reflect differences in the exposure to different possible outmarriages; for example, if single-ancestry persons are more likely to live in the same parts of the nation and/or are relatively closer residentially in cities to different single-ancestry persons than to outgroup members of mixed origin.[27]

---

[27]There is also a procedural consideration that might influence the results. If we examine the number of outmarriages that women of mixed Italian origin have with men of mixed Greek origin, all that we are concerned with at that point is that they do not share a common Italian origin. In reality, they could share a common Greek origin (after all, we have indicated what the other ancestry is for the part Italian women). Further, the true level of outmarriages between mixed persons will be overestimated because the census largely restricts itself to conditions in which only the first two origins are recorded. As a consequence a marriage involving a shared ancestry in which it is the third listed origin will appear to be an outmarriage.

Residential Propinquity

Although a definitive answer to the question of how much residential proximity influences marriage patterns cannot be pursued with the data available here, a modest analysis will be made. The residential patterns of several important groups are considered in a limited context to see if the evidence is consistent with the residential propinquity interpretation of the marriage patterns described above. If residential proximity does seem to help explain these patterns, it would be appropriate to minimize these other interpretations until such time as a direct ethnographic study shows systematic reporting shifts leading to the patterns observed above or an elegant and more extensive analysis shows that structural forces such as residential propinquity or socioeconomic differences between the mixed- and single-ancestry components could not fully explain these patterns. On the other hand, if the residential patterns fail to even partly account for the two marriage patterns of special concern, we will be inclined to consider possible distortions in the data as accounting for these patterns.

Actually, it is not easy to determine an appropriate geographical level for dealing with the influence of residential propinquity on these marriage patterns. If we assume that the influence of distance on marital choice has a nonlinear form (the gradient tapering off with increasing distance such that the reduction in inmarriage between 100 and 200 miles is far less than the reduction in inmarriage between 5 and 50 miles), it is not entirely clear what geographic units to use and the kind of subdivisions to make within them. Certainly, choice of mate will be affected by the ethnic makeup of the immediate neighborhood, but it will also be influenced by the city composition, and one could argue that even regional composition will affect exposure to different groups as potential mates.

Moreover, we know from census data only where couples currently live—we know nothing of where they were living when they first met. Also, there are other proximity factors besides residence that affect exposure to potential mates—for example, people meet in high school and college, through work, in church, or through voluntary organizations. What we can do here—and it is difficult enough—is to ask whether the intermarriage and intramarriage patterns of interest appear to be affected by the simplest of these dimensions to measure: the influence of residential contact. Fortunately, this is a good attribute since it is well known that residence influences marital choice.[28] Two different geographic bases are considered: first, the broad distribution of single- and

[28]See for example, Ceri Peach, "Ethnic Segregation and Intermarriage," *Annals of the Association of American Geography* 70 (1980):371–81.

mixed-ancestry members of four leading groups in the census divisions of the nation; second, the narrower distributions of these same four groups in the Oakland–San Francisco Standard Metropolitan Statistical Area.[29]

Outgroup Marriages

Geographic Divisions

When single-ancestry persons outmarry, is it because of spatial factors that they report outgroup mates of unmixed origin more often than mixed origins? First, we will consider the $_iP_j^*$ indexes between the groups on a broad geographic divisional basis. This index gives the probability that group I will interact with group J under the hypothetical condition that there is random mixing within the spatial units specified. The index is thus affected by both the spatial patterns of the groups and the relative size of the J group.[30] The index of .124 shown in Table 6.5 for the situation where single-ancestry English are the I group and mixed-ancestry Germans are the J group means that the average single-ancestry English person lives in a geographic division where 12.4 percent of the population are of mixed German origin. By contrast, the average single-ancestry English person lives in an area where 6.9 percent of the population is of unmixed German origin. In this case, single-ancestry English women have more marriages with single-ancestry German men than with mixed-ancestry German men *despite* the joint effect of residence and composition, which would lead to the opposite expectation.[31] In general, Table 6.5 displays higher P^* values for out-

[29]The census monograph by Michael White, *American Neighborhoods and Residential Differentiation* (New York: Russell Sage Foundation, 1988), does not provide data of the sort needed here; it analyzes data for segregation *among* the single-ancestry components and separately *among* the mixed-ancestry components. The question raised here involves proximity *between* single and mixed components. The metropolitan analysis is not at the finest level possible (blocks or tracts)—such an analysis is probably too fine-grained for choice of mate unless a distance variable is considered. On the other hand, the use of political cities and residual parts of the counties is probably all right for most of the smaller communities but too gross for the larger cities and the residual areas.

[30]Stanley Lieberson, "An Asymmetrical Approach to Segregation," in Ceri Peach, Vaughan Robinson, and Susan Smith, eds, *Ethnic Segregation in Cities* (London: Croom Helm, 1981); Stanley Lieberson and Donna Carter, "Temporal Changes and Urban Differences in Residential Segregation: A Reconsideration," *American Journal of Sociology* 88 (1982a):296–310; "A Model for Inferring the Voluntary and Involuntary Causes of Residential Segregation," *Demography* 19 (1982b):511–26.

[31]There are some obvious shortcomings to this analysis since the segregation data include persons of all ages, both sexes, and all birthplaces, regardless of their current marital status. It is unlikely, however, that the selective processes are so radical that they would significantly alter the conclusions if we had segregation data exclusively for the relevant married population.

TABLE 6.5

Segregation by Geographic Divisions, Persons of Single and Mixed Ancestry, 1980

$_iP_j^*$ Index

J

I	English		German		Irish		Italian	
	Single	Mixed	Single	Mixed	Single	Mixed	Single	Mixed
English								
Single	.128	.111	.069	.124	.047	.128	.022	.019
Mixed	.102	.118						
German								
Single	.092	.116	.100	.161	.043	.135	.029	.023
Mixed			.092	.154				
Irish								
Single	.107	.112	.074	.130	.049	.131	.036	.026
Mixed					.046	.133		
Italian								
Single	.076	.110	.075	.135	.054	.133	.063	.039
Mixed							.051	.034

TABLE 6.5 (continued)

Index of Dissimilarity

	English		German		Irish		Italian	
	Single	Mixed	Single	Mixed	Single	Mixed	Single	Mixed
English								
Single	NA	24	36	32	20	23	51	41
Mixed	24	NA	22	14	17	6	43	28
German								
Single	36	22	NA	7	26	19	45	33
Mixed	32	14	7	NA	23	12	44	29
Irish								
Single	20	17	26	23	NA	13	33	23
Mixed	23	6	19	12	13	NA	41	26
Italian								
Single	51	43	45	44	33	41	NA	15
Mixed	41	28	33	29	23	26	15	NA

NOTE: NA = not applicable.

group interactions with the mixed components than the unmixed components. (The exceptions are modest differences in the opposite direction for interaction with Italians.)

The above measure is affected by both spatial patterns and composition—an appropriate way of describing the interaction potential that exists. However, do the spatial patterns themselves, net of composition, tend to encourage single-ancestry women to outmarry more with single-ancestry men? The indexes of dissimilarity are an appropriate measure since they are not directly affected by group size. These indexes range from 0 to 100. The former value will occur if the percentage distributions for the two groups are identical in the spatial units under consideration; the latter if the presence of each group occurs only where no members of the other group are found. In the case of the index of dissimilarity, a lower value between two groups means closer proximity—opposite from the P^* index first considered. Neither extreme occurs, of course, but the indexes do vary widely for the groups under consideration. They range from a low of 6 between mixed-ancestry Germans and mixed-ancestry Irish to a high of 51 between single-ancestry English and single-ancestry Italians.

In general, the spatial patterns measured here by the index of dissimilarity do not help account for the outmarriage choices of single-ancestry women. In most paired comparisons, the single-ancestry group is more segregated from the other single-ancestry group than they are from the mixed component of that group. In Table 6.5, for example, single-ancestry members of the English group have a segregation index of 36 from single-ancestry Germans, but their segregation from mixed-origin Germans is 32. Except for the behavior of single-ancestry Italians and English vis-à-vis the Irish, all of the comparisons show that residential propinquity would not favor the marriage pattern actually observed. To be sure, the differences in many cases are small, but they are not in the direction which would account for the much greater frequency of intermarriages between the unmixed components of groups. In short, the mixed- and single-ancestry components of each group do differ in their broad geographical spatial patterns. But two different measures make it clear that these differences (alone or in combination with composition) do not help explain the outmarriage patterns for single-ancestry persons. Indeed, proximity in one form or another would lead to a gap in the opposite direction from that observed.

The Oakland–San Francisco Area

This analysis is repeated in Table 6.6 for the Oakland–San Francisco metropolitan area, the sixth largest SMSA in the nation in 1980. As the upper panel of Table 6.6 indicates, the potential for contact with the mixed members of outgroups is in general considerably greater than the potential for contact with the single-ancestry component. This is strikingly the case for outgroup interaction with the English, German, and Irish groups in the metropolitan area. For example, the P^* index for the interaction of unmixed Italians with mixed German is .123 compared with .046 with single-ancestry German.[32] When the differences between P^* for mixed and single ancestry are examined after taking composition into account, it turns out that interaction with mixed-ancestry individuals is still slightly greater than differences in composition would suggest (here this applies in two cases to interaction with Italians as well). This result also helps to undermine the hypothesis of differential contact as an explanation for the intermarriage patterns at issue.

The indexes of dissimilarity for the metropolitan area (bottom panel of Table 6.6) provide a somewhat different pattern. There are four combinations possible for outmarriages between two specific groups: mixed with mixed, single with single, and two different pairings of mixed and single ancestry. The indexes of dissimilarity for those residing in the Oakland–San Francisco area are shown in the bottom panel of Table 6.6. In all cases, the lowest intergroup index of dissimilarity is between the mixed from the two groups. In four comparisons, the single-ancestry population is less segregated from multiple-origin than single-origin members of another group. This is the case for the English and German unmixed groups when each is compared with the two components of the Irish group. And it is also the case for those two unmixed groups when each is compared with the two components of the Italian group. For example, single-ancestry Germans have an index of dissimilarity with single-ancestry Italians of 17, whereas it is only 13 with mixed Italians. But the opposite holds for the other eight comparisons; for example, single-ancestry Italians are much less segregated from single-ancestry Irish (10) than from mixed-ancestry Irish (20). Between mixed-ancestry English and Irish, for example, the index is 6—whereas it

[32]The situation is different, however, for interaction with Italians. The P^* indexes are in all cases slightly higher for interaction with single-ancestry Italians than mixed-ancestry Italians. The P^* index is influenced by composition as well as differences in spatial patterns. Thus, the specific patterns in the Oakland–San Francisco area may be affected by the distinctive ethnic makeup found in each area—a factor not at issue in the earlier analysis based on the entire nation.

TABLE 6.6

Spatial Segregation in Oakland–San Francisco, Persons of Single and Mixed Ancestry, 1980

$_iP_j$ Index

	English		German		Irish		Italian	
J								
I	Single	Mixed	Single	Mixed	Single	Mixed	Single	Mixed
English								
Single	.072	.146	.048	.133	.039	.137	.036	.035
Mixed	.073	.152						
German								
Single	.071	.145	.048	.132	.039	.137	.037	.036
Mixed			.049	.139				
Irish								
Single	.067	.135	.046	.124	.041	.130	.038	.035
Mixed					.039	.142		
Italian								
Single	.065	.133	.046	.123	.041	.131	.042	.037
Mixed							.040	.040

TABLE 6.6 (continued)

Index of Dissimilarity

	English		German		Irish		Italian	
	Single	Mixed	Single	Mixed	Single	Mixed	Single	Mixed
English								
Single	NA	8	7	10	15	10	21	15
Mixed	8	NA	8	3	18	6	23	12
German								
Single	7	8	NA	8	11	7	17	13
Mixed	10	3	8	NA	17	4	22	10
Irish								
Single	15	18	11	17	NA	15	10	17
Mixed	10	6	7	4	15	NA	20	9
Italian								
Single	21	23	17	22	10	20	NA	16
Mixed	15	12	13	10	17	9	16	NA

NOTE: NA = not applicable.

ranges from 10 to 18 in the other three combinations. At least for this metropolitan area, we find residential patterns that do favor relatively high rates of outmarriage between the mixed members of different groups.

But do these patterns explain the relatively high level of outmarriage between the unmixed members? In two cases, the answer is in the affirmative; the index of dissimilarity between English and German unmixed groups (7) is the second lowest of the four possibilities, and the index between the single-ancestry components of the Irish and Italian groups is barely higher than the index between the mixed components (10 and 9, respectively). However, the index between unmixed groups in the remaining four comparisons are not particularly low. The value of 15 for the English and Irish mixed groups is considerably higher than the analogous value for the unmixed components—6—and is actually higher than the index between English of single ancestry and Irish of mixed ancestry, albeit lower than the opposite combination. In this instance—and in the remaining three combinations—the residential segregation is relatively high between unmixed components.

Overall, then, we can conclude that the *relatively* high levels of intermarriage between unmixed components and between mixed components—compared with the rates between unmixed and mixed mates—cannot in general be accounted for on the basis of the residential patterns in the limited circumstances examined here.

Ingroup Marriages

As for the relatively low level of inmarriage between mixed- and single-ancestry members of the same group (for example, persons of unmixed French origin with those of mixed French origin), the evidence is even less ambiguous about the limited role of residential proximity in accounting for this pattern. The broad geographical divisional data (top panel of Table 6.5) and the Oakland–San Francisco data (top panel of Table 6.6) both indicate very small differences between the single- and mixed-ancestry groups in terms of their interaction potential with either other single-ancestry or other mixed-ancestry persons of the same population. On the divisional level, for example, the P^* index for English single-ancestry interactions with others of the same mix is .128, slightly higher than the P^* of .102 that mixed-ancestry English have for single-ancestry English. The gaps are even smaller for the P^* for interaction with mixed English—.111 and .118. In general, Table 6.5 indicates very slight differences in the ingroup potential each component has with mixed and unmixed compatriots.[33]

The values for interaction within the Oakland–San Francisco area likewise show virtually no difference between the unmixed and mixed components of a group in terms of their interaction potential with these segments.

Summary and Conclusion

This chapter described the rates of ethnic inmarriage in the United States and their trends over time. We have also examined the important and neglected issue of defining the boundaries to be used for the delineation of inmarriages and outmarriages and the changes which are necessary now in those definitions for European-ancestry Americans. Because the population of mixed ethnic ancestry is of growing numerical importance, these—or similar changes—will be of critical importance in the analysis of ethnic intermarriage rates. We have also examined in depth some of the marriage patterns of mixed-ancestry individuals and the differences between their marriage patterns and the patterns of single-ancestry individuals.

The overall trend is toward declining ingroup marriage for white groups in the United States. This decline in younger cohorts is largest for SCE European groups whose older cohorts had high rates of inmarriage. Blacks still experience extraordinarily high rates of inmarriage, and the rates of Hispanics and Asians are still much higher than those of European-origin groups. However, rates for all groups—even in the younger cohorts—are well in excess of what we would expect if inmarriage was a random process not influenced by ancestry at all and merely reflective of the composition of ancestry groups in the nation as a whole.

Since each new cohort of European-ancestry individuals in the United States consists of an ever larger segment of people who are themselves the product of intermarriage and are thus of mixed ancestry, we examine the marriage patterns of mixed-ancestry individuals. We found that while the mixed component of a given group generally has lower inmarriage rates than the unmixed component, they still marry individ-

---

[33]Because there is no meaningful way of using indexes of dissimilarity to describe interaction *within* a given group (except by determining their segregation from either another group or the remainder of the population), the analysis here must be different from that for outmarriages.

uals who share a common ancestry at levels much higher than we would expect by chance. In short, mixed-ancestry individuals are still influenced by their ancestral origins in their choice of mate—albeit to a lesser degree than are their single-ancestry compatriots.

In the course of examining differences in the pattern of intermarriage between mixed- and single-ancestry components, we found an interesting and puzzling distinction. For those of unmixed ancestry, intermarriage tends to occur most often with mates who are also of single ancestry and when mixed-ancestry women marry they are likely to marry men who are also of mixed ancestry. We considered two hypotheses to explain this phenomenon. The first hypothesis is that systematic reporting errors are operating across households which lead to such a pattern. The second hypothesis is that residential propinquity patterns are somehow operating to increase contact with potential mates in such a way as to cause this pattern.

In order to investigate the latter hypothesis, we exmined the distribution of single- and mixed-ancestry members in both broad census divisions and in the Oakland–San Francisco SMSA. Spatial patterns measured by the index of dissimilarity and the P^* index for census regions and the Oakland–San Francisco SMSA both failed to account for the marriage patterns observed. Overall we can conclude that these apparent preferences are not due to differences in residential proximity. Although these results are hardly conclusive, they do lend support to the possibility that the pattern reflects sytematic reporting errors. This is a matter we will return to in Chapter 8.

APPENDIX TABLE 6.1

Percentage of Endogamous Marriages, by Age Cohorts, 1980

Group	Under 25 Years Old	25–34 Years Old	35–44 Years Old	45–54 Years Old	55–64 Years Old	65 Years Old and Over
English	55.63%	51.68%	56.18%	57.13%	58.33%	61.68%
German	48.67	46.72	48.71	48.66	48.95	53.53
Irish	35.53	35.91	39.84	42.03	41.96	44.84
French	24.27	19.51	20.90	23.24	22.02	20.27
Italian	23.40	26.92	35.72	49.24	56.87	65.86
Scottish	15.68	18.33	20.04	21.44	25.39	25.01
Polish	17.82	20.21	24.94	34.25	47.34	46.59
Dutch	17.15	17.19	19.84	20.09	20.80	22.24
Swedish	9.52	9.66	13.28	13.59	17.31	22.16
Norwegian	19.15	18.29	22.63	23.06	25.84	28.35
Russian	21.08	30.49	39.87	46.83	47.00	50.72
Czech	10.48	9.01	14.23	20.24	25.75	38.95
Hungarian	4.60	8.17	7.68	11.97	24.20	23.77
Welsh	1.93	7.23	6.25	7.13	7.94	9.71
Danish	9.75	6.94	7.04	9.18	10.85	16.38
Portuguese	18.49	17.65	25.22	35.87	49.23	49.21
Black	97.77	98.58	99.08	99.01	98.57	98.66
Mexican	69.93	71.40	79.43	84.15	85.27	83.46
Puerto Rican	74.92	74.45	81.76	84.55	84.47	93.94
Spanish—Other	37.40	38.77	43.16	51.56	50.15	52.38
American Indian	27.42	26.43	27.89	24.10	25.42	24.00
American	78.51	80.52	80.30	79.45	76.72	76.38

Intermarriages, Women of Single and Mixed Origins, Aged 25–34, 1980

Wife's Ancestry	Percent Married to Husbands with Ancestry							
	English		German		Irish		French	
	Single	Mixed	Single	Mixed	Single	Mixed	Single	Mixed
English								
Single	55.25	8.29	8.78	6.84	4.39	6.19	1.79	2.14
Mixed	9.75	31.90	8.38	28.31	3.33	22.59	1.08	7.70
German								
Single	10.46	7.66	35.63	15.33	6.41	9.62	1.94	2.80
Mixed	6.81	21.96	11.41	32.85	4.06	23.75	.95	7.04
Irish								
Single	11.19	6.90	14.20	10.31	24.97	13.19	2.62	2.92
Mixed	6.72	21.57	9.18	27.99	5.73	29.42	1.18	6.86
French								
Single	13.89	6.53	12.68	8.64	6.21	7.75	22.09	8.00
Mixed	6.98	22.53	9.29	26.78	4.37	22.05	3.03	13.12
Italian								
Single	5.49	9.30	8.20	12.22	8.72	13.53	1.82	3.78
Mixed	4.50	19.05	7.31	25.23	5.62	23.58	1.57	6.90
Scottish								
Single	22.52	6.29	16.63	8.52	10.55	8.72	4.46	3.04
Mixed	7.64	23.50	8.29	25.88	4.43	27.35	.98	7.11
Polish								
Single	6.23	8.65	12.05	12.46	5.94	11.01	2.48	4.04
Mixed	4.35	16.94	8.24	26.05	3.40	19.36	1.15	5.82
Dutch								
Single	10.93	7.53	16.69	11.52	5.47	7.68	2.07	1.62
Mixed	7.24	20.16	9.32	28.31	4.42	24.01	.95	6.98
Swedish								
Single	10.92	9.05	21.37	12.95	6.08	10.92	.62	2.96
Mixed	5.88	22.24	9.59	30.34	2.70	19.90	.96	7.73
Norwegian								
Single	5.92	6.85	19.31	15.58	5.76	7.63	1.09	3.12
Mixed	4.19	18.41	13.15	31.72	2.71	18.00	1.07	6.74
Russian								
Single	4.43	7.44	7.28	10.28	3.01	6.33	.95	1.90
Mixed	2.78	15.80	6.32	21.17	2.01	16.67	.67	4.21
Czech								
Single	5.88	11.18	20.00	15.88	6.18	10.29	2.06	5.29
Mixed	5.06	22.83	10.98	30.49	4.05	20.09	.29	7.51
Hungarian								
Single	7.08	8.33	16.25	10.42	8.33	8.33	2.50	3.33
Mixed	6.12	17.02	9.59	25.12	2.81	18.02	.83	4.79
Welsh								
Single	19.44	5.56	15.28	9.03	7.64	6.25	1.39	.69
Mixed	5.86	27.43	8.29	30.86	5.14	23.00	.29	6.86
Danish								
Single	20.11	8.70	17.93	10.33	3.80	5.98	3.26	2.72
Mixed	7.93	23.28	10.34	28.10	3.10	18.97	1.72	7.24
Portuguese								
Single	8.59	9.20	6.75	8.59	6.75	11.66	1.84	9.82
Mixed	4.12	21.65	4.64	21.13	2.58	21.65	2.06	9.28

NOTE: Number of wives with husbands present include women married to men with origins not listed in the table. Percentages are based on all of these women. Also, women married to mixed-origin men are included more than once in the percentages. For example,

Wife's Ancestry	Italian		Scottish		Polish		Dutch	
	Single	Mixed	Single	Mixed	Single	Mixed	Single	Mixed
English								
Single	1.50	.67	1.20	2.40	1.01	.59	.65	1.11
Mixed	2.52	3.90	.59	7.99	1.34	3.16	.42	3.88
German								
Single	2.17	1.58	1.03	2.87	2.20	1.62	1.21	1.71
Mixed	2.69	3.82	.64	6.42	1.66	3.86	.53	4.28
Irish								
Single	5.71	2.76	1.43	3.05	2.28	1.35	.91	1.19
Mixed	3.43	4.42	.70	8.52	1.76	3.27	.46	4.09
French								
Single	3.78	1.60	1.73	2.18	2.62	1.22	1.09	1.02
Mixed	3.17	4.49	.49	6.55	1.61	3.46	.53	3.82
Italian								
Single	26.06	7.31	.76	2.57	4.26	4.29	.34	1.51
Mixed	10.12	9.75	.37	5.10	3.04	5.55	.26	3.34
Scottish								
Single	2.64	1.42	8.32	4.87	1.22	.61	.20	1.42
Mixed	1.88	3.73	1.35	17.61	1.05	2.88	.63	3.83
Polish								
Single	7.04	4.21	.92	2.83	18.22	6.75	.58	1.38
Mixed	5.54	5.91	.45	4.76	5.13	11.69	.25	3.45
Dutch								
Single	2.22	.44	.89	2.51	2.07	1.62	23.19	4.58
Mixed	1.91	3.03	.74	5.90	1.04	2.82	1.86	12.22
Swedish								
Single	2.81	1.25	1.56	3.43	2.65	1.72	1.72	1.56
Mixed	2.40	3.30	.54	7.25	1.62	3.42	.42	3.78
Norwegian								
Single	2.49	1.71	.93	2.65	1.40	1.25	1.09	2.34
Mixed	1.48	3.62	.08	6.08	.90	3.86	.74	3.86
Russian								
Single	3.80	1.74	.32	2.22	6.96	6.96	.47	1.11
Mixed	4.79	4.60	.29	4.31	3.35	12.84	.10	2.30
Czech								
Single	2.65	1.47	.29	3.82	3.82	2.35	1.18	2.94
Mixed	3.32	4.48	.72	5.49	3.90	4.62	.29	4.19
Hungarian								
Single	5.42	.83	.00	2.92	9.17	4.58	.42	2.08
Mixed	4.13	5.79	.17	5.29	3.14	7.11	.17	3.31
Welsh								
Single	3.47	.69	6.94	4.86	2.08	1.39	1.39	.00
Mixed	2.43	4.29	.43	10.14	1.00	2.71	.57	4.86
Danish								
Single	2.72	1.63	1.63	2.72	1.09	.00	2.72	.54
Mixed	1.72	3.10	1.55	6.03	.34	2.76	.34	4.14
Portuguese								
Single	5.52	6.75	.00	1.84	.00	2.45	1.23	.00
Mixed	4.12	7.22	1.03	6.70	.52	4.12	.00	2.06

the figure of 1.73 for Czech women of mixed origin and Hungarian men of mixed origin means that 1.73 percent of Czech women in first marriages with husband present are married to a mixed-origin man reporting some Hungarian ancestry.

APPENDIX TABLE 6.2 *(continued)*

Wife's Ancestry	Swedish		Norwegian		Russian		Czech	
	Single	Mixed	Single	Mixed	Single	Mixed	Single	Mixed
English								
Single	.57	.60	.46	.49	.19	.22	.30	.17
Mixed	.57	2.80	.59	1.95	.44	1.33	.29	.74
German								
Single	1.31	1.48	1.42	1.15	.57	.61	.79	.59
Mixed	.59	2.98	.81	2.51	.49	1.33	.46	1.17
Irish								
Single	.73	1.03	.75	.54	.36	.46	.38	.38
Mixed	.47	2.14	.60	1.70	.38	1.12	.31	.95
French								
Single	.77	.70	.32	.45	.32	.51	.51	.19
Mixed	.59	2.73	.53	2.05	.39	1.48	.33	1.16
Italian								
Single	.82	.89	.41	.76	1.20	1.44	.34	.69
Mixed	.37	2.36	.41	1.05	.71	2.21	.15	1.12
Scottish								
Single	1.01	.81	.20	.81	.41	.61	.00	.61
Mixed	.65	3.03	.85	1.68	.45	1.48	.40	1.10
Polish								
Single	.87	1.04	.87	.92	2.54	2.77	.58	.87
Mixed	.45	2.50	.45	1.68	2.50	6.19	.41	1.68
Dutch								
Single	1.77	1.48	1.48	.30	.74	.44	.30	.15
Mixed	.26	2.95	.91	2.17	.43	1.17	.30	.87
Swedish								
Single	5.77	3.28	5.30	1.72	.78	.62	.62	.94
Mixed	1.56	8.33	2.22	5.46	.36	.96	.48	1.74
Norwegian								
Single	4.36	4.98	16.82	7.01	.62	.00	.62	.31
Mixed	1.07	7.23	4.35	11.01	.49	1.07	.66	1.97
Russian								
Single	.32	.79	.00	.47	28.16	10.92	.32	.16
Mixed	.10	2.68	.29	1.63	7.66	17.62	.38	1.44
Czech								
Single	.88	1.76	1.47	1.76	1.47	2.35	10.88	2.35
Mixed	.87	3.18	1.30	2.75	.72	1.59	1.73	5.20
Hungarian								
Single	.00	.42	.42	.42	2.92	1.67	.83	.42
Mixed	.83	1.98	.66	1.32	2.31	6.28	.50	1.49
Welsh								
Single	1.39	2.78	.69	1.39	2.78	.00	.69	1.39
Mixed	1.00	3.71	.43	2.00	.43	2.29	.00	.57
Danish								
Single	3.26	.54	4.89	.54	.54	.54	1.09	1.09
Mixed	.86	5.69	1.03	5.34	.17	1.38	.34	2.41
Portuguese								
Single	.61	.61	1.84	.00	.61	.61	.00	.00
Mixed	.52	3.61	.00	1.55	.52	1.03	.00	.52

NOTE: Number of wives with husbands present include women married to men with origins not listed in the table. Percentages are based on all of these women. Also, women married to mixed-origin men are included more than once in the percentages. For example,

Wife's Ancestry	Percent Married to Husbands with Ancestry								Married Women (in 100s)
	Hungarian		Welsh		Danish		Portuguese		
	Single	Mixed	Single	Mixed	Single	Mixed	Single	Mixed	
English									
Single	.17	.21	.19	.35	.31	.29	.12	.07	10,384
Mixed	.23	.91	.19	1.58	.27	1.07	.20	.22	12,297
German									
Single	.39	.38	.45	.60	.40	.39	.12	.08	9,168
Mixed	.39	1.11	.25	1.40	.24	.98	.12	.22	15,756
Irish									
Single	.34	.28	.28	.38	.26	.26	.16	.24	4,960
Mixed	.27	.88	.24	1.16	.18	.80	.21	.26	14,598
French									
Single	.38	.26	.45	.77	.32	.26	.45	.13	1,562
Mixed	.28	.79	.18	1.65	.18	1.06	.18	.18	4,914
Italian									
Single	.34	.86	.31	.31	.14	.38	.38	.34	2,913
Mixed	.37	1.54	.15	1.12	.07	.45	.34	.26	2,667
Scottish									
Single	.20	.41	.61	.41	.41	.00	.41	.00	493
Mixed	.23	.78	.40	1.58	.28	.98	.10	.30	3,991
Polish									
Single	1.10	1.85	.17	.23	.35	.63	.06	.12	1,734
Mixed	.41	2.09	.16	1.39	.08	.45	.12	.21	2,438
Dutch									
Single	.44	.44	.00	.74	.59	.44	.30	.00	677
Mixed	.17	.91	.35	1.39	.13	1.04	.17	.26	2,307
Swedish									
Single	.78	.00	.62	.47	1.25	1.56	.31	.31	641
Mixed	.36	.96	.24	1.32	.48	1.80	.30	.30	1,668
Norwegian									
Single	.31	.00	.31	.16	1.25	.78	.00	.00	642
Mixed	.00	.90	.16	.66	.41	2.47	.08	.08	1,217
Russian									
Single	2.22	2.37	.32	.32	.16	.47	.00	.16	632
Mixed	.57	3.07	.19	.77	.00	.96	.10	.19	1,044
Czech									
Single	.59	1.18	.00	1.18	.59	.59	.00	.00	340
Mixed	.00	1.73	.14	1.59	.14	1.30	.00	.00	692
Hungarian									
Single	8.33	2.08	.42	.00	.00	.42	.42	.00	240
Mixed	1.49	5.79	.00	1.16	.00	.99	.00	.17	605
Welsh									
Single	.69	.00	6.25	2.08	1.39	.00	.00	.00	144
Mixed	.00	1.29	.71	6.29	.14	1.43	.00	.14	700
Danish									
Single	.00	.54	.54	1.63	5.98	1.63	.00	.54	184
Mixed	.00	1.38	.34	.86	1.90	4.83	.00	.34	580
Portuguese									
Single	.00	.61	.00	1.84	.00	.00	22.70	4.91	163
Mixed	.52	.00	.00	1.03	.52	1.03	4.12	5.15	194

the figure of 1.73 for Czech women of mixed origin and Hungarian men of mixed origin means that 1.73 percent of Czech women in first marriages with husband present are married to a mixed-origin man reporting some Hungarian ancestry.

7

INTERMARRIAGE:
CAUSES AND CHOICES

A T THIS point, based on the results observed in Chapter 6, we want to understand why ethnic groups differ in their rates of intermarriage and what leads to the growing levels of exogamy among the white ethnic groups. Also, when intermarriage does occur, what combinations are especially common or relatively infrequent? These issues are more complicated than the ones dealt with in the previous chapter and are less easily addressed exclusively with census data. Certainly, ethnic and racial groups have distinctive cultural features that affect their dispositions toward outmarriage and that also influence the dispositions of others toward having them as mates. These idiosyncratic features obviously operate; likewise, there is the possibility suggested by Warner and Srole[1] that ethnic groups vary in their cultural dissimilarities from the dominant "old-American culture," which, in turn, could affect a variety of dimensions, including intermarriage. We cannot pursue such issues with the kind of data available here. But these idiosyncratic cultural forces are affected by some broad structural factors which we can address.

As observed in the previous chapter, intermarriage for members of a group can be viewed as a function of four broad general forces: oppor-

---

[1]W. Lloyd Warner and Leo Srole, *The Social Systems of American Ethnic Groups* (New Haven: Yale University Press, 1945), pp. 283–96.

tunity, the disposition of others toward marrying members of the group, the disposition of members to seek mates from another group, and the socioeconomic characteristics—particularly education—of the group. In order to measure the influence of opportunity, we can ask if outmarriage levels are related to the composition of the population and to the level of group isolation. The composition variable refers to the relative number of men who report the origin specified, in part or whole, and hence who are possible mates. These factors clearly affect the opportunity for contact with others.

The disposition others have toward outmarrying members of a given group can be measured with the Bogardus social distance scale. We assume that the disposition to outmarry, in addition to the evidence in the previous chapter that it varies between mixed- and single-ancestry members, reflects the number of generations in the United States and that this can be tested as well. Finally, we use education as an important socioeconomic characteristic that affects outmarriage. Since we know that the outmarriage rates vary with education for all people, we can visualize its influence in two ways: affecting the disposition toward outmarriage and affecting the ability to be attractive to others. These six variables are not pure measures of any of these dispositions; they can be viewed as both causes and effects of other factors. Still, in analyzing the influence of each of these variables on the level of outmarriage, we are tapping—in varying degrees of thoroughness and adequacy—all four major influences on outmarriage.

Why Groups Differ in Their Levels of Intermarriage

The Influences of Opportunity

The *contact* members of a group have with compatriots and with others is usually a basic factor in an analysis of the forces leading ethnic groups to differ in their levels of outmarriage.[2] As noted earlier, it is impossible to construct an adequate measure for the nation as a whole of the differences between groups in the frequency and nature of their contact patterns. In turn, this means that we cannot ascertain in a to-

[2]Unless specified to the contrary, here and elsewhere in this chapter the analysis is based on data for all ages combined. Inmarriage refers to women of a given origin (combining both single and multiple ancestry) who marry a man who is also of the same origin (in part or whole). The operationalization of composition is simply the number of married men from each origin. Also, with one exception indicated in the appropriate place, data are based on American-born of both sexes in which women are in their first marriage and men in any marriage.

tally satisfactory way the influence of contact on the probability of intermarriage. But clearly demographic composition plays a central role in affecting the frequency of ingroup-outgroup contacts.[3] Among Jews, for example, those living in areas where relatively few are found have much higher rates of intermarriage than those living in places where the group's percentage is relatively high.[4]

Not only does composition influence the frequency of contact that persons of marriageable age have with potential ingroup and outgroup mates, it also has an effect throughout the childhood years before the marital ages are reached. Contact and experience with members of the ingroup and outgroup will play a role in the disposition young adults develop toward potential mates from different groups. Moreover, there is the distinct possibility that persons who live in an area with relatively few ethnic compatriots on the average have an initially weaker disposition toward ingroup maintenance. Hence this would reduce their propensity toward inmarriage for themselves or for their offspring. (In turn, it would be even more realistic to view this third dimension as nonrecursive.)

There is a sizable correlation between group size and level of inmarriage. Restricting the analysis to 16 of the largest specific white ethnic groups (see Table 7.1), the product-moment correlation is .79 between level of inmarriage and group size $(P < .005)$.[5] The regression equation, which we will come back to, is $Y = 18.1 + 1.4X_1$. There is always a danger in circumstances such as this, where a few groups are relatively large in their percentage of the population (the English, Germans, and Irish) and where many of the groups are much smaller in number, that the results are a function of some outliers. But this is not the case here; the Spearman rank-order correlation, rho, is .68 between the ranks for these 16 groups with respect to inmarriage and composition $(P < .001)$.

Of interest are the white ethnic groups who strongly deviate from this pattern (Table 7.1 compares the actual and predicted levels of inmarriage based on the regression equation reported above). Especially noteworthy among those with higher than predicted levels of inmarriage are women reporting Italian, Portuguese, and Russian origin. The lat-

---

[3]See, for example, the literature cited by Gillian Stevens and Gray Swicegood, "The Linguistic Context of Ethnic Endogamy," *American Sociological Review* 52 (1987):73–82.

[4]See, for example, the research on Jewish intermarriage in Indiana in Erich Rosenthal, "Jewish Intermarriage in Indiana," *Eugenics Quarterly* 15 (1968):277–87.

[5]Unless indicated to the contrary, single-tailed tests are used in this chapter. Also, in situations where a zero-order relationship is under consideration, the t statistic and tests of significance are identical for both the correlation and regression coefficients.

TABLE 7.1

Actual and Predicted Levels of Inmarriage, 1980

Group	Percentage of Women Inmarried	
	Actual	Predicted
English	56.12%	52.15%
German	48.56	51.88
Irish	39.49	42.86
French	21.44	25.51
Italian	39.46	25.52
Scottish	21.19	25.16
Polish	29.77	23.17
Dutch	19.32	22.20
Swedish	13.20	20.95
Norwegian	22.00	20.39
Russian	39.81	20.42
Czech	17.66	19.39
Hungarian	12.19	19.19
Welsh	6.94	19.34
Danish	9.05	19.11
Portuguese	29.24	18.50
Black	98.67	28.27
Mexican	76.05	20.39
Puerto Rican	78.72	18.67
American Indian	26.44	22.00
Other Asian	65.13	18.61

ter—who are influenced, we assume, by the Jewish component—have a level of inmarriage that is nearly double what one might expect on the basis of the group size. The magnitude of this result—albeit based on data for Russian women of all ages—is probably understated since marriages between Jews who descend from different areas of Europe might well appear to be intermarriages and, moreover, respondents insisting on reporting themselves as Jewish will be placed in a residual category. (This probably outweighs a distortion in the opposite direction which will occur whenever a Jew of Russian origin marries a non-Jew of the same origin.) The inmarriage rate among Italian women is nearly 15 percentage points greater than that predicted on the basis of composition; and Portuguese women report 29 percent inmarried compared with the 18.5 percent that the regression equation leads us to expect. By contrast, women from some of the northwestern European sources have substantially lower levels of inmarriage than the regression for all 16 groups would lead us to expect. Of note are lower levels for Danish,

Welsh, and Swedish women. Some of the larger groups—German, Irish, and French—also report lower levels of inmarriage than would be predicted, but they are only moderately lower. On the other hand, the prevalence of inmarriage among the English is actually moderately higher than expected on the basis of composition (56 versus 52 percent).

Before turning to these intriguing ethnic differences, however, we will examine the position of various non-European groups. Black, Mexican, Puerto Rican, and other Asian women have levels of inmarriage a great deal higher than would be expected on the basis of the numerical size of the group—measured as before by their male segment (Table 7.1). There are obvious differences between them in their levels of inmarriage, but all four share deviations from the regression far in excess of any observed for the specific white groups. American Indians are not particularly high in their level of inmarriage, but it is important to keep in mind that we are dealing here with persons reporting such an origin, in part or whole, on the ancestry question regardless of their response to the "race" question in the census.[6] We can see that several of the non-European groups have levels of inmarriage that are far in excess of anything found among the white groups, suggesting that even those white groups with exceptionally high levels of inmarriage are still substantially below the propensities experienced by some of the non-European groups.[7] Whatever may have occurred in earlier periods, it is reasonable to conclude that at present the barriers to intermarriage *within* the population of European ancestry are not as severe as those across other lines in the United States. As we saw in Table 6.2, intermarriage within the white population has increased substantially in successive cohorts. The divisions across white ethnic lines in the United States are at present *relatively* minuscule compared with those across the "color" lines.[8]

Clearly, composition helps account for some of the differences between the European ethnic groups—although it is not the only factor

[6]Hence many are actually people who indicate that they are white but have some American Indian ancestry. This need not be the same pattern that is found among persons who declare themselves as "American Indian" rather than "white" on the "race" question and hence are not simply whites of part Indian origin.

[7]It would be inappropriate to seriously analyze the intermarriage levels for "South Asians" or "Other Asians" because the numbers are too small to produce meaningful figures for each specific group within these categories. The separate census monograph dealing with Asian groups should provide the detailed analysis available with a much larger sample.

[8]See also Richard D. Alba, "Interethnic and Interracial Marriage in the 1980 Census." Paper presented at the American Sociological Association Annual Meeting, Washington, DC, 1985.

that is operating. In trying to determine the other factors that help account for differences between white ethnic groups in their levels of intermarriage, we will examine each factor's influence on the odds ratios reported in column 5 of Table 6.1—a ratio which describes outmarriage net of composition. These ratios were based on the odds for inmarriages versus outmarriages for each of the relevant groups compared with the ratio for the remainder of the population.[9] A high value means a greater level of inmarriage relative to the group's size. The patterns reported earlier in this chapter are largely repeated here, although there are some exceptions because of the earlier use of a regression model. Hence deviations are a function of both the discrepancies from the regression model and the inadequacy of that model. (Here, by contrast, we simply observe each group's in:out ratio.) All of the southern-central-eastern (SCE) European groups have odds ratios of at least 15. Lower ratios occur among the northwestern European groups, a number of whom report levels well below 10—although Danes and Norwegians have higher values. Overall, then, there is a fairly sharp dichotomy exhibited between these two subsets of the white population with respect to their levels of inmarriage. Why is this the case?

The two subsets of European groups differ on a number of characteristics which appear to be linked to their inmarriage odds ratios. Starting with the issue of spatial segregation, we may hypothesize that the influence of composition on inmarriage is still affected by the level of segregation; a numerically small group scattered throughout the country will be influenced by its numbers in a different way than a population of similar size that is heavily concentrated in a small number of areas and, in turn, is highly segregated within these areas. This proposition is examined with a crude measure—the indexes of divisional dissimilarity reported in Table 3.2. (This is "crude" in the sense that a more narrowly delineated set of spatial units would probably be a better approximation of the impact of spatial segregation on intermarriage.) Nevertheless, a linkage is found in the hypothesized direction between this measure and the odds ratio (natural logarithms). The correlation coefficient is .79 and the regression coefficient is 1.38 ($P < .005$). A group's level of spatial concentration is positively correlated with the frequency of its inmarriages (after population composition is taken into account). Again, considering the crudeness of the segregation measure, this is an impressive result.

---

[9]For example, the Italian ratio of 19.0 means that the odds for an Italian woman being married to an Italian husband are 19 times greater than the odds that a non-Italian woman will be married to an Italian husband.

Disposition of Others Toward a Group

The Bogardus social distance scale is a widely used measure of a group's acceptability to others in activities of varying levels of contact:

close kinship by marriage

personal chums in respondent's club

neighbors on the same street

employment in respondent's occupation

citizenship in the country

visitors only to the country

exclusion from the country[10]

A group acceptable to everyone for all seven of these activities would get a score of 1.0; higher scores indicate progressively greater social distance. Bogardus scores were available for 12 of the 16 white ethnic groups under consideration.[11] There is a correlation between odds ratios for inmarriage (arithmetic) and these Bogardus scores of .83 ($b = 39.0$, $P < .005$). White groups with relatively low levels of acceptability, as measured by the scale, are indeed groups with relatively high levels of in-group marriage. This is not surprising since one of the scale items is measuring the acceptability of marriage (although attitudes and behavior are by no means the same).

Generation

Since the groups vary greatly in their average number of generations in the United States and because one might expect the strength of ethnic ties to decline over time, there is good reason to consider the influence of generation on the odds ratios. In this case, the logarithm of the odds of inmarriage is indeed linked to generational length (the percentage of the ethnic group with four or more generations' residence in the United States). The correlation is $-.78$, and the regression coefficient is

---

[10]For a discussion of this measure and the data used in 1966, see Richard T. Schaefer, *Racial and Ethnic Groups*, 2nd ed. (Boston: Little, Brown, 1984), pp. 66–70.

[11]Data for Hungarians, Welsh, Danish, and Portuguese are unavailable. This exclusion probably does not alter any of the regressions with the Bogardus scale since other relationships are not particularly altered when these four groups were dropped for purposes of comparison.

−.03 $(P < .005)$. Groups that have, on the average, a relatively lengthy residence in the United States are also more likely to outmarry.[12]

Education as an Influence on Outmarriage

The relationship between education and intermarriage is complicated. We expect the more educated segment to have higher levels of
intermarriage because we assume that education works to increase the
propensity toward outmarriage by weakening ethnic attachments *and*
by increasing contact with potential mates from other groups. Education
often leads to greater movement away from an individual's local areas
of residence and later will affect occupational contacts. Further, we assume that outmarriage increases with age; hence more educated individuals would be more likely to outmarry just because of the correlation
between age at first marriage and educational attainment.[13]

The cross-sectional results do show a connection between educational attainment and intermarriage (see Table 7.2). In the youngest age
cohort, there is a progressive decline in the percentage inmarrying with
each succeeding educational level. For all of the cohorts, there is a progressive decline through at least high school graduates and, in several
cases, beyond this category as well. At the very least, then, we can say
that educational attainment through early college appears to be inversely linked with outmarriage in the fashion suggested here.[14]

[12]See, for example, Richard D. Alba, "Social Assimilation Among American Catholic
National-Origin Groups," *American Sociological Review* 41 (1976):1030–46; Robert
Schoen and Lawrence E. Cohen, "Ethnic Endogamy Among Mexican American Grooms:
A Reanalysis of Generational and Occupational Effects," *American Journal of Sociology*
86 (1980):359–66; an exception is Douglas T. Gurak and Joseph P. Fitzgerald, "Intermarriage Among Hispanic Ethnic Groups in New York City," *American Journal of Sociology*
87 (1982):921–34.
  Some technical problems exist since the generational data are based on sample surveys conducted by the National Opinion Research Center in their General Social Surveys
through 1980 and refer to all members of the ethnic group living in the United States. By
contrast, the marriage data refer to only American-born. Also, there is a certain type of
ecological correlation here since it would be more appropriate to examine this hypothesis
by determining whether the level of intermarriage varies within each group by generation.
However, that is not possible since two different data sets are being used here.
  [13]Susan Hill Cochrane, *Fertility and Education: What Do We Really Know*, World
Bank Staff Occasional Papers no. 26 (Baltimore: Johns Hopkins University Press, 1979),
p. 8.
  [14]This is not to rule out the possibility that some part of the inverse association
between inmarriage and educational attainment is a function of ethnic reporting errors
(particularly toward simplification and homogeneity of spouses) that are correlated with
education. See Stanley Lieberson and Mary C. Waters, "Ethnic Groups in Flux: The
Changing Ethnic Responses of American Whites," *Annals of the American Academy of
Political and Social Science* 487 (1986):79–91.

TABLE 7.2
Inmarriage Rates, by Age and Education of Wife, 1980

Age	Eight Years of School or Less	High School		College			All
		Some	Graduate	Some	Graduate	Beyond	
Under 25	71.2%	60.5%	55.7%	50.3%	49.2%	46.4%	55.5%
25–34	71.3	63.0	55.2	48.5	49.0	47.7	53.3
35–44	73.0	62.6	56.6	52.3	52.7	52.1	56.7
45–54	70.2	60.9	56.4	55.2	56.4	55.4	58.3
55–64	67.4	61.4	55.4	55.5	56.4	55.5	58.6
65 and Over	66.8	60.6	56.8	56.8	57.9	59.3	60.7

These results notwithstanding, there is no linkage between the level of an ethnic group's educational attainment and their odds of outmarriage (whether considered in linear or nonlinear form).[15] Groups with relatively high levels of education were no more likely than those with lower levels to outmarry ($r = -.29$, $P > .10$). For example, of the 16 groups considered, Portuguese and Russians had the highest inmarriage ratios; yet the Portuguese were lowest in educational attainment and the Russians were highest of all groups. Eliminating these two outliers has no effect on the conclusion; there is still no significant linkage in the direction hypothesized. Given the general association observed in Table 7.2 between educational attainment and intermarriage, how do we explain this apparent contradiction? The most likely interpretation is that the influence of education is relatively small compared with ethnic dispositions per se. This implies that within a group there is a linkage between education and intermarriage, but the regressions are different for each group and hence the group effect overshadows the educational factor operating within the group. Another possibility is that the results in Table 7.2 reflect all sorts of spurious linkages between ethnic origin, education, and generation—rather than any meaningful connection between the factors of concern here. Finally, the gross linkage between education and intermarriage could be misleading and not correct. It could reflect a linkage between ethnic distortions and

---

[15]The educational attainment of each group was measured by computing the Index of Net Difference between all women in the United States and the educational attainment of women of the specified origin who were born in the United States (in both cases aged 25 and over in 1980). See Stanley Lieberson, "Rank-Sum Comparisons Between Groups," in David Heise, ed., Sociological Methodology 1976 (San Francisco: Jossey-Bass, 1975). A positive value means that the group in question exceeds the national level. No attempt is made to adjust for the part-whole problem in comparisons; use of the total population simply provides a standard for determining each group's position with respect to their distribution.

education such that less educated people are especially likely to warp their ethnic reports in the direction of marital homogeneity—a factor that we do think operates to some unknown degree.[16] At any rate, ethnic differences in educational attainment do not help us to understand differences in the ethnic groups' levels of intermarriage.

Mixed Ancestry and the Likelihood of Outmarriage

Finally, since we know that persons of mixed origin are more likely to outmarry than are compatriots of unmixed origin (Chapter 6), it is appropriate to consider the role of this factor in accounting for ethnic differences in outmarriage. Are the inmarriage ratios lower for those groups with relatively large percentages of mixed-ancestry members? (This is an ecological correlation and is not a substitute for the issue of whether single and mixed persons within the same group differ in their levels of outmarriage. The latter is a question that was addressed directly in the preceding chapter.) The level of inmarriages does indeed tend to be lower for those groups that have relatively large percentages with mixed ancestry. The correlation between the log of the odds ratio and percentage mixed is $-.71$ $(P < .005)$. This makes sense, of course, in terms of several factors: the probability that those of mixed origin will have weaker ethnic identification and emphasis; the possibility that, among the lower ranking white ethnic groups, persons of mixed European origins are less stigmatized than unmixed persons; and the more diverse ethnic pulls that operate on ancestry persons, even if their identification is the same as single-ancestry persons. Moreover, in a certain sense, the presence of this negative correlation confirms a certain level of temporal continuity in the positions of the groups with respect to their relative rates of inmarriage and/or attractiveness to others as potential mates. For, in fact, the presence of mixed-ancestry people is due to previous intermarriage in some earlier generation. The percentage in a group who are of mixed ancestry reflect the combined influence of five factors: the levels of intermarriage for earlier cohorts, the number of generations in the country, differences between mixed and unmixed in their rates of outmarriage, differences in fertility and mortality between the mixed and unmixed components of each group, and the incidence of reporting errors. The absence of such a negative correlation would mean that the groups with relatively few members who are of single ancestry are also the groups who at present are less likely to outmarry.

[16]Lieberson and Waters, "Ethnic Groups in Flux."

Intercorrelations

Too much can be made of these results, impressive as they appear to be. This is because the four independent variables that seem to affect the level of inmarriage—generations in the United States, multiple ancestry, regional segregation, and Bogardus social distance score—tend to be intercorrelated (Table 7.3). The first three are highly intercorrelated, and the Bogardus scale is correlated significantly with one of the three as well. The level of a group's educational attainment, by contrast, both fails to account for intergroup differences in intermarriage *and* is also uncorrelated with any of these other independent variables. Essentially, then, the cross-sectional causal linkages that we find really involve a set of intercorrelated variables.

This cluster of intercorrelated independent variables means that basically we are observing an old-new distinction operating with respect to inmarriage rates (net of composition). The newer white ethnic groups have a shorter average residence in the United States, are less likely to be of mixed origin, are more segregated regionally, and tend to have lower Bogardus scores (see the Mann-Whitney U Test results in Table 7.4). By contrast, not only does educational attainment fail to correlate significantly with the other independent variables (Table 7.3), but there is not a significant difference between the old and the new groups as well (Table 7.4). Trying to separate the effect on intermarriage of each of these variables is inappropriate with the cross-sectional data reported above. It is difficult enough under optimal conditions to separate the "basic" causal factor (or factors) from those variables which are "superficial" causes; and with cross-sectional data it is virtually impossible to accomplish this.[17]

TABLE 7.3

Product-Moment Correlations Between Independent Variables

Variables	(1)	(2)	(3)	(4)	(5)
(1) Percentage Fourth Generation	—	$-.69^a$	$.73^b$	$-.80^b$	.0
(2) Bogardus Social Distance	—	—	$-.36^c$	.40	.3
(3) Multiple Origins	—	—	—	$-.63^b$	.3
(4) Regional Dissimilarity	—	—	—	—	$-.1$
(5) Educational Attainment	—	—	—	—	—

NOTE: N = 16, except for correlations involving Bogardus, where N = 12.

[a] $P < .01.$

[b] $P < .001.$

[c] $P \geq .10.$

TABLE 7.4

Mann-Whitney Test of Old-New Differences

Variables	Single-Tailed Probability
Percentage Fourth Generation	<.001
Bogardus Social Distance	.014
Multiple Origins	.001
Regional Dissimilarity	<.05
Educational Attainment	>.05

Changes Through the Years

It still must be noted that group differences in inmarriage are indeed linked to their differences in these independent variables. If a true causal linkage is operating, we would expect to find *changes* in these variables helping to account for shifts in the levels of inmarriage for the groups.[18] This is a rather different matter than the cross-sectional variables analyzed above. The question posed is whether changes in these attributes are linked with changes in levels of ingroup marriage. This is particularly of concern since we have seen that the independent variables are correlated with one another and hence it is difficult to separate them.

Most of the causal factors considered above can be examined longitudinally to see if there is some linkage between their actual changes and shifts in the levels of inmarriage. Shifts in the regional segregation measure will not be examined; it requires either ethnic data for earlier periods or age-specific residential data for 1980. Because of the cross-sectional results reported above, the influence of educational changes on ingroup marriages will also not be considered. We can determine if shifts in the other variables over time are linked to changes in the inmarriage levels of the groups.[19]

[17]Stanley Lieberson, *Making It Count* (Berkeley: University of California Press, 1985a), pp. 185–94.

[18]Ibid., p. 180.

[19]Because the marriage data are analyzed by age of respondent rather than age of occurrence of the marriage, we are unable to separate those people whose marriage occurred one day prior to the census from those in the same cohort who married when they first reached their mid-teens. It is therefore necessary to make some estimates of the appropriate periods for the independent variables to compare over time with changes in the age groups. However, we can assume that the vast majority in each age cohort were married in a relatively narrow span of years and that, moreover, the periods were different for each age cohort. This is an assumption that can be made comfortably since we have restricted the analysis to women in their first marriage.

Ethnic Composition

Although the ethnic composition of the United States is continuously changing it is unlikely that these changes are primarily responsible for the increases in outmarriage of the magnitude observed during the half century or so under consideration. As a matter of fact, during this period when the level of inmarriage declined substantially for many of the groups, the compositional shift for a number of the white groups was in the opposite direction such that the component of the relevant married male population *increased*. To formalize the matter, we consider the percentage outmarried for the 16 white groups, asking whether changes in these percentages between the cohorts aged 65 and over and those aged 25–34 are linked in any way to changes in each group's percentage of the relevant male population.[20] We approach the problem by first considering the regression of outmarriage on composition for the older cohort, and then again for the younger cohort. If declines in outmarriage are purely a function of compositional changes for the groups under consideration, the regressions would be identical in the two cases. This is clearly not the case. For women aged 65 and over in 1980, $b_{yx} = 103.0$, where y is the percentage of women in a given group who inmarry and x is the percentage of all reporting the origin specified. The analogous results for the 25-to-34-year-old cohort yields a significantly larger regression coefficient (148.6).[21] There is evidence that the relationship between composition and inmarriage has shifted between the two cohorts.

The linkage, by the way, between composition and percentages inmarried is particularly close for the younger of the cohorts, r is .90, whereas it is .51 for those aged 65 and over in 1980 ($Z = 2.32$).[22] Two factors could account for this result. First, since the analysis is confined to women in their first marriage, the older cohort has been decimated to a greater extent by both divorce and death. As a consequence, any ethnic differentials in divorce or mortality would have had the greatest chance to affect progressively older populations. Another possibility is substantive: namely, that the idiosyncratic differences between groups in their propensities to inmarry, as well as differences between them in other factors which may influence outmarriage (for example, genera-

[20]The odds ratios are not used here because we do not wish to purge the intermarriage measure of the influence of composition.

[21]$P < .01$, based on an analysis of covariance test of the hypothesis that the two age cohorts can be represented by the same regression.

[22]Separate tests are necessary here. Although the level of significance for a zero-order correlation is identical to that for a zero-order regression (see footnote 5 above), tests of the difference for two independent samples between their zero-order regressions do not apply to the significance of the difference between their zero-order correlations.

tion), are weaker in the progressively younger cohorts. As a consequence, composition plays a stronger role as the other factors disappear ("disappear" not in the sense that they no longer influence inmarriage rates, but rather in the sense that the groups differ less from each other on these factors than they once did). For example, the groups probably differ less from one another now than they once did in the propensity to favor inmarriages.

To examine further the issue at hand, changes in composition were considered several different ways, using both absolute and percentage shifts. Likewise, changes in the inmarriage rates were examined several different ways. In all cases, we were unable to find any evidence that changes in composition affected the decline in endogamy. Many of the groups that experienced massive drops in endogamy also experienced slight increases in their male component of the population and hence, ceteris paribus, composition alone should have led to an increase in endogamy. We can safely conclude that the major declines in inmarriage are *not* a function of changes in the ethnic and racial composition of the United States.

Social Distance

Changes in the Bogardus social distance scale for the 12 ethnic groups, when considered for the broadest span of time that is appropriate for the available studies, leave a somewhat unclear result. Changes in outmarriage between the 55-to-64-year-old cohort and the 25-to-34-year-old cohort (measured by the ratio of the two relevant log odds ratios),[23] when considered with numerical differences in the Bogardus social distance scores reported in major surveys of 1946 and 1977 (and hence presumably at periods when the vast majority of each cohort were getting married for the first time), at first glance seem to indicate a certain impressive linkage.[24] The correlation is .57 and b is .23 ($P < .05$). This seems to suggest that shifts in the Bogardus scale are linked to shifts in outmarriage in the direction expected if changes in the "acceptability" of a group are affecting the propensity of others to marry their

---

[23]Given the limited number of groups being analyzed, here and later in this section, we have used crude change scores even though this entails assumptions that are less than ideal. See, for example, Jacob Cohen and Patricia Cohen, *Applied Multiple Regression/ Correlation Analysis for Behavioral Sciences* (Hillsdale, NJ: Lawrence Erlbaum Associates, 1975), pp. 378–93.

[24]Based on data reported in Carolyn A. Owen, Howard C. Eisner, and Thomas R. McFaul, "A Half-Century of Social Distance Research: National Replication of the Bogardus Studies," *Sociology and Social Research* 66 (1981):80–98.

members. However, there are two bothersome features to the observed linkage. First, much of the relationship appears to be a function of the change for Italians. Their Bogardus score shifted in a spectacular manner during this period, dropping from 2.28 to 1.65—a shift far greater in magnitude than that experienced by any of the remaining 11 groups. Likewise, their drop in outmarriage was the greatest of all observed. In itself, this should be exactly what we might expect if the linkage is in the direction hypothesized. However, it is more than that. For without this one group, the linkage fairly much disintegrates ($r = .26, P > .20$). The second problem derives from the nature of the 1976 Bogardus social distance study. Similar to the earlier studies, it is based on a sample that is doubly nonrandom. First, a small number of colleges and universities were selected and, in turn, selected classes were used in these colleges to get student rankings. The 1977 study included a substantially larger black component of raters than did the earlier ones (19 versus 10 percent), and there is a danger that this change affected the ratings reported of different white groups. At any rate, for whatever the reason, we are somewhat cautious about the results for 1977 (the earlier static analysis of Bogardus was based on the 1966 survey).

As a consequence, the issue was re-examined with changes in the scale scores for the 20-year period between 1946 and 1966 compared with changes in outmarriage for these groups for the cohorts in 1980 who were aged 25–34 and 45–54. The results are again in the direction expected such that the groups with the greatest inmarriage declines are also the ones with the most favorable shifts in their Bogardus scores ($b = .10, r = .45, .10 > P > .05$). However, here too the linkage observed is largely a reflection of the Italian outlier. Once this group is excluded, the observed linkage is essentially nil for the remaining 11 groups ($r = -.09, b = -.05$). In conclusion, then, there is little reason to believe that the declines in outmarriage are responding to a drop-off in the general disposition toward these groups. Any barriers that existed because of negative attitudes are more or less intact during a period when inmarriage declines rather substantially for the white ethnic groups under consideration.

Generational Effects

Generation is clearly a central consideration in the analysis of European groups in the United States. The groups vary greatly in their migration patterns, as we saw in Chapter 2, and in turn this has consequences for their behavior many years later. When we compare Americans of Greek origin with those of Dutch origin, for example, we are also comparing two groups with radically different average lengths of residence in the country. As a consequence, comparisons which fail to consider generational differences overlook a central force affecting a variety of group patterns that has nothing to do with culture or other idiosyncratic group features. Generational factors are important for understanding the position of other immigrant groups as well, such as those from various parts of Asia. And it even has a relevant counterpart when considering the patterns for blacks in the North.[25] Almost certainly, where generational factors do operate, the influence is not linear, but declines in significance after the first few generations such that the social changes experienced between the grandchildren of immigrants and the immigrants themselves (third and first generations, respectively) is far greater than the changes between third and fifth, with the latter gap still greater than the differences between fifth and seventh, and so on. At some point—unknown at present because we generally do not have such detailed data—generational effects would decline to the point where they are essentially nil.

Earlier in this chapter we observed a static correlation for a number of groups between the generational factor and their levels of outmarriage. The issue is whether shifts over time in this generational factor can help us to understand the substantial declines in intermarriage found for these groups. In the cohort aged 65 and over in 1980, the percentage with at least three generations in the United States varies greatly (Table 7.5). Only 10 percent of persons aged 65 and over from the more recent European groups—Poles and Italians—are of at least three generations' residence in the United States; about a third of the two Scandinavian groups are third generation; two thirds of German elderly fall in this category; and more than four fifths of the English, Irish, Scottish, and Dutch who are aged 65 and over are of at least three generations' residence in the country.[26] The figures are radically different for those aged 25–34 in 1980. The percentages have risen for all ten of

[25]Stanley Lieberson, "Generational Differences Among Blacks in the North," *American Journal of Sociology* 79 (1973):550–65.

[26]In the static analysis, we employed data on the percentage with four or more generations in the United States. These data were obtained from the General Social Survey conducted by the National Opinion Research Center, using a procedure described by Richard D. Alba and Mitchell B. Chamlin, "A Preliminary Examination of Ethnic Identification Among Whites," *American Sociological Review* 48 (1983):240–47. Because of the small numbers involved, it is not possible to use that data source for the generational analysis here; instead data from the 1979 Current Population Survey are employed to determine the percentage of persons in specific age cohorts who are of at least three generations' residence in the country. The 1980 census provides no delineations by generation and our age-specific analysis based on the 1979 survey is limited to ten leading white groups. Also, because of numerical restrictions, we are still obliged to employ ecological correlations for the analysis over time since we cannot investigate intermarriage rates for generation-specific categories within each ethnic population. Below it will be possible to consider the behavior of mixed- versus single-ancestry persons, but in that case not with generational cross-tabulations.

TABLE 7.5

*Percentage with Three or More Generations' Residence
in United States, by Age, 1979*

Group	65 Years Old and Over	25–34 Years Old
English	85%	93%
German	68	95
Irish	84	96
French	74	91
Italian	10	83
Scottish	82	93
Polish	10	89
Dutch	87	94
Swedish	31	94
Norwegian	38	91

the groups, but much more for the newer groups. As a consequence, the gaps between the European groups have narrowed greatly—albeit the recency of some groups is still reflected in their slightly smaller percentages with three generations' residence.

Groups that have changed most in their percentage with three or more generations' residence are also the groups that have declined most in their percentage inmarried. The dependent variable for each group is the percentage inmarried aged 25–34 divided by the percentage inmarried among those aged 65 and over—the greater the decline in inmarriage, the smaller the ratio that will result. The independent variable is the percentage with at least three generations' residence among those aged 65 and over divided by the comparable figure for those aged 25–34. Here too, a small ratio means a big increase in the component with at least three generations' residence in the country. A positive coefficient means that in marriage tends to decline most sharply for those groups with the greatest relative increase in the percentage with three or more generations in the country. The association is indeed positive, with Y best described as an exponential function of X ($r = .91$, $b = .89$, $P < .005$). Thus, we can conclude that shifts in the generational makeup of the groups are linked to changes in their inmarriage rates over time.[27] A decline in the propensity toward inmarriage occurs as the generational distance between the immigrants and their descendants widens. The

[27]To be sure, differences between the groups are not entirely revealed by these figures for three generations or more since the category cannot distinguish grandchildren of immigrants from those with many ancestors going back to the pre-Revolutionary times. Obviously, the ethnic groups will vary in their generational makeup within this broad category.

later descendants lose the intensity of their ethnic attachments, thereby weakening (although not eliminating) the earlier propensity toward marital endogamy. Ironically, during the period when a number of writers were arguing that the melting pot was not occurring and that there was a resurgence of ethnic loyalties, the rates of outmarriage were rising with each successive cohort.[28]

Mixed Versus Single

Earlier in the chapter we observed a static cross-sectional linkage between the degree of mixture in different ethnic groups and their rates of outmarriage. Such a pattern could simply mean that groups who have intermarried more in the past are also continuing to have higher intermarriage levels at present. The question is whether actual changes over time in the mixed component of each group can account for shifts in the levels of outmarriage.[29] The answer is more complicated than one might think.

To be sure, the mixed-origin component has increased for all 16 groups. Indeed, the ratio of single- to mixed-origin members for those aged 25–34 is, on the average, only about a third of the ratio for those aged 65 and over (the mean ratio is .34, with the values ranging from .09 to .81). Barring massive immigration of single-ancestry persons, the decline in the unmixed single-ancestry component is inevitable over time if there is intermarriage and if the ethnic labeling system in the society is receptive to mixed delineations. The latter is not always the case, as illustrated rather clearly by current responses to white-black offspring in the United States (a practice that could well change in the future). Insofar as interbreeding is an almost certain consequence of interethnic contact, in the long run we can expect to have a growing population who are of mixed origins. If such components are less disposed toward endogamy and/or are more acceptable to others, the ethnic levels of intermarriage can be expected to go up. This, too, is the case; except for Scots (and a minor reversal for Swedes of mixed origin), single-ancestry members of each group do exhibit higher levels of inmarriage (Table

[28]Michael Novak, *The Rise of the Unmeltable Ethnics* (New York: Macmillan, 1971).

[29]The current rate of mixed marriages for various groups need not be a simple linear function of the percentage of the group that is of mixed origin. Aside from differences in fertility and self-identification, the generational shifts observed above would have a greater impact on some groups than others and in turn affect the intermarriage rates for the mixed. But also at issue is the marital behavior of persons of mixed origin; there is no a priori reason to expect that the level of outmarriage for mixed persons of different combinations will be uniform.

TABLE 7.6

Inmarriage, by Age and Mix of Ancestry, 1980

| | Percent Inmarried | | | |
| | 65 Years Old and Over | | 25–34 Years Old | |
Group	Ancestry Single	Ancestry Mixed	Ancestry Single	Ancestry Mixed
English	69%	50%	64%	42%
German	60	45	51	44
Irish	49	43	38	35
French	35	13	30	16
Italian	69	23	33	20
Scottish	20	26	13	19
Polish	50	25	25	17
Dutch	33	17	28	14
Swedish	26	13	9	10
Norwegian	35	13	24	15

7.6; compare column 1 with 2, and 3 with 4.)[30] (This was also discussed in Chapter 6.)

The question, then, is whether each group's intercohort changes in the pure:mixed ratio are indeed correlated with changes in the group's outmarriages. The coefficient of correlation for intercohort changes between those aged 65 and over and those aged 25–34 is .87 (b = .25, P < .005).[31] Thus, the shifts in the ratio of pure to mixed appear to be operating in the hypothesized direction, providing longitudinal support for the cross-sectional linkage reported earlier. However, these results may overestimate the influence of single-mix changes on the decline in inmarriages; the analysis is based on ecological correlations. Intercohort comparisons for persons of single ancestry reveal a decline in endogamy for all ten groups. For example, 60 percent of single-ancestry Germans aged 65 and over are inmarried, whereas 51 percent of those aged 25–34

[30]We are concerned here with endogamy involving only one of the groups specified. In other words, for the data delineating Italians, we know how many women of mixed Italian-German origin marry a man who is partly or entirely Italian, but we ignore at that point marriages with men who are in some part German. Hence we are describing the degree that mixed Italian women are married to men who are also Italian, but not the entire range of possible inmarriages for such women. Likewise, when examining inmarriage rates for women of mixed German origin, at that point only marriages with German men are being considered—and all we can say is whether their rates of marrying such men are different from those of single-ancestry German women. Later in this chapter, marital choices will be considered in terms of both origins at the same time.

[31]The regression is in the form of $Y = a + b(\log X)$, where X is the ratio of pure to mixed in the younger cohort divided by the analogous ratio for the older cohort; Y is the ratio of percentage inmarriages for the younger cohort divided by the analogous figure for the older cohort.

are inmarried (Table 7.6). For some groups the declines are far greater; Italians decline from 69 to 33 percent and Poles from 50 to 25 percent. There is also an intercohort decline among mixed-origin women, although the declines are not as substantial—indeed, there are small increases among two of the ten groups. Thus, something more is operating to increase intermarriage than simply a growth in the mixed component of each group—granted that such a shift does occur and will itself increase outmarriage. Something more is going on because the unmixed component is itself outmarrying to a far greater extent than was the case for the older cohorts. There are two possible interpretations. The first is simply that young cohorts cannot be compared with older cohorts because we are dealing with surviving marriages rather than with the actual rates of outmarriages. The second interpretation is that there are changes over time in outmarriage rates of single-ancestry individuals that reflect societal shifts that cannot be explained by taking various background factors into account.

There is evidence that at least a substantial part of the decline in endogamy among persons of single ancestry reflects the generational influence observed earlier (Table 7.5). This is a period during which those of single ancestry experience substantial changes in their generational makeup. Among Poles, for example, about 10 percent of those aged 65 and over were of third generation compared with nearly 90 percent of those aged 25–34. This occurs for some of the other groups as well— Swedes, Italians, Norwegians, and Scots to a lesser degree. In the case of the single-ancestry changes in inmarriage, we can assume that a good part of the drop-off in inmarriages is a function of this generational shift. The increase in outmarriage among single-ancestry women is associated with increases in the component of such women who have resided in the United States for at least three generations. The correlation coefficient is .89 ($b = .56$, $P < .005$), where Y is the percentage inmarrying among women aged 25–34 divided by the analogous percentage for women aged 65 and over; and X is the percentage of unmixed ancestry aged 65 and over who are third generation or more divided by the analogous percentage for those aged 25–34. Similar results are not found for the changes in the mixed-origin component. There is no reason to believe that intercohort shifts in outmarriage among the mixed component are related to generational changes in that component ($b = .14$, $r = .42$, $P > .10$).[32]

---

[32]Variables are the same as those reported for the single-ancestry population other than that they refer to inmarriages of the *mixed-origin* segment and the size of the generational component of the *mixed-origin* cohorts. Reported regression is based on a non-linear model, $Y = aX^b$. The fit is even poorer with the simple linear model used successfully with the single-ancestry component. In both cases, these are ecological correlations and hence are subject to certain alternative interpretations.

There is also little question that declines in the size of each group's unmixed-ancestry component are closely tied to changes in the group's generational composition. The correlation is $-.96$ ($b = -.59$, $P < .005$) in the nonlinear regression, $Y = a(X^b)$, where X is the ratio of third generation or more to earlier generations for those aged 25–34 divided by the analogous ratio for the population aged 65 and over; Y is the ratio of pure:mixed for the young cohort divided by the analogous ratio for the older cohort.

Summary

Generational changes in the makeup of each ethnic group are a key factor in helping us to understand why the groups differ in the degree of decline in endogamy observed in the United States during the period under consideration. This is a prosaic variable because such changes are essentially assured for each ethnic group unless it experiences progressively larger immigration through time (or if there is a substantial out-migration of the later generations to another country). The latter has not been the case for the European groups of American birth, and the former has not been possible for most of these groups since the cessation of large-scale immigration in 1924. As a consequence the white population is developing progressively longer roots in the United States, and this seems to greatly affect the levels of inmarriage.

Several of the other variables considered do not help us to understand why the groups differ in their relative increases in exogamy. As for propinquity, however, we cannot examine changes in propinquity for progressive age cohorts and therefore are unable to draw any conclusions about its possible influences on changes in outmarriage. It is also difficult to decide if increases in the mixed segment of each group help account for the observed declines in endogamy. Clearly, the mixed are more likely to outmarry, but we cannot separate the influence of this factor from its connection to changes in the generational makeup of the groups and the impact that has on intermarriage. The decline in endogamy among the single-ancestry component could possibly be accounted for by their changing generational makeup. On the other hand, changes in endogamy among the mixed-ancestry component are not readily explained by this factor—albeit it is an ecological correlation. Accordingly, we are inclined to speculate that the growth in the mixed component of these groups affected changes in their outmarriage levels independently of the generational factor. A further step toward reaching a more definitive answer will occur when data cross-tabulating third-generation status by both age and marital choice are developed for women of mixed and single origins separately.

Patterns of Intermarriage

To a striking degree, contemporary ethnic relations in the United States are marked by marriages across ethnic lines.[33] There are 240 different pairings of single-ancestry men and women in the 16 x 16 matrix shown in Table 7.7, excluding the cases of inmarriage found on the main diagonal. *In slightly more than 60 percent of these combinations, intermarriage across specific ethnic lines is in excess of the number that would be expected on the basis of composition.* For example, in column 1 we see that 22.5 percent of all single-ancestry Scottish women have single-ancestry English husbands. Since men of English origin amount to 11.8 percent of all husbands (bottom of column 1), it is clear that such inmarriages occur in excess of the numbers expected simply on the basis of the ethnic composition of husbands of wives in their first marriages. On the other hand, only 5.5 percent of Italian women are married to English men—a figure far less than the 11.8 percent that would occur if ethnic origin had no direct or indirect linkage to marital choice.

This figure of slightly more than 60 percent is obtained even though there has been no adjustment for the ingroup marriages experienced by each ethnic population, "the main diagonal effect." A major factor contributing to this finding is the relatively infrequent combinations in which one mate is of single ancestry and the other is of mixed ancestry. As observed in Chapter 6, when single-ancestry people outmarry, they tend to marry mates of single—rather than mixed—ancestry. Hence, we would almost certainly find many outmarriage combinations between a single-ancestry wife and a mixed-ancestry husband that are well below compositional expectations. Infrequent matings with some of the non-European groups is another factor that makes it possible to have high inmarriage rates *and* also outmarriage levels in excess of chance with a number of other white ethnic groups.

There are important differences between groups in both the frequency of outmarriage and the groups selected. Outmarriage is most common for single-ancestry women of German, Irish, French, Polish, Dutch, Swedish, and Welsh origin (where from 11 to 13 of the remaining 15 white ethnic groups are picked in excess of the husbands' distribu-

[33]Our analysis is restricted to the marital behavior of women aged 25–34 in 1980 belonging to any of 16 leading white groups, who are American-born, have American-born husbands, and are currently married to their first husband. Also, for reasons explained earlier, we confine our analysis to the single-ancestry components of each of these groups. (Later in this chapter we will consider the marital behavior of women reporting multiple ethnic origins.) The compositional data refer to all American-born husbands of the specified women, and therefore none of the rows add to 100 percent because mates of other single-ancestry origins as well as all multiple-origin mates are included in the denominators.

TABLE 7.7
Husbands by Wives, Single Ancestry, 1980

Wives	Husbands							
	(1)	(2)	(3)	(4)	(5)	(6)	(7)	(8)
(1) English	55.3%	8.8%	4.4%	1.8%	1.5%	1.2%	1.0%	.7%
(2) German	10.5	35.6	6.4	1.9	2.2	1.0	2.2	1.2
(3) Irish	11.2	14.2	25.0	2.6	5.7	1.4	2.3	.9
(4) French	13.9	12.7	6.2	22.1	3.8	1.7	2.6	1.1
(5) Italian	5.5	8.2	8.7	1.8	26.1	.8	4.3	.3
(6) Scottish	22.5	16.6	10.6	4.5	2.6	8.3	1.2	.2
(7) Polish	6.2	12.1	5.9	2.5	7.0	.9	18.2	.6
(8) Dutch	10.9	16.7	5.5	2.1	2.2	.9	2.1	23.2
(9) Swedish	10.9	21.4	6.1	.6	2.8	1.6	2.7	1.7
(10) Norwegian	5.9	19.3	5.8	1.1	2.5	.9	1.4	1.1
(11) Russian	4.4	7.3	3.0	1.0	3.8	.3	7.0	.5
(12) Czech	5.9	20.0	6.2	2.1	2.7	.3	3.8	1.2
(13) Hungarian	7.1	16.3	8.3	2.5	5.4	.0	9.2	.4
(14) Welsh	19.4	15.3	7.6	1.4	3.5	6.9	2.1	1.4
(15) Danish	20.1	17.9	3.8	3.3	2.7	1.6	1.1	2.7
(16) Portuguese	8.6	6.8	6.8	1.8	5.5	.0	.0	1.2
All Husbands	11.8	10.7	5.1	1.6	3.2	.7	1.9	.7

TABLE 7.7 (continued)

	(9)	(10)	(11)	(12)	(13)	(14)	(15)	(16)
(1) English	.6%	.5%	.2%	.3%	.2%	.2%	.3%	.1%
(2) German	1.3	1.4	.6	.8	.4	.5	.4	.1
(3) Irish	.7	.8	.4	.4	.3	.3	.3	.2
(4) French	.8	.3	.3	.5	.4	.5	.3	.5
(5) Italian	.8	.4	1.2	.3	.3	.3	.1	.4
(6) Scottish	1.0	.2	.4	.0	.2	.6	.4	.4
(7) Polish	.9	.9	2.5	.6	1.1	.2	.6	.1
(8) Dutch	1.8	1.5	.7	.3	.4	.0	.6	.3
(9) Swedish	5.8	5.3	.8	.6	.8	.6	1.3	.3
(10) Norwegian	4.4	16.8	.6	.6	.3	.3	1.3	.0
(11) Russian	.3	.0	28.2	.3	2.2	.3	.2	.0
(12) Czech	.9	1.5	1.5	10.9	.6	.0	.6	.0
(13) Hungarian	.0	.4	2.9	.8	8.3	.4	.0	.4
(14) Welsh	1.4	.7	2.8	.7	.7	6.3	1.4	.0
(15) Danish	3.3	4.9	.5	1.1	.0	.5	6.0	.0
(16) Portuguese	.6	1.8	.6	.0	.0	.0	.0	22.7
All Husbands	.7	.8	.7	.4	.3	.2	.2	.2

tions). At the other extreme, English, Russian, and Portuguese women have levels of outmarriage that are in most cases (10 to 12 groups) below the frequency expected on the basis of composition alone. The English are rather surprising to us, and we are still inclined to speculate that at least a substantial part of this finding represents ethnic misreporting which leads toward homogeneity (a rather high level of inmarriage is reported for this group, which reduces the opportunities for outmarriages in excess of the compositional expectations).

As noted earlier, the data are not entirely suitable for considering gender differences in the patterns of outmarriage. Nevertheless, the affinities (defined as being in excess of compositional expectations) are nearly always slightly different between the men and women in a given ethnic group. These differences are, on the whole, fairly modest and not much can be made of them because of shortcomings in the data. The most extreme gender differences are for Scots and Russians (presumably heavily Jewish). In both cases, men from those groups have a wider range of outmarriages (in excess of composition) than do women. Seven other groups of women marry Scottish men in excess of their composition; whereas Scottish women marry only four groups of non-Scottish men in excess of their composition (compare the row for Scottish women with the column for Scottish men in Table 7.7). Exactly the same difference occurs for Russian men and women. The problem is intriguing, but we are not in a position to evaluate the variety of possible interpretations of these gender gaps. Stevens and Swicegood[34] have observed "a general tendency for women to be more likely than men to have spouses of the same ethnic descent."

Intermarriage with Non-Europeans

Dealing as we are with interethnic marriages, let us consider briefly the marriages that European groups have with such major non-European populations as blacks, Mexicans, American Indians, and Asians. What is the frequency of such intermarriages, particularly compared with what might be expected under random choices of mate? Do the European groups differ much among themselves in their levels of outmarriage with specific non-European populations? We can learn much about race and ethnic relations in the United States by answering these two questions.

Blacks are 7.0 percent of all men married to women who are still in

[34]"Linguistic Context of Ethnic Endogamy."

TABLE 7.8

Levels of European Ethnic Outmarriage with Non-European Groups, 1980

Wives		Husbands			
	Black	Mexican	Puerto Rican	American Indian	Other Asian
English	.11%	.22%	.03%	.52%	.04%
German	.11	.30	.03	.64	.05
Irish	.11	.33	.06	1.24	.06
French	.12	.33	.03	.89	.07
Italian	.18	.18	.18	.22	.05
Scottish	.10	.29	.00	.52	.10
Polish	.09	.16	.05	.15	.05
Dutch	.07	.31	.03	.82	.00
Swedish	.11	.28	.00	.32	.11
Norwegian	.14	.21	.00	.25	.00
Russian	.09	.06	.00	.03	.12
Czech	.11	.22	.00	.61	.00
Hungarian	.08	.16	.00	.40	.00
Welsh	.00	.35	.00	.35	.00
Danish	.11	.00	.00	.33	.00
Portuguese	.14	1.81	.70	.42	.97

their first marriage.[35] For women from most of the white groups, the levels of outmarriage with blacks run from one to two tenths of 1 percent (Table 7.8), substantially below the 7.0 percent that would occur in a society where there was no direct or indirect influence due to the race of husband. Moreover, these rates are generally so small that it would be inappropriate to try to make much of the differences between white groups in this regard. *There are essentially no substantial differences among the leading white ethnic groups in their levels of intermarriage with black men in the United States.*

[35]The analysis is based on women of all ages in their first marriage, but is restricted to women and men of unmixed ancestry. The inclusion of all ages is done to maximize the numbers which are often small for some of the groups and because the relevant outmarriages are so infrequent. Analysis is restricted to unmixed ancestry in order to avoid the problem of assuming outmarriages when they are not fully occurring—for example, if a woman of part English ancestry appears to be married to a man who is black, it may reflect the fact that the woman is also of part black origin and that black mixes with English are more frequent than with some other European origins. Of course, this means we cannot consider intercohort shifts, adjust for ethnic differences in age composition, or separately consider the patterns for whites of mixed origins. But it does provide the reader with a quick and reasonably precise picture of white ethnic differences in their outmarriages with these groups.

The rates of outmarriage with Mexican men (again, only those of single origin) are for the most part higher than the rates for black men (see Table 7.8), but they are well below the Mexican component of relevant married men (1.54 percent). There are no grounds, based on these data, for concluding that the white ethnic groups differ substantially in their levels of marriage with Mexican men. (Women of Portuguese origin appear to have an exceptionally high level of intermarriage with Mexican men, but the percentage is based on 13 cases of inmarriage with Mexicans.) The basic conclusion is that there is more intermarriage with Mexican Americans than with blacks, a fact which is even more significant since the number of black men married to women in their first marriage is much larger. But, again, there are no paticular ethnic differences in these propensities. Intermarriage with Puerto Ricans is also uniform (Table 7.8) and extremely low (men of that origin constitute 0.4 percent of the relevant men, well above the actual percentages of women marrying such men). There appears to be a slightly higher level of marriage—again, based on very small numbers—with Puerto Rican women for Portuguese men.

The results are different for white marriages with American Indians: The levels are higher in both an absolute sense and relative to the number of men in the population; also, there appear to be meaningful differences between the white groups in their levels of intermarriage with Native Americans.[36] At one extreme, 1.2 percent of Irish women and slightly less than 1.0 percent of French and Dutch women in their first marriage have mates of American Indian origin. At the other extreme, 0.5 or 0.6 percent of English, German, Scottish, and Czech women have such single-ancestry mates, and the levels are much lower for Poles, Italians, and Russians. Almost without exception, these figures are still higher than those reported for marriages with blacks. Since men of unmixed American Indian origin are 0.8 percent of all husbands in the study, the single-ancestry component of some of the white groups have levels of intermarriage with Indian men in excess of their proportions of the population—although it does not apply to other groups. It is our general impression that the groups with relatively high levels of intermarriage are those that tend to be located in parts of the country where relatively large concentrations of American Indians are found. Likewise, the groups with the lowest levels of intermarriage are those

---

[36]Since the number of whites reporting mixed American Indian ancestry exceeds by far the number of persons who report only Indian ancestry, it is important to keep in mind that the analysis here has been restricted to persons reported as being of only Indian ancestry. Although this is not the same as persons reporting themselves as American Indian on the "race" question, the results are still based on rather restrictive criteria in this regard.

with special concentrations in the industrial states of the Northeast and eastern part of the Midwest.[37]

Regarding marriages with such major Asian groups in the United States as Asian Indians, Chinese, Filipinos, Japanese, Koreans, and Vietnamese, all but the Asian Indians are included in the "Other Asian" category along with a number of smaller ethnic groups. Unmixed "Other Asia" men amount to 0.3 percent of all American-born men married to American-born women. With Portuguese again providing the only exception, women from other specific white groups are uniformly low in their marriage rates with men of these origins (see Table 7.8). However, the specific white groups were generally lower than composition would lead us to expect in their marriages with Asian women. One possibility here is that a fair segment of the white-Asian marriages observed entail foreign-born Asian women who met their husband overseas while the husband was serving in the military.

Several features of Portuguese history in the United States[38] may help account for their somewhat higher levels of intermarriage with non-European groups. Some of their early settlements were in areas that increased the probability of such outmarriages. For example, there were early immigrants from the Azores and Cape Verde who migrated to the Hawaiian Islands and San Francisco. In addition, beginning in 1878 contract laborers arrived in Hawaii from the Madeira Islands. Another factor is that several Portuguese groups are not entirely of European ancestry and hence may have found such intermarriages both more attractive and possible. The Cape Verdeans are a racially mixed group of African as well as Portuguese heritage. Likewise, there was a small settlement of Luso-Sino-Americans from Macao (near Hong Kong) in California immediately after World War II. Finally, Rogers observes an early tendency in the United States to consider at least some Portuguese as nonwhites (p. 815).

Overall, however, these results indicate that whites do not differ on ethnic lines very much with respect to marriages with these leading

---

[37]In the "ethnic ancestry" question on the 1980 census, 1.9 million are reported as single-ancestry American Indian—a figure far less than the 4.8 million persons reporting part American Indian ancestry. Still this is proportionately well in excess of the 1.4 million reporting themselves as American Indian on the "race" question in the same census. As a consequence, some unknown percentage of the American Indian women analyzed here (conceivably up to a quarter) could have given white as their "race." Regretfully, we are not in a position to delve into this further. It is almost certain that additional refinements would still not undercut the relative intermarriage position of American Indians compared with the other non-European groups considered in Table 7.8.

[38]Reported in Francis M. Rogers, "Portuguese," in Stephan Thernstrom, ed., *Harvard Encyclopedia of American Ethnic Groups* (Cambridge, MA: Belknap Press, 1980), pp. 813–20.

non-European groups. The intermarriage rates are low and, for the most part, fairly uniform among the white groups. If there is an "ethnic effect," it is largely drowned out by the general "white effect" on marriages across these lines. The numbers are too small to make much of this, but the overall patterns suggest that the small differences between ethnic groups are as likely to be a reflection of proximity as of anything else. On the other hand, the results in Table 7.8 do show that there are genuine differences in the outmarriage levels that white groups have with men of these different origins—particularly when composition is taken into account.

Religious and Spatial Influences on Intermarriage

Religious Influences

Above and beyond the relative sizes of the ethnic groups, two of the factors most widely mentioned as affecting intermarriage are religion and spatial proximity. Interest in the influence of religion goes back to the pioneering work of Ruby Jo Reeves Kennedy,[39] whose studies of New Haven, Connecticut, showed ethnic intermarriage among whites increasing through the decades, but in a nonrandom way such that ethnic intermarriages tended to be within religious lines—that is, Protestants disproportionately outmarry other Protestants, Roman Catholics select other Catholics, and Jews select other Jews. From a different perspective, Duncan and Lieberson and Lieberson[40] observed that the level of a group's residential segregation influenced the apparent frequency of intermarriage experienced by the group ("apparent" because the measure was necessarily rough).

More recently, Peach[41] has re-examined these two basic results, arguing that the latter studies have implications that contradict Kennedy's thesis: Since the Irish are highly segregated from some of the heavily Roman Catholic groups from SCE Europe but are not very segregated from the largely Protestant groups of northwestern Europe (for example, British and Scandinavians), Peach[42] questions the idea of a triple melting

[39]"Single or Triple Melting Pot? Intermarriage Trends in New Haven, 1870–1940," *American Journal of Sociology* 49 (1944):331–39; and "Single or Triple Melting Pot? Intermarriage in New Haven, 1870–1950," *American Journal of Sociology* (1952):56–59.

[40]Otis Dudley Duncan and Stanley Lieberson, "Ethnic Segregation and Assimilation," *American Journal of Sociology* 64 (1959):364–74; Stanley Lieberson, *Ethnic Patterns in American Cities* (New York: Free Press, 1963a).

[41]Ceri Peach, "Ethnic Segregation and Ethnic Intermarriage: A Reexamination of Kennedy's Triple Melting Pot in New Haven, 1900–1950," in Ceri Peach, Vaughan Robinson, and Susan Smith, eds., *Ethnic Segregation in Cities* (London: Croom Helm, 1981).

[42]Peach, "Ethnic Segregation," pp. 194–95.

pot on the basis that segregation patterns would prevent such an outcome. Moreover, since some of the Catholic SCE European groups are
highly segregated from all other white ethnic groups, there is also the
question of whether there would be much intermarriage at all for such
groups.

Clearly, Peach has performed a great service in reopening the triple
melting pot hypothesis, a perspective that he correctly argues is more or
less taken for granted as a point of departure for many scholars.[43] In our
estimation, the religious issue and the segregation question are not necessarily contradictory if we subscribe to the possibility that both are
independently affecting the choices of mates. The extensive data on intermarriage that have been drawn from the 1980 census—albeit still less
than ideal—provide an exceptional opportunity to consider the influence of these factors on intermarriage between specific ethnic combinations. Rather than talk about separate melting pots for Protestants
and Roman Catholics, we will examine the role of religion (and later
segregation) for each specific group in terms of the mates chosen from
other ethnic groups.

In its most general form, the ideal way of determining the influence
of religion on marital choice would entail learning of each person's religious upbringing along with religious practices when the person and
his/her future mate first met. Religion at the time of marriage—let
alone as reported afterward by married couples, is too easily distorted by
adjustments and changes that reflect the marital experience, preferences
of mates, plans for children, and so on. We are unable to consider this
issue here in this way. The census obtains no information about religion, let alone in the form that would be most appropriate. Instead we
resort to a reasonable approximation through ecological correlations
based on the percentages reporting themselves as Roman Catholic in the
National Opinion Research Center (NORC) General Social Surveys
through 1980 (in which respondents were asked: "In what religion were
you raised?") The figures ranged widely from only 5 and 6 percent for
those of Scottish, English, and Welsh origin to 90 percent and higher for
Italians and Portuguese (see Table 7.9).

In a number of cases religion plays an important role in the outmarriage patterns. We determined the percentage of women from different ethnic groups who have husbands from some specific predominantly
non-Catholic ethnic group. We then considered whether these figures
correlated (inversely) with the percentage Roman Catholic in the 15
groups. For example, the percentage of women aged 25–34 who are married to Scottish men ranges from 0 for single-ancestry Hungarian and
Portuguese women to 6.94 for Welsh women. Since only 5 percent of

---

[43]Peach, "Ethnic Segregation," p. 194.

Scots are Roman Catholic, we would expect the percentage of women marrying Scottish men to correlate inversely with the Roman Catholic percentage of their group. This is precisely what happens; the Spearman rank-order correlation is $-.63$ between the degree of Catholicism in a group and the percentage marrying Scottish men ($P = .005$). Significant negative correlations are found for the men from several other groups that have minimal Roman Catholic affiliation—namely, Welsh, English, and Danes (Table 7.9, column 2). In addition, the correlation for Swedes is barely above the .05 level ($P = .06$). At the other extreme, for two groups that are heavily Roman Catholic—Poles and Italians—there are significant *positive* correlations between the propensity of women to marry men of either of these origins and the degree of Catholicism reported for their group.

This pattern does not show up in the marital choices involving either Norwegian or Dutch men; in both groups less than 10 percent report themselves as Roman Catholic, but the percentages of women who marry such men do not correlate particularly with the women's level of Catholic affiliation. The situation is ambiguous for men of German, Irish, and French origin since they are not overwhelmingly associated with one religion or the other; the NORC study finds a substantial segment that is Protestant and another that is Roman Catholic in each of these groups.[44] Germans, who are 20 percent Roman Catholic, do show a negative correlation (almost significant) between the percentage of women marrying German men and the percentage Catholic of the women's ethnic group (Table 7.9, column 2). On the other hand, the correlations for the Irish and French are not significant. It is unfortunate that we cannot analyze marital choice separately for the Catholic and Protestant subsets of the German, Irish, and French groups in the same way as Greeley examined socioeconomic differences between such ethnoreligious combinations.[45] Furthermore, a stronger analysis beyond the purview of this study, and probably unjustified by the limited data, would entail a more detailed analysis of the religious composition of these groups. (For example, the Lutheran component of the Protestant population varies considerably by ethnic group.)

Overall, religion has a distinct impact on contemporary patterns of ethnic intermarriage. The evidence is clear that the level of outmarriage

---

[44]The Irish may be a surprise, but there clearly is a numerically important segment of the population who report Irish ethnic origin and are Protestants. Bear in mind the substantial Irish population located in the South. Also a sizable segment of the Irish have been in the United States a long time and, with intermarriage, their descendants have had the opportunity to shift away from the Catholic church. Finally, in the ambiguous situation faced by a significant number of whites when asked to indicate their ethnicity, there may be a propensity to differentially emphasize Irish as a response.

[45]Andrew M. Greeley, *Ethnicity in the United States* (New York: Wiley, 1974), chap. 3.

TABLE 7.9

Influence of Religion and Spatial Segregation (Census Divisions)
on Intermarriage with 15 Other European Groups, 1980

| | | Spearman Rank-Order Correlations | |
Group	Percentage Catholic	Percentage Catholic	Divisional Segregation from the Groups
English	6.4%	−.57[b]	−.62[b]
German	20.4	−.40	−.63[b]
Irish	39.0	.22	−.20
French	44.2	.07	−.15
Italian	90.4	.61[b]	−.52[a]
Scottish	5.0	−.63[b]	−.55[a]
Polish	79.6	.46[a]	−.79[b]
Dutch	9.8	−.11	−.13
Swedish	7.2	−.41	−.77[b]
Norwegian	6.5	.08	−.50[a]
Russian	13.4	.34	−.42
Czech	67.1	−.03	−.49[a]
Hungarian	39.0	.15	−.72[b]
Welsh	6.4	−.47[a]	−.24
Danish	6.5	−.60[b]	−.89[b]
Portuguese	96.7	.23	−.34

[a] $p < .05$.

[b] $p \leq .01$.

between different ethnic groups is affected by this religious factor. This
is best summarized by considering the direction and strength of the set
of rank correlations reported in Table 7.9, column 2. There is a rank
order correlation of .81 between the percentage of the group reporting
themselves as Roman Catholic (column 1) and the sign and direction of
the correlations reported in column 2. In other words, groups with relatively few Catholics tend to have large negative correlations in the propensity of their men to be married to "Catholic groups"; groups with a
sizable percentage Catholic tend to have large positive correlations with
Catholicism in their outmarriages.

Spatial Influences

Spatial segregation between the groups also influences the frequency of various marital combinations. For each of the 16 groups, there
is a negative correlation between their level of segregation from each of
the remaining 15 groups and the percentage of women in each of these

15 groups who marry men from the origin under consideration (Table 7.9, column 3).[46] The Spearman correlations vary considerably, from − .13 for the Dutch to − .89 for the Danish, with the vast majority being statistically significant. In view of this connection between spatial proximity and the levels of intermarriage with specific white groups, the apparent long-term maintenance of distinctive spatial patterns attains added significance (reported in Chapter 3). If the ethnic groups continue to maintain their distinctive current patterns of residential concentration in the United States, we can expect differential levels of intermarriage between various ethnic combinations in the nation—with certain combinations being far more common and others less so—even if the groups were to be fully indifferent to the ethnic origins of their prospective mates.

Further Issues

Questions raised by these results can be posed here even if the answers await further work. Although most of the ethnic groups exhibit intermarriage patterns that are affected by their spatial patterns and/or religious makeup, the Irish, French, Dutch, and Portuguese respond to neither. We can only speculate about why these groups are exceptions. The Portuguese pattern may reflect the relative recency of the bulk of their migration; hence they may not be as assimilated as the other groups. The Irish are a heterogeneous and complicated category in the United States. On the one hand, there are the Scotch-Irish, an important stock in the early peopling of the United States; on the other hand, there are the Irish Catholics who migrated in such substantial numbers beginning in the mid-nineteenth century. We are unable to distinguish these two subsets very easily, except when the Scotch-Irish give a mixed-ancestry response rather than simply reporting themselves as "Irish." But a fairly substantial number of all persons giving a single-ancestry Irish response do reside in the South. Indeed, 35 percent do, a figure exceeded only by the English (52 percent) and equaled only by the French. Thus, this uncontrolled heterogeneity may be the reason for the difficulty in finding these spatial patterns operating. The inability to tabulate census data by religion may be a severe problem for a group with such an overall split in their rates. In terms of the issues raised by Peach, it may well be that the absence of such a correlation for the Irish

---

[46]The reader is again reminded of the various cautions discussed earlier about the proximity issues generally, let alone when such broad areal units as the census Geographical Divisions are used.

reflects two pushes toward intermarriage that operate in different directions; a push toward marrying persons with a common religion and a push toward marrying persons close at hand. Since, for the Irish, these may well not be the same groups, the zero-order correlations are relatively weak for this group.

As for the French, there may be a problem of a similar nature; namely, several fundamentally different components located in different parts of the nation are all confused and pooled under this rubric. This includes French Canadians who migrated to New England and elsewhere in the nineteenth and early twentieth century; French in Louisiana, who are the descendants of both earlier forced migrants from Canada as well as those migrating from Europe at the time of French control; and the descendants of early French migrants and explorers to elsewhere in the United States in the colonial periods and later. Finally, we are unable to even speculate about the reasons for the low correlation that Dutch show with either religion or spatial patterns in terms of the factors affecting their relative levels of outmarriage with different groups.

There is evidence that a considerable amount of intermarriage is occurring between the single-ancestry ethnic components of the white population of the United States. This pattern of intermarriage is found even though inmarriage is still occurring far above the levels expected if only population composition was affecting choice. Nevertheless, outmarriage combinations vary greatly—even when the size of the available male segment of each group is taken into account. In this regard, both the spatial distribution and the religious makeup of the groups affect which of the combinations are especially likely or unlikely to occur.

The Behavior of Selected Mixed Combinations

What are the marital choices made by white women of mixed ethnic origins?[47] Table 7.10 indicates the mates of such women for a limited number of major combinations. As an illustration of what these data mean, consider the first combination shown in the table: women of mixed English-German ancestry. For ease of comparison, the mixed combination is sandwiched between the relevant groups. The three relevant columns allow us to compare the husbands of such women with

[47]This section is based in part on Stanley Lieberson and Mary C. Waters, "Ethnic Mixtures in the United States," *Sociology and Social Research* 70 (1985):43–52. The analysis here is restricted to currently married women in their first marriages who are married to men who are also in their first marriages.

TABLE 7.10

Marriages of Specific Multiple-Origin Women Compared with Those of Single-Origin Women

Husband	Wife		
	English Only	English-German	German Only
English	67.00%	46.00%	18.00%
German	15.00	44.00	54.00
Neither	21.00	28.00	32.00
Odds of English	2.03	.85	1.17
German		.79	

Husband	Wife		
	German Only	German-Italian	Italian Only
German	54.00%	41.00%	15.00%
Italian	3.00	19.00	50.00
Neither	43.00	42.00	36.00
Odds of German	1.17	.69	1.00
Italian		.23	

Husband	Wife		
	English Only	English-Irish	Irish Only
English	67.00	44.00	17.00
Irish	10.00	37.00	44.00
Neither	24.00	35.00	41.00
Odds of English	2.03	.79	.79
Irish		.59	

Husband	Wife		
	German Only	German-Polish	Polish Only
German	54.00	45.00	18.00
Polish	3.00	20.00	40.00
Neither	44.00	42.00	44.00
Odds of German	1.17	.82	.67
Polish		.25	

TABLE 7.10 (continued)

	English Only	English-Italian	Italian Only		Irish Only	Irish-Italian	Italian Only
English	67.00	37.00	11.00	Irish	44.00	36.00	16.00
Italian	2.00	16.00	50.00	Italian	6.00	24.00	50.00
Neither	31.00	49.00	40.00	Neither	51.00	43.00	35.00
Odds of English	2.03	.59	1.00	Odds of Irish	.79	.56	1.00
Italian		.19		Italian		.32	

	English Only	English-Polish	Polish Only		Irish Only	Irish-Polish	Polish Only
English	67.00	33.00	9.00	Irish	44.00	34.00	13.00
Polish	1.00	13.00	40.00	Polish	3.00	14.00	40.00
Neither	32.00	57.00	51.00	Neither	53.00	54.00	48.00
Odds of English	2.03	.49	.67	Odds of Irish	.79	.52	.67
Polish		.15		Polish		.16	

	German Only	German-Irish	Irish Only		Italian Only	Italian-Polish	Polish Only
German	54.00	46.00	23.00	Italian	50.00	28.00	8.00
Irish	16.00	37.00	44.00	Polish	6.00	17.00	40.00
Neither	34.00	34.00	38.00	Neither	45.00	57.00	52.00
Odds of German	1.17	.85	.79	Odds of Italian	1.00	.39	.67
Irish		.59		Polish		.20	

NOTE: The percentages sum to more than 100 because some husbands have both of the ancestries specified.

the marital patterns among women of unmixed German ancestry and of unmixed English ancestry, what might be called the two "root groups." For women who are of part English and part German ancestry, the appropriate column shows the percentages in their first marriage with husbands reported to have at least some English ancestry. These can be compared with the marital choices made by women of either unmixed English origin or unmixed German origin. (The comparisons between mixed and single members in Table 7.10 are not affected by composition since the same men are eligible for a marriage with any of these sets of women.) At present 46 percent of mixed English-German women in their first marriage have a husband who has at least some English ancestry (the percentages married to men who are English only, mixed English and German, mixed English and some non-German group, and English-German-Irish triplets are, respectively, 11, 16, 17, and 1). Also, 44 percent of such women are married to men who report at least some German ancestry. And, finally, 28 percent of women of mixed German-English ancestry are married to men who report neither German nor English ethnic origin.[48]

The two root groups, women of single English ancestry and women of single German ancestry, provide appropriate comparisons for the mixed-ancestry women. They permit us to see how far the marital choices of mixed persons are from the appropriate single-ancestry compatriots. Mixed English-German women favor English men to a lesser degree than do women of unmixed English ancestry (46 versus 67 percent); likewise, they favor German men to a lesser degree than do women of unmixed German ancestry (44 versus 54 percent). Nevertheless, it is clear that their ties are still strong with men of both groups. Whereas, 18 percent of single-ancestry German women are married to men with some English ancestry, the figure is considerably higher for the mixed women. The same pattern also holds when the propensity of mixed women to marry German men is compared with the marital behavior of women with only English ancestry. In this particular situation, we see that mixed German-English women still show strong ties to both ancestry groups, albeit the ties are weaker than those for women with a single ancestry. The net effect is that 28 percent of such mixed-ancestry women are married to men who report neither English nor German ancestry. This is somewhat higher than the figure for single-ancestry English women (21 percent) and it is actually *lower* than the figure for single-ancestry German women (32 percent).

[48]The figures can sum to more than 100 percent here and elsewhere in Table 7.10. This occurs when women are married to men who appear in both the first and second rows. In this case, husbands who are of both German and English ancestry will be reported twice, as is appropriate.

240

Without exception, this pattern is repeated with all of the combinations considered; the level of ingroup marriage for women of mixed ancestry falls between the levels found for the root groups. Among women of mixed German-Irish ancestry, for example, 46 percent have husbands with some German ancestry; a figure that is lower than the German ingroup propensity (54) but distinctly above the unmixed Irish propensity to marry Germans (23). Likewise, 37 percent of the mixed women are married to men with some Irish ancestry—again, a value which falls between the single-ancestry Irish women (44 percent) and the single-ancestry German women (16 percent). Thus, mixed-ancestry persons occupy intermediate positions between their root ancestry groups in their propensity to marry endogamously.

The groups, however, are not equally strong in their relative pulls and a variety of outcomes are found. Women of part German or part Irish origin—in the combinations examined here—always show rather strong pulls toward inmarriage with German or Irish men, respectively. The rate toward their own group is more akin to the single-ancestry women of their root group than it is like the other root group. For example, women reporting unmixed Irish ancestry have Irish husbands 44 percent of the time; women reporting unmixed Italian ancestry have Irish husbands 16 percent of the time. The relevant rate for mixed Irish-Italian women is 36 percent, far closer to the rate for the Irish root group than for the Italian root group. The opposite holds for women of mixed Italian and mixed Polish ancestry. In all of the combinations examined here, their propensity toward marrying Italian or Polish men, respectively, is less like the root group's propensity than it is like the other group's. Thus, women of mixed Irish-Italian origin select Italian men 24 percent of the time, a figure closer to the 6 percent for single-ancestry Irish women than the 50 percent for single-ancestry Italian women. The pattern for women of part English ancestry fluctuates; in some combinations their propensity to marry English men is closer to the behavior of single-ancestry English women, and in other cases it is closer to the rate for the other group.

We can examine this more formally by considering for each specific group the odds for mixed members selecting a mate who also matches that group (in part or whole). In the case of single-ancestry German women, 54 percent are married to men with at least some German ancestry. Accordingly, the odds of their picking someone of German origin, as we saw in Chapter 6, is $54/(100-54) = 1.17$. The odds for a woman of mixed German origin picking a mate with some German ancestry is uniformly high, running from about 60 to 70 percent of that figure in each of the combinations considered. For example, in the case of English-German combinations, 44 percent have husbands with some

German ancestry. Hence their odds of inmarriage are 44/56 = .79, which is 67 percent of the odds for single-ancestry German women. The results for Irish women are only slightly higher, ranging from 65 to 74 percent in each combination from the inmarriage ratio for unmixed Irish women. The average is lower and the dispersion greater for women of mixed English ancestry. The odds of selecting an English husband runs from about 42 to 24 percent of the odds for unmixed English women, depending on the particular mixture involved.[49] Polish women have a somewhat lower level of conformity with their unmixed compatriots, but their variation is narrower than the English, running from 24 to 32 percent of the ingroup odds for single-ancestry Polish women. The results for Italians are very close to that for Poles with respect to both the average and the dispersion about the average.

Marital Patterns

These ethnic differences mean that there are several distinctive marital patterns resulting from the intermixing of the population—a far more complicated situation than has hitherto been envisioned. One pattern, which is well illustrated by the Irish-German mixture, involves rather strong pulls toward inmarriage with each root group. These mixed-ancestry women are married to Irish men at close to the frequency found for women of unmixed Irish ancestry. However, their rate of marriage with German men is close to the level for single-ancestry German women. The net effect, given these double pulls, is not much of an increase in their propensity to marry persons who are of neither German nor Irish ancestry (34 percent versus 34 and 38 percent for single-ancestry German women and single-ancestry Irish women, respectively). This pattern, with a double strong pull, is also found among women of mixed English-Irish ancestry and mixed English-German ancestry. Marriage to the remaining population falls somewhere between the rates for the root groups. These three combinations represent situations in which relatively strong pulls toward the inmarriage patterns of the root group continue to operate. It is particularly striking for the Irish and Germans.

Another pattern is found among mixed-ancestry women when one ancestry component is German or Irish and the other component is Polish or Italian. In these cases, the ancestry tie with either the German or Irish group is relatively close to the root group's rate, but the choice of

[49]Formal tests of the differences in means and dispersion are not appropriate because the number of cases is so small.

Italian or Polish mates is much weaker than that for the Italian or Polish root group. This was observed earlier for Irish-Italian women and is repeated for women of mixed Irish-Polish, German-Italian, and German-Polish origins. In the last combination, for example, Table 7.10 shows that the propensity to marry German men has not dropped off from the propensity of single-ancestry German women anywhere as greatly as has the decline in the propensity of women of Polish ancestry to marry Polish men. A third pattern exists for the English-Italian, English-Polish, and Italian-Polish mixes. Here there is a much more pronounced decline in inmarriage rates for both root groups and an especially strong propensity to marry mates who share neither of these origins. In the English-Polish example, the propensity to marry men of English origin (33 percent) is closer to the rate for women of single Polish ancestry and the propensity to marry men of Polish origin (13 percent) is closer to the rate for the English root group. As a consequence, the percentage of English-Polish women who marry men of neither ancestry (57) is higher than for either of the root groups.

An interesting result in Table 7.10 is that mixed-ancestry women do not necessarily have levels of outmarriage in excess of those experienced by both of the root groups. The behavior of mixed Italian-Polish women represents the kind of pattern that we expected in general; their level of outmarriage (57 percent) is greater than that for either of the single-ancestry roots (45 and 52 percent).[50] Such a result should occur if women of mixed origin are, by virtue of their being mixed, less strongly identified with their ethnic roots. In addition, we know that mixed-ancestry people are on the average of greater generational length of residence in the United States than single-ancestry people and hence likely to have weaker ethnic ties. However, such a result is found in only four of the ten situations considered in Table 7.10. In addition to the Italian-Polish mixture, English-Polish, English-Italian, and Irish-Polish women marry men of neither root origins more frequently than do either of the single-ancestry compatriots. In one case, German-Polish mixes, the women are less likely to outmarry (42 percent of the time) than are single-ancestry German or Polish women (44 percent of the time). This difference is small, to be sure, but certainly it is in the opposite direction from what one might expect. In any case, the outmarriage rates for

[50]Although the marriage of a single-ancestry Italian woman to a non-Italian man with Polish origins does not count as an inmarriage by any criterion, we include such marriages here in order to cope with the fact that women of mixed Italian-Polish origin do have inmarriages when mated with non-Italian husbands with at least some Polish ancestry. This procedure is used throughout in order to have directly comparable measures of outmarriage that are not affected by shifts in population composition. Thus, in discussing outmarriage for a given mixed combination, an identical definition of outmarriage is used for the relevant root groups.

mixed women occupy an intermediate position in the remaining five combinations—higher than those for one root group but lower than the others.

Speculations About Marital Patterns

The most striking finding is that, in some mixes, there is not a very sharp decline from the ethnic endogamy patterns exhibited by unmixed persons with a common ancestry. This appears to be the case for two of our most important groups, the Germans and the Irish, and the rate for the mixed-ancestry English is still high in some cases, albeit there is more of a downward shift from the level reported for the single-ancestry English. So there is by no means any indication that mixed ethnicity leads to rapid disintegration of ethnic influences on choice of mate. On the other hand, for at least the two SCE European groups considered, there is a strong shift in that direction. The reasons for these differences between certain groups and/or combinations remain to be determined, but it will take better data and cross-tabulations than have hitherto been used. The point, however, is that the marital choices of the mixed persons examined here are in all cases still influenced by their ancestral roots. Continued intermarriage will lead to an increasing number of mixed persons within the white population and, in turn, such mixed persons have different marital patterns than the unmixed root groups. However, in varying degrees for mixed persons, the choice of mate is still strongly affected by their origins.

Because social conditions are not similar for the mixed and unmixed components of a given ethnic group with respect to such key factors as geographic location, parental dispositions, and socioeconomic position, we are unable to attribute differences between mixed and unmixed persons entirely to the effect of mixing per se. Likewise, there are important generational differences between women of mixed and single ancestry—the former on the average having more generations in the United States and hence more exposure to assimilation. This could mean that the propensity of mixed persons still to follow the marital choice patterns of their unmixed compatriots is—if anything—probably underestimated from what would appear if generational effects were also considered.

In terms of the original questions raised in this section, we conclude that ethnic forces are still strong among those of mixed ancestry. The act of intermarriage is certainly an appropriate indicator, ceteris paribus, of assimilation and identification. However, the offspring of many such combinations are still very much affected by their parental ancestry in their choice of mate. The contrast between the modest decline for some of the larger northwestern European groups and the relatively massive shifts experienced recently for the SCE European populations, however, could be due to a variety of factors. The generational progression among the newer European groups probably played a central role in their sharper decline; movement from first to second and third generation has more impact than changes between, say, third and fifth generations. Another possibility is that single-ancestry members of the German and Irish groups have relatively moderate tendencies toward endogamy at present and there is likewise relatively little aversion toward them by others. This means that there is not a drastic reduction for those persons who are only partly affiliated with these groups. A very different possibility is that mixed persons tend to identify strongly with the German or Irish element and hence the effect of mixing is to reduce only moderately the group's influence while largely reducing the other group's impact.

Yet another possibility is that there are important and systematic reporting errors operating such that there are distortions in the genealogical roots in a nonrandom way. This is difficult to ascertain with the data available, although Chapter 8 provides strong evidence of intragenerational shifts in the ancestry declared by persons. In such a case there could be some remarkable shifts in the ancestries that white Americans *report* as opposed to the genealogical roots that they have. The fact remains, however, that many persons reporting themselves as belonging to two ethnic ancestries also report that their spouse shares with them a common ancestry. Such pairings still operate to an impressive degree in the United States even as the mixed nature of the population increases.

Summary

Several major issues about intermarriage are raised in this chapter. First, why do the ethnic groups differ in their rates of intermarriage? In part, the levels of exogamy reflect group differences in their numerical size and their geographical distribution in the country. Additionally, after these factors are taken into account, the SCE European ethnic groups have relatively higher levels of inmarriage than those from northern and western Europe. This gap between the old and new Europeans is linked with a cluster of attributes (at least on the cross-sectional basis) that are not easily analyzed separately: generation, degree of mix, social attitudes toward the groups, and so on.

Second, why has intermarriage been increasing substantially in successive cohorts for all of these European groups? Changes in composition do not account for the declines in inmarriage—indeed, some of the groups with the sharpest drops in endogamy are groups that have actually increased slightly in their proportion of the population. The changing generational makeup of the groups is an important force in accounting for these increases. With successive cohorts, even the newer European groups are increasingly of at least three generations' residence in the United States. The results for changes in the Bogardus social distance scale as well as for the rise in the proportion who are of mixed ancestry, are unclear. The intercohort shifts for those of single ancestry provide some evidence of a broad societal shift in recent decades in a stronger disposition toward intermarriage.

Finally, among those who do outmarry, who are they outmarrying? It is certainly not non-Europeans; at present, there is still very little marriage across racial lines in the United States. Moreover, although the groups differ with respect to which specific white ethnic groups they are especially likely to marry, they are consistently low and rather uniform with respect to their tendencies to outmarry across racial lines. Among the European groups examined, religion and spatial segregation account for the choice of mate when outmarriages occur.

Because a growing segment of the population is outmarrying, the behavior of the offspring of such marriages is of increasing relevance. Are persons of mixed origin no longer affected by their ancestral roots? Or do they still lean toward the marital patterns of one or another of their root groups? The answer is not easily summarized since the patterns are quite complicated and vary between ethnic groups. Some mixed-ancestry people behave more like their fellow single-ancestry compatriots and some groups exhibit rather different patterns. Because this is the first time that data are available on the marital choices made by persons of specific mixed origins, much more will be learned when it is possible to analyze changes in such marital choices in future censuses.

8

CONCLUSIONS:
THE PRESENT AND THE FUTURE

Melting Pot Versus Cultural Pluralism

ALMOST all discussions of ethnic and racial groups in the United States ultimately address the issue of the melting pot versus cultural pluralism.[1] To what degree are the groups alike, and to what degree do they maintain their separate identities? More precisely, are the initial differences between the groups disappearing such that the groups are becoming indistinguishable for all purposes? The answer is too complicated for a simple yes or no.

First of all, it makes a difference which groups are being considered. Differences among white groups are for the most part dwarfed by comparison with the gaps we observe between whites and other groups. On most attributes, the most important division is between whites and non-European groups such as blacks and Hispanics, as well as peoples from Asia, Latin America, and the Caribbean. A principal finding of this study is that white ethnics, while different from one another on a variety of measures, are still much more similar to each other than they are

---

[1]Parts of this chapter appeared in Stanley Lieberson, "Unhyphenated Whites in the United States," *Ethnic and Racial Studies* 8 (1985b):159–80; and Stanley Lieberson and Mary C. Waters, "Ethnic Groups in Flux: the Changing Ethnic Responses of American Whites," *Annals of the American Academy of Political and Social Science* 487 (1986): 79–91.

to blacks, Hispanics, American Indians, and Asians. This gap is evident in our socioeconomic data and startlingly clear in our findings on intermarriage. While there still is a much higher degree of endogamy among white ethnic groups than one would expect by chance, the big gaps in who marries whom are between whites and nonwhites. The conclusion is inescapable: For whatever the cause(s), a European–non-European distinction remains a central division in the society.

As for the white groups, the answer to the melting pot question depends on the measure. In the preceding chapters, we have found that these white ethnic groups have become for all intents and purposes indistinguishable from one another on some dimensions. Nevertheless, on other measures the white groups retain very distinctive profiles which in some cases—such as residence and certain occupations—can be traced to their immigrant beginnings.

In this monograph we also considered a question which guided much of the previous research in the area of white ethnic groups: How relevant is the distinction between the old immigrant groups, primarily from northern and western Europe, and the newer European immigrant groups, primarily from southern-central-eastern (SCE) Europe? On this issue, too, we find a variety of outcomes. For the most part the wide gaps found between these groups in earlier decades in the United States have disappeared. This is true on measures such as education, occupation, and income. Yet some old-new differences are found in intermarriage levels, especially among older cohorts. Northern and western European groups had much higher levels of exogamy than groups from SCE Europe.

Timing and initial conditions of immigration still have lasting effects on some variables. The geographical distribution of ethnic groups is an example. As we have seen in Chapter 3, the initial location of European immigrants in the United States has strong influences on the ancestry distribution of the population in the various regions and metropolitan areas of the country. Such influences may last well into the future, for we found that ethnic ancestry still affects the location and destination of internal migrants in the nation. Moreover, there are still differences among these groups in the propensity to marry that can be traced back at least 50 years to patterns observed among the children of immigrants to the United States. (To be sure, we are unable to determine if the differences in ethnic intermarriage reflect distinctive generation- and age-specific propensities for white groups, or are strictly a function of their socioeconomic and opportunity differences partly generated by their different locations in the nation.) There is also remarkable evidence, reported by Salamon, of ethnic persistence and distinctiveness with respect to certain farming practices in the Midwest.

Comparing German and Irish farming communities in East Central Illinois, Salamon finds the persistence of ethnic values for family behavior and inheritance[2] and type of farming operation.[3] She also reports important differences between German Catholic and Yankee farmers in South Central Illinois:

> Despite similar farm soils and separation by only 20 miles, significant differences exist between the communities in farm size and organization. German farms are smaller and diversified with dairy, hogs and beef, and grain in contrast to the larger Yankee monoculture grain operations. Farming strategies are demonstrated as selected within a context of ethnically derived family and farming goals, more complex than short-run profit optimization. Germans are motivated to replicate family farm and family land ownership in each generation, while Yankees are driven by more entrepreneurial motives. These contrasting farming strategies, it is argued, represent persistent parallel patterns in midwestern agriculture.[4]

We also reported some distinctive occupational patterns in 1980 that can be traced back to immigrant concentrations occurring 80 years earlier.

We have addressed another aspect of the melting pot question through our examination of the increasing proportion of people in the United States who are of mixed ethnic ancestry. (A substantial and growing segment of the white population is of mixed ethnic ancestry; in 1980, 37 percent of those giving at least one specific ancestry gave a multiple one.) The persistence of the ethnic factor in American life is also seen in the marital choices made by persons who are themselves of mixed ethnic origin. The evidence indicates that the component ancestries of mixed whites still influence the mates chosen by such individuals. In fact, persons of multiple origin are the embodiment of the mixed results we have found with reference to white ethnic groups. By their very existence mixed-ancestry individuals are evidence of a high degree of assimilation—marital assimilation among their parents, if not earlier generations. Yet the fact that these mixed-ancestry individuals display at least some similarity in behavior and characteristics with their single-ancestry compatriots attests to the continuing influence of ethnic membership on American individuals. The 1980 census, by al-

---

[2]Sonya Salamon, "Ethnic Differences in Farm Family Land Transfers," *Rural Sociology* 45 (1980):290–308.

[3]Sonya Salamon, "Sibling Solidarity as an Operating Strategy in Illinois Agriculture," *Rural Sociology* 47 (1982):349–68.

[4]Sonya Salamon, "Ethnic Communities and the Structure of Agriculture," *Rural Sociology* 50 (1985):323–40.

lowing mixed-ancestry responses, provides a new and valuable source of information on whites of later generations' residence in the United States. This is the first time researchers have been able to address questions about the status and behavior of mixed-ancestry individuals on so large a scale. (While we have done some analyses of these very interesting mixed-ancestry people—especially with reference to intermarriage—there are important research questions about this population waiting to be addressed.)

Yet while white ethnic groups do maintain these distinctive patterns, on other measures the differences among them have disappeared. In Chapter 4 we saw that the rather large differences among immigrant women in their levels of fertility and the much higher fertility of European immigrant women compared with native-born American women has disappeared. The daughters and granddaughters of the European immigrants display fertility levels which are indistinguishable from one another and from the fertility of the United States as a whole.

On socioeconomic measures, too, what used to be a wide gulf between northwestern Europeans and SCE Europeans has all but disappeared. We find relatively little variation in the median years of schooling among the 16 specific white ethnic ancestries—the exception being the high educational median of Russian men. The gap in educational attainment between the SCE and northwestern European immigrants has disappeared. We find the same developments in the socioeconomic achievement of white ethnic groups. White groups are more like each other than unlike on income, occupation, and education measures. Again, the gap between whites and non-Europeans by comparison is still quite large.

The overall decline in socioeconomic and cultural differences between white ethnic groups—as well as the very high level of intermarriage across ethnic lines within the white population—is linked to an ethnic flux that we believe is occurring in contemporary America. As ethnic identity declines as a sociopolitical issue for white groups and as it loses the influence it once had on major life chances and behaviors, two processes seem to result. First, a proportion of the population also change their identification—identifying as "American" or "unhyphenated white." Second, although the majority of the population still report at least one European ancestry, many of these reports appear to involve distortions of the full array of their ancestral roots. For many respondents, the ethnic origin(s) they choose to report is becoming a choice made from within the set of ancestries in their histories. So the flux we describe below is made possible by, and in turn contributes to, the processes we have described throughout this book: the lessening of differences between white groups due to their assimilation. However, we are not simply concluding that these groups are assimilating; it is a much more complicated process than that; people assimilate on some attributes and not others—for example, income but not residence. Not only do variables differ, but so do people. Only some people lose their ancestral identification(s); many keep track of complicated multiple ancestries and report them in the census.

The 1980 census is the first to provide such extensive data on later generations. These data show two different processes operating at the same time within the white population: massive assimilation to the point of no longer knowing, or at least reporting, one's European origins; and continued identification such that many people report very detailed ancestries. This raises questions about measuring ancestry which are substantive as much as they are methodological: How is ancestry determined for people who are many generations removed from the original immigrants or who have ancestors from a variety of European sources? How do patterns of ethnic identification shift in the United States, and how can a census or other surveys measure such shifts? In any case, the flux and inconsistencies we report below would not be possible without the increasing generations of residence in the United States for European groups, a rather high level of intermarriage, and both the cultural and socioeconomic changes chronicled in earlier chapters.

Ethnic Flux

There is evidence of tremendous flux, uncertainty, and ethnic intermixing among the white groups we have studied. It is likely that this flux and ambiguity will be of increasing importance in the decades ahead, at least for the population of European origin. We also believe that this flux is contributing to the development of a growing proportion of the population who do not recall or do not declare a European ancestry but instead are "unhyphenated whites" who claim an American ancestry. In other words, a new ethnic category may be evolving in the United States; people who are able or willing to identify themselves solely as whites, and who have little or no interest in or knowledge of their European ancestry or origin. Of those who do not report a specific ancestry, it is impossible to determine how many do not know where their immigrant ancestors come from—compared with those who either reject any identification or feel it has no relevance for their own lives.

In this monograph we have looked at differences and similarities among the 33 ethnic and racial groups we defined in Chapter 1. But we have also been forced to consider the boundaries and definitions of these groups themselves. This is appropriate because these groups should be viewed not merely as static entities, but also as products of labeling and identification processes that change and evolve over time. Obviously, differentials in fertility, mortality, and migration will affect the size of a group. But beyond this, gradual shifts occur in the sets and subsets of groups found in a society such as to lead to both new combinations and new divisions. A continuous process of combining and recombining means that the very existence of a given group is not to be taken for granted; groups appear and disappear. Ethnic groups such as Mexicans or Puerto Ricans are essentially very recent, resulting from interethnic contacts only since the expansion of Europe into the New World. In similar fashion, the Coloured population in South Africa is a recent group. Older ethnic groups are also hybridized populations; the English ethnic population in the United Kingdom, for example, consists of the descendants stemming from European contact and expansion involving a number of different populations.

In short, when examining the racial and ethnic groups found in a given society, there is a tendency to take for granted their existence. In point of fact, a given racial or ethnic group does not go back to the origins of the human species. Rather, each ethnic group was created out of dynamic processes that may have taken place over periods far longer than a given individual's lifespan. Just as various species in the plant and animal worlds are continuously changing—even though it is normally possible to point to this species or that—so, too, ethnic groups are under continuous flux in terms of their birth, maintenance, and decline.

If people are asked for their ethnic ancestry at a given time, they are apt to give answers that largely fit under the rubrics established and conventional at the time. Responses that do not fit these rubrics tend to be viewed as "errors" or as failures of the enumeration instrument or the enumerator. And often that is the case. But, in addition, there is a continuous flux in the categories themselves and in the population of those who define themselves, or are defined by others, as belonging. And in this manner, there are shifts in racial and ethnic populations. It is possible—particularly at some intermediate stage of change—for some persons of X ancestry to identify themselves as belonging to ethnic group X while an increasing proportion with X ancestry are now reporting themselves as Y.

What we have then are processes that run counter to the goals and desires of both census takers and quantitative researchers. Through both intergenerational and intragenerational shifts of a nonrandom nature, changes occur that can mean inconsistency and less than full reliability—terms that are counter to the goals of most empirical instruments. Ethnic origin, from this point of view, is both a status and a process. At any given time, we are more likely to see the state of affairs reported by the population—it is less easy to see the process of ethnic change that is also going on. Indeed, some of the difficulties that researchers and census takers experience in using data on racial and ethnic groups are due not to problems of instrumentation or execution—such as might occur if a question was constructed incorrectly through, say, some vagueness or ambiguity of meaning. Rather some of the difficulties and inconsistencies reflect the processes of ethnic and racial change themselves; the "errors" are telling us something about the flux in the concepts and identifications themselves.

We believe that some of the "irregularities" we have discovered in the 1980 ancestry data are due to these processes of ethnic flux and development. The meanings of responses to the ancestry question are less sharp now than they were in the past and probably will be even less "accurate" in the future. In part this may be because the census question and the other indicators we use to test ancestry are not designed well enough to cope with the flux and changes occurring in American ethnic processes. The census question, specific instructions, and treatment of mixed-ancestry respondents are all discussed in Chapter 2. But even with the confusion we found in the design of the 1980 ancestry question, the responses to the census, in our opinion, do reflect real social phenomena that are occurring in the United States.

We present here three types of distortion and inconsistency in the 1980 data which can be interpreted as representing flux in the ethnic categories themselves, rather than simply as conventional respondent or enumeration errors. These are differences in the age distribution of persons of single and mixed ancestries, inconsistencies within families in the ancestry labeling of children and parents, and the association of education and marital status with the nature of the reported ancestry. The data indicate that there are shifts in ethnic affiliation through two different processes, both changes over the lifetime of an individual as well as intergenerational changes between parent and child.[5]

Age Distribution

Ethnic identification may change within someone's lifespan through a variety of ways. A complicated ancestral history can slowly change and be simplified by forgetting or unlearning some parts of it. Even some details of a relatively simple ancestral history could be distorted and changed during a person's lifetime. In either case, there would be a deterioration in

[5]Lieberson, "Unhyphenated Whites."

the detail with which ancestral history is reported. Certainly, too, there is the question of self-identification, particularly after people reach an age where they are removed from parental pressures and control. At such a point, certain changes in self-identification may be freer to come out and, in turn, can affect the ancestral roots reported by the respondent.

There is a certain natural drift mechanism causing simplification and distortion. Namely, indifference to one's ethnic origin will lead to the loss of detailed or even partly accurate information on ancestry. Once this occurs, it is unlikely that the details will be recovered in later generations, although there is the possibility via grandparents or from other relatives such as aunts or uncles. Hence, for the most part, any de-emphasis or loss of interest in ethnic origins will lead to permanent losses of information and, as a consequence, possibly newer, vaguer, and simpler identification schemes. In that sense, change can occur only in the direction toward distortion, and inaccuracy, and new delineations. Whether new delineations or distortions of old ones result is an open question at this point, with no clear principles operating.

An examination of age data suggests that there is significant simplification and distortion of ethnic ancestry at the point where sizable numbers of children leave home and begin to report ancestry on their own, as opposed to having their parents provide the ethnic labels. Because intermarriage among white groups has increased, we would expect the percentage of the population reporting multiple ethnic origins as opposed to a single ethnic ancestry to be progressively larger for younger age groups. In fact, there was a very sharp increment in the single-ancestry component beginning with those aged 18–24 (Table 8.1). The

TABLE 8.1

Type of Ancesty Response, by Age, 1979

| Age | Percentage Reporting | | |
	Single	Mixed	Other
Under 5	34.5%	49.2%	16.3%
5–13	33.9	50.2	15.9
14–17	32.3	49.2	18.5
18–24	40.6	40.5	18.9
25–34	48.0	34.9	17.1
35–44	48.7	33.2	18.1
45–54	50.8	31.8	17.5
55–64	52.1	31.2	16.8
65 and Over	55.9	27.0	17.2

SOURCE: Stanley Lieberson and Mary C. Waters, "Ethnic Groups in Flux: The Changing Ethnic Responses of American Whites," *Annals of the American Academy of Political and Social Science* 487 (1986):79–91, table 1.

TABLE 8.2

Ancestry Response for Persons with at least Three Generations of Residence in the United States

Age	Type of Ancestry Reported			
	Single	Double	Triple	All Other
Under 5	41.0%	47.0%	5.7%	6.3%
5–9	40.6	46.8	6.2	6.4
10–14	39.3	49.0	5.9	5.8
15–19	40.2	46.0	6.4	7.4
20–24	50.0	37.3	4.0	8.7
25–29	52.8	35.5	2.8	8.9
30–34	53.3	35.3	3.0	8.4
35–39	52.9	34.7	3.3	9.1
40–44	53.3	34.5	3.3	8.9
45–49	53.5	34.1	3.8	8.6
50–54	53.7	34.0	3.2	9.1
55–59	52.6	35.3	4.3	7.8
60–64	54.1	34.2	3.7	8.0
65 and Over	56.9	31.2	3.8	8.1

SOURCE: Stanley Lieberson and Mary C. Waters, "Ethnic Groups in Flux: The Changing Ethnic Responses of American Whites," *Annals of the American Academy of Political and Social Science* 487 (1986):79–91, table 2.

percentage of the population with single ancestry jumped up sharply in the young adult ages from 32 percent at ages 14–17, to 41 percent at ages 18–24, and then to 48 percent at ages 25–34. It was relatively stable in the younger ages, when parents did the ethnicity reporting for their offspring, as well as in the later ages.

This tendency toward the simplification of ethnic origins is dramatically demonstrated in Table 8.2, where the analysis is confined to the population with at least three generations' residence in the United States. This generational restriction reduces the disturbance on the cross-sectional age data due to immigration patterns.[6] Going from youngest to oldest respondents, we find the percentage with single ancestry to be relatively stable up through respondents aged 15–19. Immediately after that point, however, there was a sharp increase from 40 to 50 percent in the single-ancestry component of those aged 20–24. Accompanying these changes was a sharp decline in the numbers reporting either two ancestries or one of the triple-ancestry combinations used in the census, such as English-German-Irish.

[6]The relative distribution of the categories in Table 8.2 is different from Table 8.1 not only because the former is restricted to the third generation, but also because Table 8.1 includes people who have not specified any generation.

The triple ancestries which the census allowed show a linkage with age which is both dramatic and compatible with the thesis advanced here. The high point for triple ancestry among those of at least three generations' residence in the nation was at ages 15–19, where 6.4 percent of the respondents were reported to have one of the 17 triplets reported by the census. In the next oldest group, ages 20–24, triple ancestry was reported by 4.0 percent, followed by 2.8 percent among those aged 25–29. This sharp drop in the early adult ages is then followed by a relatively constant level of persons reporting these triple origins—albeit lower—among the older ages. These results also support the conjecture that American whites tend to simplify their more complex ancestral history as they move away from home and define themselves in their own, rather than their parents', terms.

Detailed analyses are consistent with this general pattern. For example, we examined the U.S. population who in 1980 reported either single or mixed German ancestry. Looking at the German-origin population by single year of age, those aged 17 and younger in 1980 who reported mixed German ancestry ranged narrowly from 12.2 to 12.8 percent. At the ages of separation, this percentage moved downward from 12.6 for those aged 17 to 10.5 for those aged 25. For approximately the same age group, the percentage of those who claimed single German ancestry increased from 4.0 at age 16 to 6.4 at age 25. The total percentage reporting themselves as German either exclusively or in combination with some other ancestry changed far less during the ages of early adult independence—from 16.6 at age 17 to 17.0 at age 25—than did the percentages for either of these two components separately. This pattern is repeated for a number of other large white ethnic groups as well.

A further analysis of the 1979 Current Population Survey[7] provides more support for this hypothesis. Table 8.3 reports the influence of living arrangements on the ancestry reported for third generation and later nonblack young adults. The young adults who are living on their own have a consistently higher percentage of single-ancestry responses, regardless of age. For instance, among 20-to-24-year-olds still living with relatives, 31.6 percent are reported to have a single ancestry; by contrast, a single ancestry is reported for 51.7 percent of those living on their own or with a spouse. The number of triple-ancestry responses is also dramatically higher among those living at home with their parents (7.3 percent of those aged 20–24 living at home compared with 2.8 percent of those living on their own). Finally, Waters also shows that the

[7]Mary C. Waters, "The Process and Content of Ethnic Identification: A Study of White Ethnics in Suburbia," unpublished doctoral dissertation, University of California, Berkeley, 1986.

TABLE 8.3

Age by Type of Ancestry by Living Arrangements,
Third Generation and Later, Nonblacks, 1979

Age	Ancestry			No Response	Total
	Single	Double	Triple		
INDEPENDENT:					
15–19 years	723	524	33	206	1,486
	(48.6%)	(35.3%)	(2.2%)	(13.9%)	
20–24 Years	4,655	3,108	251	988	9,002
	(51.7%)	(34.5%)	(2.8%)	(11.0%)	
25–29 Years	5,907	4,590	331	1,246	12,074
	(50.0%)	(38.0%)	(2.7%)	(10.3%)	
LIVING AT HOME:					
15–19 Years	4,050	7,523	1,099	1,011	13,683
	(29.6%)	(55.0%)	(8.0%)	(7.4%)	
20–24 Years	1,839	3,176	423	384	5,822
	(31.6%)	(54.6%)	(7.3%)	(6.5%)	
25–29 Years	575	770	85	105	1,535
	(37.4%)	(50.2%)	(5.6%)	(6.8%)	

SOURCE: Mary C. Waters, "The Process and Content of Ethnic Identification: A Study of White Ethnics in Suburbia," unpublished doctoral dissertation, University of California, Berkeley, 1986, table 5.6.

percentage of young adults unable or unwilling to give an ancestry response is much higher among those living away from their parents.

A note of caution is appropriate because the cross-sectional age data we are obliged to use here and elsewhere in this analysis are less than ideal and can be interpreted in other ways. A totally appropriate analysis of age-linked distortion requires comparisons between two different periods, a step that is not possible at this time because of data limitations that we hope will be remedied with the inclusion of a similar ethnic question in the 1990 census. So these results, although compatible with the perspective taken here, should be viewed as only one part of the array of evidence that points toward simplifications of ethnic heritage. Incidentally, a longitudinal analysis during an 11-year period of ethnic identification in the Soviet Union is compatible with our conclusions for the United States. Net reidentification occurred and was most common among those aged 9–18 at the initial period, followed by lesser shifts among those in their 20s and 30s.[8]

[8]See the analysis of ethnic distortions in the Soviet Union by Barbara A. Anderson and Brian B. Silver, "Estimating Russification of Ethnic Identity among Non-Russians in the U.S.S.R.," *Demography* 20 (1983):474–75.

Intergenerational Inconsistency

Intergenerational transmission of ethnic identity will also be severely distorted by the common situation in which children spend at least part of their life in a household in which at least one of the parents is absent through divorce, desertion, or death. Intergenerational knowledge can also be affected in situations where children are abandoned, children are raised by relatives on one side of the family, or promiscuity leads to no knowledge of father's origins. Finally, there is the possibility of intentional discontinuities between parents and children in which parents attempt to hide certain "less desirable" ethnic origins or in some way deemphasize or shift the ancestral history—as they know it to be—in terms of what is passed on to their offspring. To be sure "intentional" and "unintentional" are polar types in a continuum and many changes of this sort do not neatly fall into one category or the other.

In addition, some children may have only a modest interest in their ancestral origins. Others become interested too late to obtain accurate information from parents, who, by then, are deceased. In similar fashion, some parents may have little or no interest in discussing ancestral histories with their offspring. In all of this, intergenerational shift will occur largely in one direction—that is, from knowledge to ignorance, from detail to blur. Thus, unless exceptional effort is made, it is unlikely that knowledge about ancestral origins will be reclaimed in later generations. Such events can mean not only that members of later generations will be unable to respond, but also that responses are so inaccurate that a question on ancestry for some respondents begins to approximate a sociological form of the inkblot test.

There is considerable inconsistency in 1980 when the ethnic origins reported for children are compared with the origins indicated for their parents. One would expect complete consistency if biological parents report on their children. Hence, if the father is an X and the mother is a Y, then all of the children should be reported as XY, if ethnic origins are simply a matter of tracing known roots. If both parents are Zs, then each child ought to be a Z. A marriage between an AB and a CD should lead to reporting children as ABCD, and so forth. To examine the consistency between white parents and children we restricted our analysis to those children living at home, under age 18, in families where both father and mother were American-born, both were present, and both were in their first marriage. We also excluded families in which the number of children present exceeded the number ever born by the wife; this exclusion was a way of partly eliminating cases in which the child was adopted or otherwise not the biological offspring. Also eliminated

TABLE 8.4

Percentage of Correctly Labeled Children in Families
Where Each Parent Is of a Different Single Ancestry, 1980

| | Ancestry | |
Group	Father	Mother
English	57.7%	55.7%
German	65.4	65.9
Irish	65.3	66.3
French	62.3	60.5
Italian	71.5	72.9
Scottish	63.9	57.7
Polish	68.1	72.3
Dutch	60.3	62.1
Swedish	61.9	64.7
Norwegian	63.9	64.1
Russian	57.5	54.3
Czech	66.7	64.4
Hungarian	62.3	61.9
Welsh	59.2	58.8
Danish	62.8	57.7
Portuguese	60.9	62.9
Black	50.0	25.6
Mexican	41.3	46.6
Puerto Rican	37.9	43.4
Spanish[a]	40.8	38.1
American Indian	45.5	49.1

SOURCE: Stanley Lieberson and Mary C. Waters, "Ethnic Groups in Flux: The Changing Ethnic Responses of American Whites," *Annals of the American Academy of Political and Social Science* 487 (1986):79–91, table 3.

[a]Spanish-Other.

were those cases in which either parent reported more than one ancestry.[9]

In cases of intermarriage where the spouses each have a different single ethnic origin—say, the mother is an X and the father is a Y—a consistent response requires a multiple ethnic entry such that the children are reported to be XY. The consistency in these cases is remarkably low;

[9]Census procedures make it hard to examine the offspring when one or both parents report multiple origins. With certain exceptions described earlier, the census truncated the ethnic histories of persons reporting multiple ancestries, listing only the first two ancestries. As a consequence, we do not know if parents with two ancestries had listed additional ancestries for themselves and/or their children.

between only 50 and 65 percent of the children are labeled by their parents with the expected ancestries. For example, when a German father is married to a woman of single non-German ancestry, in only 65 percent of the cases do we find the children labeled with both parents' ancestries. Consistency is similarly low when the wife is of German ancestry and the husband is of some other single origin. Table 8.4 provides this information for a number of the larger groups, indicating high levels of inconsistency in all of the husband-wife combinations. Since intermarriage across ethnic lines has been an increasingly common phenomenon within the white population, a large number of offspring are reported in terms that are inconsistent with their parents. To be sure, inconsistent patterns could mean distortions in the origins reported for the parents rather than the offspring. Moreover, this result does not tell us how children describe their ethnic origins after they leave home. Still, the figures leave little doubt that a substantial number of the offspring of mixed marriages are not being correctly described in terms of what we know about their parental origins.

Consistency is far more common in what is probably the most ideal situation for maintaining intergenerational continuity, namely, in families where mother and father both report the same single ethnic ancestry. Under these circumstances, in the larger white groups we find ethnicity consistently reported for up to 95 percent of the children. In most cases it is in the low 90s, and in some cases a bit lower than that. Still, in homes where there was a reported first marriage between two parents of the same single ethnicity, at least 5 percent—and usually more—of the children are not reported as having the same single ethnicity. For example, among the children living in homes where both parents reported themselves to be of single unmixed German origin, only 94 percent of the children were also reported with the same single German ancestry. Of the remaining children, 3 percent were reported as having unknown ancestry, 1 percent as American, and 2 percent as having some other ethnicity such as a single non-German origin or a multiple ancestry that may or may not include German. The reader may be tempted to interpret this result as reflecting the existence of situations where indeed at least one of the reported parents is not the biological parent of the child. Although the distortions affected by divorce and remarriage are eliminated and some cases of adoption are excluded, we were still not able to avoid children born out of wedlock to a mother who later marries a different man, nor can we exclude all adopted children. However, in the case of mixed marriages, the inconsistencies observed above are of a magnitude far too great to be explained by such factors.

Education and Marital Status

The association between reported ancestry and both education and marital status suggests further examples of inconsistency and flux. Starting with education, we find that the attainment level of American-born women affects the complexity of the ethnic origin that they report. Simply stated, those with less education are more likely to simplify their ethnic origins. Among women aged 25–34, for example, the ratio of single ancestry to multiple ancestry is 1.71 for those with less than a high school education, but 0.96 for women who are high school graduates and 0.71 for those with at least some college education. This pattern is repeated in all of the age groups and is also found within most of the specific white groups. For instance, the propensity for women aged 45–54 to report only German as their ancestry, as opposed to German and at least one other origin, varies from a ratio of 0.79 for those least educated to 0.71 for high school graduates and 0.48 for the most educated. The patterns vary by group and age since the true level of the mixing of ancestry groups likewise is different, and there are exceptions, but the overall pattern indicates a linkage with education of a magnitude that is unlikely to be explained by any true association between the complexity of ethnic origins and educational attainment. We also find that less educated segments of the population are more likely to either not respond or give a new non-European response such as "American" (see below).

At present, there is no adequate empirically supported explanation for why education appears to affect either the complexity of ethnic responses or even knowledge of a European origin. On the one hand, it may be that more highly educated respondents are simply more likely to know what their ancestry is and/or to know it in greater detail—or think that they do—because it is a part of the family history that is passed down through the generations. Or it may be that the higher socioeconomic segments find it improper or even embarrassing to have no answer to a question about family background. Not to be ruled out is the possibility of a differential interest in the subject—in no small way a function of stimulation from the educational experience itself—or a differential in recall. Of course, more than one of these factors could be operating. Finally, it is also possible that the more educated are generally more apt to give complex answers to many sorts of questions. In any event, educational attainment seems to affect both the ability to respond with any origin as well as distortions in the ones that are reported.

Marriage itself seems to affect the ethnic origins reported by the population in two different ways. The first way is through simply the enumeration procedure itself. In many homes it is likely that one person is primarily responsible for filling out the census forms. Hence, there is simplification when a respondent filled out the ancestry question for his or her spouse. Women of a given origin who were currently married— and with a husband present—were compared with those who were either not currently married or whose husband was not present. For the larger white ethnic groups, in each age and educational category, a single ancestry is far more often reported for women living with their spouse. Moreover, the differences are by no means trivial. Among English-origin women aged 25–34 who are high school graduates and living with their husband, for example, the ratio of unmixed to mixed is 0.926; by contrast the ratio is 0.619 for English-origin women who are unmarried. For German-origin women in the same age and educational category, the unmixed to mixed ratio is likewise higher among the married—0.622 versus 0.433. As we have noted, there are a few exceptions, but generally married women are more likely to be reported as unmixed than are unmarried women.

On this score, evidence gathered by Tom W. Smith of the National Opinion Research Center (NORC) is of great relevance. In the 1985 General Social Survey, a question was added on ethnicity of spouse. Overall, the respondent's self-reported ethnicity is more detailed and complicated than the ethnicity he/she described for the spouse. For example, nearly 50 percent of respondents report that they were of two or more different origins, whereas comparable complexity is reported for only a third of the spouses.[10] This distortion of the spouses' ethnicity does indicate true shifts of a modest magnitude insofar as it suggests that mates have less than full knowledge about the ancestry of their spouses and hence will give incomplete information to their offspring about the latter's heritage—a situation that can be relieved only through discussions between offspring and both of their parents.

There is a second and even more powerful way in which marriage may be warping the intergenerational transmission of accurate ethnic knowledge. Namely, spouses may be emphasizing common heritages either by dropping other heritages when they have a common ancestral tie or by introducing a spurious ancestry. This would help explain the high levels discussed earlier in the volume of apparent intragroup marriage among those reporting unmixed ancestry. Obviously it is impossible to separate the impact of marriage on ethnic distortions—particularly when these work toward generating similarities—from the

---

[10]Information based on personal communication from Tom W. Smith, for which we are most grateful.

opposite process, whereby persons marry others with common origins. All that we can say here, given the information available, is that some of the rates of inmarriage lead us to suspect such distortions.

Of special note are two facts. There is an enormous concentration of ingroup marriages reported for persons of unmixed single ancestry. For example, in an earlier chapter we saw that 72 percent of the single-ancestry women in the lowest educational category are reported as married to men of the same single ancestry. Moreover, for some of the ethnic groups, the data seem to show that ingroup marriage was relatively high and had not declined in recent age cohorts. In both the English and the German ethnic groups, the percentage of ingroup marriages had not declined with progressively younger age cohorts. This pattern is radically different from that experienced for most groups.[11] We do not yet know what accounts for this, but possibly there is a tendency to distort origins in the direction of these two groups when any common English or German bond exists in the couple or if there is even a vague notion of such a bond. At any rate, it seems unlikely that the cross-sectional age-specific intermarriage rates would remain so flat for these groups at a time when other white segments were experiencing declining homogamy.

A second fact is the level of inmarriage reported between people with common multiple origins. For example, among women aged 35–44 in 1980 and in their first marriage, 4 percent of those who were of German origin reported husbands who were of mixed German-Irish ancestry. Likewise, 4 percent of unmixed Irish women reported husbands of mixed German-Irish ancestry. However, among mixed German-Irish women, 15 percent had husbands who were also of the same mix. Of mixed English-German women, 14 percent are married to husbands with the same ethnic mixture, whereas only 3 percent of either unmixed German or unmixed English women have such husbands. Obviously, selective mating operates and a propinquity factor is not to be overlooked as well; but our suspicion is that the concentration of such marriages is beyond what might be reasonably expected on that basis. Rather, these data, as well as the unchanging levels of ingroup marriage reported previously for the English and Germans, suggest a certain propensity for couples to distort their origins in the direction of homogeneity.[12] If this is the case, we must ask whether certain origins are more resistant to change and which groups are the net gainers in these shifts.

---

[11]Stanley Lieberson and Mary C. Waters, "Ethnic Mixtures in the United States," *Sociology and Social Research* 70 (1985):43–52; table 2.

[12]For evidence that husbands and wives do sometimes distort ancestries in order to match each other, see Colleen Leahy Johnson, *Growing Up and Growing Old in Italian American Families* (New Brunswick, NJ: Rutgers University Press, 1985).

A New Ethnic Group?

Finally, there is evidence suggesting that this flux in ethnic categories and identification is leading to the growth of a population which is quite different from other ethnic groups in the United States. Namely, there are a substantial number of people who recognize that they are white, but lack any clear-cut identification with, and/or knowledge of, a specific European origin. Such people recognize that they are not the same as some of the existing ethnic groups in the country such as Greeks, Jews, Italians, Poles, or Irish. Their actual origins are assumed to be predominantly from the older northwestern European groups, but there are some persons from newer European sources of immigration who are shifting into this group. This population has been labeled "unhyphenated whites," differentiating them from the more pejorative term WASP (which is not used because of its negative connotations and because a sizable proportion of this population is not Protestant).[13]

The evidence for the existence of this population comes from census and survey data about Americans in the 1970s and 1980s. The NORC General Social Survey, the 1979 Current Population Survey, and the 1980 census all include data that show that a sizable proportion of the population either cannot or will not give an answer to the ancestry or ethnic identification question. A quite sizable proportion (12 percent) in the 1980 census also give "American" as a response to the ancestry question. This is true even though the response was specifically discouraged by the Census Bureau. This population of respondents who give American as their ethnic response are the group we will examine for evidence of the creation and formation of a new ethnic group.

That this population appears in the 1970s and 1980s is in itself a surprising development because it seems to go against the prevailing wisdom about the state of ethnicity in the United States. Much commentary has held that the 1970s were characterized by the rise of the "new ethnicity" which trumpeted the role of diversity of ethnic cultures in the overall culture and identity of Americans. This growth of ethnic consciousness and advocacy of ethnic identification stressed the pluralism and diversity of ethnic groups in the United States. However, against just such a backdrop of this heightened ethnic consciousness and identification, there is evidence that a quite sizable proportion of Americans are unaware of their ethnic origins, choose to identify with none of the known ethnic groups and to identify themselves as Americans, or refuse to state an ancestry.

Of a total U.S. population of 226.5 million in 1980, 13.3 million

[13]Lieberson, "Unhyphenated Whites."

gave "American" or "United States" as their ancestry. Just under 6 percent of the population could not name any specific ancestries—or chose not to; in the 1979 survey, the percentage was slightly higher—6.3.[14] To appreciate the importance of this number, consider three additional facts. First, American is a major ethnic response—ranking fifth in the nation. To be sure, it trails by a large amount those reporting English (50 million), German (49 million), Irish (40 million), and black (21 million), the actual number indicating black on the direct census "race" question is nearly 8 million greater than the number obtained on this ethnic item. But American narrowly edges out such groups as French and Italian, and, by much greater margins, exceeds other leading ancestry responses such as Scottish, Polish, Mexican, American Indian, and Dutch.[15]

Whites are only about 45 percent of the respondents indicating "American" on the General Social Survey and they are about 74 percent of the much larger number who cannot name any ancestral country. Between these two categories, it means that 9 percent of the entire population are whites who are either unable to report an ancestral nation or indicate simply that they are American. Confining ourselves to NORC survey data only for whites, we find that the American component amounts to 10 percent of all whites in the period between 1972 and 1980. Thus, the number of whites who respond as Americans or who report that they are unable to name any ancestry is still an important component of the entire white population of the United States. In terms of the nonblack population of the United States in 1979, then, approximately 15.4 percent either did not report an ancestry or indicated "American."[16]

The NORC survey permits a distinction in terms of four generations, applying the procedure described by Alba and Chamlin.[17] Some 57 percent of the entire U.S. population is at least fourth generation; that is, the United States is the country of birth for themselves, both of their parents, and all four of their grandparents. Among "unhyphenated whites" (those unable to name any ancestral country or choosing "American"), 97 percent were of at least fourth generation ancestry. Thus, unhyphenated whites make up 16 percent of all Americans with

[14]U.S. Bureau of the Census, *1980 Census of Population, Supplementary Report,* "Ancestry of the Population by State: 1980," PC80-51-10 (Washington, DC: U.S. Government Printing Office, 1983a), table E, p. 4.

[15]See U.S Bureau of the Census, p. 2.

[16]Admittedly, this last set of census figures includes people who are neither white nor black, but the form of the census procedure in 1979 makes it desirable to calculate in this way and the numerical impact is certainly minor.

[17]Richard D. Alba and Mitchell B. Chamlin, "A Preliminary Examination of Ethnic Identification Among Whites," *American Sociological Review* 48 (1983):240–47.

at least four generations' residence in the United States. By contrast, unhyphenated whites are 1 percent or less of the third, second, and first generations. (This sharp difference by generation—with such small percentages for earlier generations—suggests that the data are quite meaningful. One would be suspicious if many of the immigrants or their offspring were unable to state the countries or part of the world from which their ancestors came and/or if the American response was given after such a short generational stay in the United States.)

Compared with all whites, unhyphenated whites are especially likely to be found in the South, particularly in the South Atlantic states (38 percent of all unhyphenated whites are found in the South Atlantic states and 67 percent are in the entire South). By contrast, only about 30 percent of the entire white population surveyed by NORC lives in the South. (Given the southern concentration, it is not surprising that 87 percent of unhyphenated whites were raised as Protestant compared with 64 percent for all whites in the country.) Not only is the new white ethnic population disproportionately located in the South, but it is concentrated in rural areas. In the United States as a whole, 33 percent of all unhyphenated whites are located in what NORC refers to as "open country," compared with 17 percent of all whites. This is more than a reflection of regional differences and the concentration of unhyphenated whites in the South. Some 27 percent of all whites living in the South are found in open country compared with 42 percent of unhyphenated whites. We could speculate that there is such a concentration of these individuals in the rural areas of the South because these places have experienced relatively little immigration for more than a century. Thus, because there is a great deal of homogeneity in terms of ethnic ancestry, attention to ethnicity is minimal and shift is thereby encouraged.

Education not only affects the complexity of the ethnic response—as we observed earlier—but in this case it also appears to affect the ability or willingness of whites to give any specific European origins at all. Restricting the analysis to whites living in the rural South, with at least four generations' residence in the nation, we applied data gathered by the NORC through 1980 to determine the more subtle linkages between education and the absence of any claim to a specific European heritage. Even in the rural South education has a distinct effect on the response. Whereas 29 percent of those with at least a high school education could not name any ethnic ancestry or selected American, 46 percent of those with less education gave a similar response. As a general rule, the unhyphenated white population tends to be of lower socioeconomic status than the entire white population in the United States. However, this is by no means exclusively a class phenomenon. It is still the case, even among rural fourth-generation southern whites who do not give one or more specific European ancestries, that 38 percent have at least a high school diploma.

It may well be the case that the melting pot is working in a different way than has been discussed in the literature. In addition to different groups acting increasingly alike, it may be that a new population is in the process of forming. Whether this is the case or not requires considerably more evidence than can be presented here. For one, the strongest test will occur in the 1990 census, when it will be possible to make longitudinal comparisons over time. Such comparisons can address the question of whether there is an increase in the "unhyphenated white" type of response for the same age- and generation-specific cohort as they age (cross-sectionally, at the present time, the proportions giving such responses seem to be concentrated in the older age groups, but with data for one period it is impossible to separate the age, cohort, and period effects).

A second issue pertains to the meaning of the responses. Given the relatively low socioeconomic status of the unhyphenated white population, as measured with NORC data, there is always the possibility that people giving these responses are selective on various characteristics and do not represent a "new" ethnic thrust. Is it merely a convenient label for those people who do not know or are not interested in their ethnic background? Or is it a specific "ethnic character," something which other ethnic groups are trying to assimilate into? In this regard, the two subsets of the population defined as unhyphenated white with NORC data—those reporting themselves as American as opposed to those unable to name a group—do differ on some dimensions. For example, the specifically American subset do appear to be relatively higher in socioeconomic status, less likely to reside in the South, and more likely to be Catholic compared with the other subset. But they are still different from all whites.

Conclusion

In our estimation, three central types of ethnic flux are occurring within the white population. The first is well known among whites; this is the development of new ethnic categories that evolve soon after immigration to the United States. For example, people who viewed themselves as members of a town or province prior to immigration gradually gain a broader identification—say, as Italians or Poles—that is both imposed on them by the dominant society and chosen by them as their contacts increase and as earlier cleavages become secondary. This process is largely over for white European groups, although it will continue for newer groups migrating to the United States as well as other non-European groups. In particular, there may well be further changes in the delineations among Hispanic groups or among Southeast Asian groups, possibly emphasizing commonalities among groups that initially saw themselves as quite distinct from one another. Certainly, that is the case for the "American Indian" concept, which is essentially the pooling together under a single rubric tribes (basically ethnic groups) with distinctive cultures, languages, and historical traditions.

The second shift, we believe, will be of growing relevance in the years ahead for the white population. As the distance from the immigrant generation widens for the vast majority of the white population, we expect increasing distortion in the true origins of the population. This assumes that intermarriage will continue at a high level, that ethnic enclaves will diminish, and that there will be a relatively modest degree of discrimination and prejudice against various white ethnic groups. In other words, central to the projection is the assumption that ethnic origin among whites will decline as a sociopolitical issue. If these conditions occur, we believe that ethnic responses will be of declining reliability in terms of a means of tracing true ancestral roots. This, however, need not preclude reported ethnic origins from being significantly related to all sorts of other social phenomena—only that the correlations may be increasingly due to a reverse causal order such that people with different social characteristics vary in the probability of reporting certain social origins. To be sure, at this point there is still reason to take the ethnic data at face value more often than not. Hence we can still have confidence that the social characteristics observed for different ethnic groups do indeed largely reflect the influence of the latter on the former.

The third shift that we expect to find is that all of this flux and uncertainty in ethnic origins should lead to an expansion in the segment of the population whose members are unable to provide any picture of their ethnic origins, but simply know that they are unhyphenated whites. In other words, we expect to find a complete circle. Just as the immigrant groups who migrated here were the product of earlier mergers of different peoples in Europe, so, too, their descendants in the United States generations later will form the strands of a new American ethnic group in this country.

Bibliography

Abramson, Harold J. "Interethnic Marriage Among Catholic Americans and Changes in Religious Behavior." *Social Analysis* 32 (1971):31–44.
—— *Ethnic Diversity in Catholic America.* New York: Wiley, 1973.
Adams, Romanzo *Interracial Marriage in Hawaii.* New York: Macmillan, 1937.
Alba, Richard D. "Social Assimilation Among American Catholic National-Origin Groups." *American Sociological Review* 41 (1976):1030–46.
—— "Interethnic and Interracial Marriage in the 1980 Census." Paper presented at the American Sociological Association Annual Meeting, Washington, DC, 1985.
—— *Italian Americans: Into the Twilight of Ethnicity.* Englewood Cliffs, NJ: Prentice-Hall, 1986.
——, **and Mitchell B. Chamlin** "A Preliminary Examination of Ethnic Identification Among Whites." *American Sociological Review* 48 (1983):240–47.
Alba, Richard D., and Reid M. Golden "Patterns of Ethnic Marriage in the United States." *Social Forces* 65 (1986):202–23.
American Council of Learned Societies "Report of Committee on Linguistic and National Stocks in the Population of the United States." *Annual Report of the American Historical Association, 1931*, vol. 1. Washington, DC: U.S. Government Printing Office, 1932.
Anderson, Barbara A., and Brian D. Silver "Estimating Russification of Ethnic Identity among Non-Russians in the U.S.S.R." *Demography* 20 (1983):474–75.
Archdeacon, Thomas J. "Problems and Possibilities in the Study of American Immigration and Ethnic History." *International Migration Review* 19 (1985):112–34.
Australian Bureau of Statistics *The Measurement of Ethnicity in the Australian Census of Population and Housing.* Fyshwick, A.C.T.: Canberra Reprographics, 1984.
Bartholomew, D. J. *Stochastic Models for Social Processes*, 2nd ed. London: Wiley, 1973.
Becker, Gary S. *The Economics of Discrimination.* Chicago: University of Chicago Press, 1957.
Beijbom, Ulf "Swedes." In Stephan Thernstrom, ed. *Harvard Encyclopedia of American Ethnic Groups.* Cambridge, MA: Belknap Press, 1980.
Blau, Peter M., and Otis Dudley Duncan *The American Occupational Structure.* New York: Wiley, 1967.
Carpenter, Niles *Immigrants and Their Children: 1920*, Census Monograph 7. Washington, DC: U.S. Government Printing Office, 1927.
Center for Political Studies *American National Election Study, 1984: Appendix: Notes and Questionnaire* (Ann Arbor, MI: Inter-university Consortium for Political and Social Research, 1986).

Chenkin, Alvin "Jewish Population in the United States, 1982." In Milton Himmelfarb and David Singer, eds. *American Jewish Year Book, 1983.* New York: American Jewish Committee, 1983.

Choldin, Harvey M. "Statistics and Politics: The 'Hispanic Issue' in the 1980 Census." *Demography* 23 (1986):403–18.

Cochrane, Susan Hill *Fertility and Education: What Do We Really Know,* World Bank Staff Occasional Papers no. 26. Baltimore: Johns Hopkins University Press, 1979.

Cohen, Jacob, and Patricia Cohen *Applied Multiple Regression/Correlation Analysis for the Behavioral Sciences.* Hillsdale, NJ: Lawrence Erlbaum Associates, 1975.

Cohen, Steven M. "Socioeconomic Determinants of Intraethnic Marriage and Friendship." *Social Forces* 55 (1977):997–1010.

Davis, James A. "Up and Down Opportunity's Ladder." *Public Opinion* 5 (1982):11–51.

Duncan, Beverly, and Otis Dudley Duncan "Minorities and the Process of Stratification." *American Sociological Review* 33 (1968):356–64.

Duncan, Otis Dudley; David L. Featherman; and Beverly Duncan *Socioeconomic Background and Achievement.* New York: Seminar Press, 1972.

Duncan, Otis Dudley, and Stanley Lieberson "Ethnic Segregation and Assimilation." *American Journal of Sociology* 64 (1959):364–74.

Featherman, David L. "The Socioeconomic Achievement of White Religio-Ethnic Subgroups: Social and Psychological Explanations." *American Sociological Review* 36 (1971):207–22.

———, **and Robert M. Hauser** *Opportunity and Change.* New York: Academic Press, 1978.

Glazer, Nathan, and Daniel Patrick Moynihan *Beyond the Melting Pot.* Cambridge, MA: MIT Press, 1963.

Gordon, Milton M. *Assimilation in American Life: The Role of Race, Religion, and National Origins.* New York: Oxford University Press, 1964.

Greeley, Andrew M. *Ethnicity in the United States.* New York: Wiley, 1974.

Gurak, Douglas T., and Joseph P. Fitzpatrick "Intermarriage Among Hispanic Ethnic Groups in New York City." *American Journal of Sociology* 87 (1982):921–34.

Handlin, Oscar *Race and Nationality in American Life.* Garden City, NY: Doubleday Anchor Books, 1957.

——— *Boston's Immigrants,* rev. and enl. ed. Cambridge, MA: Belknap Press, 1959.

Heer, David M. "The Marital Status of Second-Generation Americans." *American Sociological Review* 26 (1961):233–41.

——— "Intermarriage." In Stephan Thernstrom, ed. *Harvard Encyclopedia of American Ethnic Groups.* Cambridge, MA: Belknap Press, 1980:513–21.

Higham, John *Strangers in the Land.* New Brunswick, NJ: Rutgers University Press, 1955.

Hirschman, Charles "America's Melting Pot Reconsidered." *Annual Review of Sociology* 9 (1983):397–423.

Horowitz, Donald L. *Ethnic Groups in Conflict.* Berkeley: University of California Press, 1985.

Hutchinson, E. P. *Immigrants and Their Children: 1850–1950.* New York: Wiley, 1956.

Johnson, Charles E., Jr. *Consistency of Reporting of Ethnic Origin in the Cur-*

rent Population Survey. Technical Paper no. 31, Current Population Survey. Washington, DC: U.S. Government Printing Office, 1974.

Johnson, Colleen Leahy *Growing Up and Growing Old in Italian American Families.* New Brunswick, NJ: Rutgers University Press, 1985.

Jones, Maldwyn Allen *American Immigration.* Chicago: University of Chicago Press, 1960.

Kennedy, Ruby Jo Reeves "Single or Triple Melting Pot? Intermarriage Trends in New Haven, 1870–1940." *American Journal of Sociology* 49 (1944):331–39.

———— "Single or Triple Melting Pot? Intermarriage Trends in New Haven, 1870–1950." *American Journal of Sociology* 58 (1952):56–59.

Klein, George, and Patricia V. Klein "United States and Yugoslavia: Divergent Approaches Toward Ethnicity." In Chester L. Hunt and Lewis Walker, eds. *Ethnic Dynamics: Patterns of Intergroup Relations in Various Societies.* Holmes Beach, FL: Learning Publications, 1979.

Kobrin, Frances E., and Calvin Goldscheider *The Ethnic Factor in Family Structure and Mobility.* Cambridge, MA: Ballinger, 1978.

Kralt, John M. "Ethnic Origin in the Canadian Census, 1871–1981." In W. R. Petryshyn, ed. *Changing Realities: Social Trends Among Ukrainian Canadians.* Edmonton, Alberta: Canadian Institute of Ukrainian Studies, 1980.

Labov, Teresa, and Jerry A. Jacobs "Intermarriage in Hawaii, 1950–1983." Paper presented at the Annual Meeting of the Population Association of America, Boston, 1985.

Lieberson, Stanley "A Societal Theory of Race and Ethnic Relations." *American Sociological Review* 26 (1961):902–10.

———— *Ethnic Patterns in American Cities.* New York: Free Press, 1963a.

———— "The Old-New Distinction and Immigrants in Australia." *American Sociological Review* 28 (1963b):550–65.

———— "The Price-Zubrzycki Measure of Ethnic Intermarriage." *Eugenics Quarterly* 13 (1966):92–100.

———— "Stratification and Ethnic Groups." *Sociological Inquiry* 40 (1970a):172–81.

———— *Language and Ethnic Relations in Canada.* New York: Wiley, 1970b.

———— "Generational Differences Among Blacks in the North." *American Journal of Sociology* 79 (1973):550–65.

———— "Rank-Sum Comparisons Between Groups." In David Heise, ed. *Sociological Methodology 1976.* San Francisco: Jossey-Bass, 1975.

———— "A Reconsideration of the Income Differences Found Between Migrants and Northern-Born Blacks." *American Journal of Sociology* 83 (1978):940–66.

———— *A Piece of the Pie: Blacks and White Immigrants Since 1880.* Berkeley: University of California Press, 1980.

———— "An Asymmetrical Approach to Segregation." In Ceri Peach, Vaughan Robinson, and Susan Smith, eds. *Ethnic Segregation in Cities.* London: Croom Helm, 1981.

———— *Making It Count.* Berkeley: University of California Press, 1985a.

———— "Unhyphenated Whites in the United States." *Ethnic and Racial Studies* 8 (January 1985b):159–80. Reprinted in Richard D. Alba, ed. *Ethnicity and Race in the U.S.A.: Toward the Twenty-First Century.* London: Routledge & Kegan Paul, 1985b.

————, **and Donna Carter** "Temporal Changes and Urban Differences in Residential Segregation: A Reconsideration." *American Journal of Sociology* 88 (1982a):296–310.

—— "A Model for Inferring the Voluntary and Involuntary Causes of Residential Segregation." *Demography* 19 (1982b):511–26.

Lieberson, Stanley, and James F. O'Connor "Language Diversity in a Nation and Its Regions." In Stanley Lieberson, ed. *Language Diversity and Language Contact.* Stanford, CA: Stanford University Press, 1981.

Lieberson, Stanley, and Lawrence Santi "The Use of Nativity Data to Estimate Ethnic Characteristics and Patterns." *Social Science Research* 14 (1985):31–56.

Lieberson, Stanley, and Mary C. Waters "Ethnic Mixtures in the United States." *Sociology and Social Research* 70 (1985):43–52.

—— "Ethnic Groups in Flux: The Changing Ethnic Responses of American Whites." *Annals of the American Academy of Political and Social Science* 487 (1986):79–91.

National Opinion Research Center *General Social Surveys, 1972–1980: Cumulative Codebook.* Chicago: NORC, 1980.

—— *General Social Surveys, 1972–1986: Cumulative Codebook.* Chicago: NORC, 1986.

Neidert, Lisa J., and Reynolds Farley "Assimilation in the United States: An Analysis of Ethnic and Generation Differences in Status and Achievement." *American Sociological Review* 50 (1985):840–50.

Novak, Michael *The Rise of the Unmeltable Ethnics.* New York: Macmillan, 1971.

Owen, Carolyn A.; Howard C. Eisner; and Thomas R. McFaul "A Half-Century of Social Distance Research: National Replication of the Bogardus Studies." *Sociology and Social Research* 66 (1981):80–98.

Passel, Jeffrey S. "Undocumented Immigration." *Annals of the American Academy of Political and Social Science* 487 (1986):181–200.

Peach, Ceri "Ethnic Segregation and Intermarriage." *Annals of the Association of American Geography* 70 (1980):371–81.

—— "Ethnic Segregation and Ethnic Intermarriage: A Re-examination of Kennedy's Triple Melting Pot in New Haven, 1900–1950." In Ceri Peach, Vaughan Robinson, and Susan Smith, eds. *Ethnic Segregation in Cities.* London: Croom Helm, 1981.

Petersen, William "The Classification of Subnations in Hawaii: An Essay in the Sociology of Knowledge." *American Sociological Review* 34 (1969):863–77.

Price, Charles A., and J. Zubrzycki "The Use of Inter-Marriage Statistics as an Index of Assimilation." *Population Studies* 16 (1962):58–69.

Rogers, Francis M. "Portuguese." In Stephan Thernstrom, ed. *Harvard Encyclopedia of American Ethnic Groups.* Cambridge, MA: Belknap Press, 1980.

Rosenthal, Erich "Jewish Intermarriage in Indiana." *Eugenics Quarterly* 15 (1968):277–87.

Ryder, Norman B. "The Interpretation of Origin Statistics." *Canadian Journal of Economics and Political Science* 21 (1955):466–79.

Salamon, Sonya "Ethnic Differences in Farm Family Land Transfers." *Rural Sociology* 45 (1980):290–308.

—— "Sibling Solidarity as an Operating Strategy in Illinois Agriculture." *Rural Sociology* 47 (1982):349–68.

—— "Ethnic Communities and the Structure of Agriculture." *Rural Sociology* 50 (1985):323–40.

Schaefer, Richard T. *Racial and Ethnic Groups,* 2nd ed. Boston: Little, Brown, 1984.

Schoen, Robert, and Lawrence E. Cohen "Ethnic Endogamy Among Mexican American Grooms: A Reanalysis of Generational and Occupational Effects." *American Journal of Sociology* 86 (1980):359–66.

Schoup, Paul A. *The East European and Soviet Data Handbook: Political, Social and Developmental Indicators 1945–1975.* New York: Columbia University Press, 1981.

Simmel, Georg "Social Interaction as the Definition of the Group in Time and Space." In Robert E. Park and Ernest W. Burgess, eds. *Introduction to the Science of Sociology.* Chicago: University of Chicago Press, 1921.

Simon, Julian L. "Basic Data Concerning Immigration into the United States." *Annals of the American Academy of Political and Social Science* 487 (1986):12–56.

Snipp, C. Matthew "Who Are American Indians? Some Observations About the Perils and Pitfalls of Data for Race and Ethnicity." *Population Research and Policy Review* 5 (1986):237–52.

Statistics Canada *1981 Census of Canada, Population.* Vol. 1: *Ethnic Origin.* Ottawa, Ontario: Statistics Canada, 1984.

Stevens, Gillian, and Gray Swicegood "The Linguistic Context of Ethnic Endogamy." *American Sociological Review* 52 (1987):73–82.

Taeuber, Alma F., and Karl E. Taeuber "Recent Immigration and Studies of Ethnic Assimilation." *Demography* 4 (1967):798–808.

Thompson, Warren, and P. K. Whelpton *Population Trends in the United States.* New York: McGraw-Hill, 1933.

U.S. Bureau of the Census *Seventh Census of the United States: 1850.* Washington, DC: U.S. Government Printing Office, 1853.

—————— *A Century of Population Growth: 1790–1900.* Washington, DC: U.S. Government Printing Office, 1909.

—————— *Fifteenth Census of the United States: 1930, Population.* Vol. 2: *General Report, Statistics by Subject.* Washington DC: U.S. Government Printing Office, 1933a.

—————— *Fifteenth Census of the United States: 1930, Population. Special Report on Foreign-Born White Families by Country of Birth of Head.* Washington, DC: U.S. Government Printing Office, 1933b.

—————— *Sixteenth Census of the United States: 1940, Population. Differential Fertility, 1940 and 1910. Women by Number of Children Ever Born.* Washington, DC: U.S. Government Printing Office, 1945.

—————— *1950 Census of Population.* Vol. 2: *Characteristics of the Population,* pt. 1: *U.S. Summary.* Washington, DC: U.S. Government Printing Office, 1953.

—————— *1950 Census of Population.* Vol. 4: *Special Reports,* pt. 3: *Nativity and Parentage of the White Population.* Washington, DC: U.S. Government Printing Office, 1954.

—————— *1960 Census of Population. Subject Reports. Women by Number of Children Ever Born,* PC(2)-3A. Washington, DC: U.S. Government Printing Office, 1964.

—————— *Historical Statistics of the United States: Colonial Times to 1970,* Bicentennial Edition, pt. 1. Washington, DC: U.S. Government Printing Office, 1975a.

—————— *Historical Statistics of the United States: Colonial Times to 1970,* Bicentennial Edition, pt. 2. Washington, DC: U.S. Government Printing Office, 1975b.

———— *November 1979 CPS Interviewer's Instructions,* CPS Interviewer's Memorandum no. 79-18. Washington, DC: U.S. Bureau of the Census, 1979.

———— *Statistical Abstract of the United States: 1980.* Washington, DC: U.S. Government Printing Office, 1980.

———— "Money Income of Families and Persons in the United States: 1979." *Current Population Reports,* Series P-60, no. 129. Washington, DC: U.S. Government Printing Office, 1982.

———— "Ancestry and Language in the United States: November, 1979." *Current Population Reports,* Series P-23, No. 116. Washington, DC: U.S. Government Printing Office, 1982.

———— *1980 Census of Population. Supplementary Report,* "Persons of Spanish Origin by State: 1980," PC80-S1-10. Washington, DC: U.S. Government Printing Office, 1983a.

———— *1980 Census of Population. Supplementary Report,* "Ancestry of the Population by State: 1980," PC80-S1-10. Washington, DC: U.S. Government Printing Office, 1983a.

———— *1980 Census of Population. U.S. Summary,* "Number of Inhabitants," PC80-1-A1. Washington, DC: U.S. Government Printing Office, 1983b.

———— *1980 Census of Population. U.S. Summary,* "Characteristics of the Population," PC80-1-A1. Washington, DC: U.S. Government Printing Office, 1983c.

———— *Statistical Abstract of the United States: 1984.* Washington, DC: U.S. Government Printing Office, 1983d.

———— *1980 Census of Population and Housing: Public-Use Microdata Samples, Technical Documentation.* Washington, DC: Bureau of the Census, 1983e.

———— *1980 Census of Population.* Vol. 1: *General Social and Economic Characteristics,* pt. 1. *U.S. Summary.* Washington, DC: U.S. Government Printing Office, 1983f.

———— *1980 Census of Population.* Vol. 2: *Subject Reports,* "Earnings by Occupation and Education," PC80-2 8B. Washington, DC: U.S. Government Printing Office, 1984.

———— *1980 Census of Population and Housing, Evaluation and Research Reports,* "Content Reinterview Study: Accuracy of Data for Selected Population and Housing Characteristics as Measured by Reinterview," PHC80-E2. Washington, DC: U.S. Government Printing Office, 1986.

U.S. Census Office *Compendium of the Eleventh Census: 1890,* pt. 3, 1897.

U.S. Department of Justice *1970 Annual Report, Immigration and Naturalization Service.* Washington, DC: U.S. Government Printing Office, 1971.

U.S. Senate *Reports of the United States Immigration Commission: Occupations of the First and Second Generations of Immigrants in the United States,* 61st Cong., 2nd Sess. Document no. 282. Washington, DC: U.S. Government Printing Office, 1911.

Warner, W. Lloyd, and Leo Srole *The Social Systems of American Ethnic Groups.* New Haven: Yale University Press, 1945.

Waters, Mary C. "The Process and Content of Ethnic Identification: A Study of White Ethnics in Suburbia." Unpublished doctoral dissertation, University of California, Berkeley, 1986.

Wells, Robert V. *The Population of the British Colonies in America Before 1776.* Princeton, NJ: Princeton University Press, 1975.

Willcox, Walter F. *International Migrations,* vol. 1. New York: Gordon and Breach, 1969.

APPENDIX

THE GEOGRAPHICAL DIVISIONS
OF THE UNITED STATES

New England:
  Maine
  New Hampshire
  Vermont
  Massachusetts
  Rhode Island
  Connecticut

Middle tlantic:
  New York
  New Jersey
  Pennsylvania

East North Central:
  Ohio
  Indiana
  Illinois
  Michigan
  Wisconsin

West North Central:
  Minnesota
  Iowa
  Missouri
  North Dakota
  South Dakota
  Nebraska
  Kansas

South Atlantic:
  Delaware
  Maryland
  District of Columbia
  Virginia
  West Virginia
  North Carolina
  South Carolina
  Georgia
  Florida

East South Central:
  Kentucky
  Tennessee
  Alabama
  Mississippi

West South Central:
  Arkansas
  Louisiana
  Oklahoma
  Texas

Mountain:
  Montana
  Idaho
  Wyoming
  Colorado
  New Mexico
  Arizona
  Utah
  Nevada

Pacific:
  Washington
  Oregon
  California
  Alaska
  Hawaii

Name Index

A

Abramson, Harold J., 163n, 180
Adams, Romanzo, 163
Alba, Richard D., 5, 18n, 50n, 163n, 208n, 211n, 219n, 265n
American Council of Learned Societies, 38, 40
American Philosophical Society, 3
Anderson, Barbara A., 257n
Archdeacon, Thomas J., 35n
Australian Bureau of Statistics, 23n

B

Bartholomew, D. J., 77n
Beijbom, Ulf, 40n
Blau, Peter M., 95n
Burgess, Ernest W. 42n

C

Carpenter, Niles, 25n, 43n, 63, 101
Carter, Donna, 189n
Center for Political Studies, 24n
Chamlin, Mitchell B., 163n, 219n, 265n
Chenkin, Alvin, 73n
Choldin, Harvey M., 16n
Cochrane, Susan Hill, 211n
Cohen, Jacob, 217n
Cohen, Lawrence E., 211n
Cohen, Patricia, 217n
Cohen, Steven M., 180
Connecticut Academy of Arts and Sciences, 3

D

Davis, James A., 122
Dillingham Commission, 119

Duncan, Beverly, 95n
Duncan, Otis Dudley, 95n, 232

E

Eisner, Howard C., 217n

F

Farley, Reynolds, 11n, 12n, 143
Featherman, David L., 95n, 143
Fitzgerald, Joseph P., 211n
Franklin, Benjamin, 30

G

Glazer, Nathan, 75n
Golden, Reid M., 18n, 163n
Goldscheider, Calvin, 105n
Gordon, Milton M., 163
Greeley, Andrew M., 10, 163n, 234
Gurak, Douglas T., 211n

H

Handlin, Oscar, 15n, 30n
Hauser, Robert M., 95n
Heer, David M., 102–103, 163
Heise, David, 27n, 44n, 61n, 109n, 131n, 212n
Himmelfarb, Milton, 73n
Hirschman, Charles, 5n
Horowitz, Donald L., 2n
Hunt, Chester L., 82n
Hutchinson, E. P., 3, 123n

J

Jacobs, Jerry A., 163n
Johnson, Charles E., Jr., 48

Subject Index

Boldface numbers refer to figures and tables.